TRUMPET AT A DISTANT GATE

TRUMPET AT A DISTANT GATE

The Lodge as Prelude to the Country House

Tim Mowl & Brian Earnshaw

WATERSTONE · LONDON
1985

Copyright © 1984 Timothy Mowl and Brian Earnshaw

Published 1985 in Great Britain by Waterstone and Company Ltd., London.

All rights reserved. No part of this publication may be reproduced, stored in a retrieval system or transmitted, in any form or by any means, electronic, mechanical, photocopying, recording or otherwise, without the prior permission of Waterstone and Company Ltd.

This book is sold subject to the condition that it shall not, by way of trade or otherwise, be lent, re-sold, hired or otherwise circulated without the publisher's prior consent in any form of binding or cover other than that in which it is published and without a similar condition being imposed on the subsequent purchaser.

Distributed (except in the USA) by Thames and Hudson Ltd.

Designed by Nancy Slonims and James Beveridge.

Set printed and bound by Imago Productions Far East Pte. Ltd.

ISBN 0 947752 05 6

CONTENTS

Introduction

CHAPTER ONE
Antecedents and Origins *Page 1*

CHAPTER TWO
'Procul O Procul Este Profani' *Page 16*

CHAPTER THREE
The Gothick Lodge as Mood Setter *Page 36*

CHAPTER FOUR
The Lodge in the Pattern Books 1740–1830 *Page 56*

CHAPTER FIVE
The Arc of Triumph as a Garden Gate *Page 77*

CHAPTER SIX
The Long Reign of the Classical Box 1740–1800 *Page 95*

CHAPTER SEVEN
The Columned Temple at the Park Gate *Page 107*

CHAPTER EIGHT
A Carriage Drive to the Castle Perilous *Page 126*

CHAPTER NINE
'That Peculiar Mode of Building which was Originally the Effect of Chance' *Page 137*

CHAPTER TEN
A New Florence in the West — the Lodge as an Episode in the Italianate *Page 146*

CHAPTER ELEVEN
The Lodges of High Victorian Historicism *Page 159*

CHAPTER TWELVE
The Last Lodges *Page 172*

CHAPTER THIRTEEN
One River and Two Parks of Lodges *Page 184*

Notes to the Text *Page 207* List of Illustrations *Page 215*
Glossary *Page 219* Bibliography *Page 225* Index *Page 229*

II

ACKNOWLEDGEMENTS

Lodges are often set in lonely, isolated places. It would be ungenerous not to open with a general tribute to literally hundreds of friendly lodge dwellers who received us with a manifest pride in, and an awareness of, the highly individual character of their houses. As lodge enthusiasts we tended to investigate a less chronicled world than the authors of most architecture books, so our thanks go out with real sincerity to the people who allowed us into their back gardens to get the best angle on a pediment, or who shared with us their speculative architectural attributions and dating.

As typical of so many others we remember Mr. and Mrs. Hill and Mrs. Mary Page, whose interest in old engravings and the brickwork of their cellars helped us with William Kent's archetypal twin lodges on Esher Green, and the landlord of the Edgehill Tower Inn who let us tramp through his best bedroom to reach Sanderson Miller's viewing room at the top of that multi-purpose fortress lodge.

Documentary evidence relevant to the building dates and architects of lodges is often slender, so Edward Hubbard's precise and factual information on the lodges of Cheshire was outstanding. We wish then to offer our particular thanks to Roger White for reading our manuscript and affording us his cautious good sense. The enthusiasm and interest at our publisher's office of Roderick Brown, Bridget Sleddon and Celia Van Oss was a pleasure and an encouragement.

May we then thank, in no other order than the alphabetical, the following for their information, their help and their advice: Rene Baker, Geoffrey Beard, Viscount Camrose, T.H. Carter, Howard Colvin, Stephen Croad, Sue Cummings, Ian Gow, Eileen and John Harris, Richard Hewlings, Charles Hind, Peter Howell, Clare Howes, Morrice Jennings, Francis Kelly, Charlotte Kennett, Nicholas Kingsley, Peter Leach, the Hon Robin Neville, John Newman, Julian Orbach, Canon T.W. Pritchard, Peter Reid, Alwyn J. Roberts, J. Hesketh Roberts, Phyllis Rogers, Peter Smith, Nigel Temple and Charles Wynne Eaton.

Tim Mowl, Brian Earnshaw. Bristol July 1984

DEDICATION

To Bristol — the last English city in which it is possible to be architecturally optimistic.

INTRODUCTION

Writing in a slim illustrated volume *Rural Residences,* published in 1818 to press the merits of his own designs, the Regency architect John Papworth told an anecdote. It concerned 'an old nobleman' who must have been the summer terror of the landed gentry. Each year his vacations were spent touring stately homes: 'He amused himself with speculations upon the character of the individuals from the entrances to their several properties as he met with them upon the road', pre-judging, in fact, the owners' characters by the look of their lodges. In prose heavier than any of his own classical terraces Papworth continued the story. The old aristocrat became so proficient in these character tests that at length he declined to visit owners 'if he thought he perceived characteristics objectionable to him in the entrances to their domains. "It is very easy", said he, "to say which belongs to the proud and lofty, and which to the vain and conceited; which to the liberal, the prodigal, the penurious, the courteous, the frivolous, the reserved, or the nervous; and it matters not that they may have been made by the predecessors of the present occupiers; had there been great differences of nature in them, the entrances would have been altered." '

The lesson, of course, to be drawn from this was to commission one of Papworth's own lodges or, 'to effect greater symmetry and convenience', two of them.[1]

Papworth's sales talk can be taken lightly but he wrote in the golden age of the lodge when three separate architectural idioms — the neo-classical, the Gothic and the *Cottage Orné* — divided the aristocratic fancy, and he does stress one role of the park gate lodge which can easily be forgotten in their present eclipse. Humphry Repton had made just the same point in his *Observations* of 1803.[2] Lodges were not merely garden structures, they were designed as entrances, garden buildings on the perimeter to lure respectable visitors to view similar pleasures within. As key note elements to park and house they were a serious subject of architectural design, and to their individual qualities and variety must be added their sheer numerical weight.

There were about fifty old style counties in England and Wales. At a considered guess each of these averaged one hundred parks apiece, Herefordshire alone has almost one hundred and fifty; and each park has, on average, two lodges. Most of these lodges have survived the lean 1950s and weathered, though not unchanged, the property hungry 1970s. This means that there is a body of at least ten thousand small houses, ambitiously designed, often by famous architects, to reflect in concentrated form, the changing architectural fashions of the last two hundred and fifty years.

The mystery is that no one has yet given this group of buildings anything more than the most cursory attention. Some lodges, like the one at Rendlesham Hall in Suffolk with a flying Gothic crown on its roof, or the Gothic Gates to Ballysaggartmore at Waterford, make a regular appearance in books on follies and grottoes.[3] A few, like Kent's great Worcester Lodge at Bad-

1
Woodbridge Lodge, Rendlesham Hall, Suffolk. A late 18th century Gothick work, more folly than lodge, (Rumsey Collection).

minton, Gloucestershire, are honourably appraised in all the relevant studies. The rest, for complex reasons, pass ignored. Even the new books on park and garden architecture, which appear regularly in bookshops each Christmas, seem deliberately to ignore the lodges which protect the entrances to their subject material.

One reason for this may be psychological. The British delight in their uniquely preserved class structure. Most visitors who pass through park gates do so in a spirit of near reverential preparation for the unashamedly upper class aesthetic experience which they are about to enjoy. Lodges held lower class families who had not even the cachet of being intimate house servants. So they are visually ignored as car or coach drives on to the inner class-sanctum of the great house itself.

There is also a reason why books have been published on subjects such as topiary and ornamental hedges or the details of Edwardian pubs while nothing has appeared to appreciate ten thousand small houses of quality. The subject is a minefield: architectural historians are cautious souls, happy when the attribution of a building to an architect is firmly proven by documentary evidence. Such evidence is rarely available to link an architect to a lodge. As a result many of the attributions in this book have had to be made on stylistic likeness and on judicious use of source books. This inevitably leaves the authors open to some critical attack.

To take an example; the volumes in the invaluable Pevsner series *The Buildings of England* vary in the range of structures they choose to describe. But when the excellent and far from lodge-blind revised volume on the West Riding reaches Wentworth Woodhouse, a park with six lodges, three of them buildings of real distinction, it ignores the lot. Faced with an unusual lodge of great presence — the north lodge pair to Carden Hall, Cheshire — the Cheshire Pevsner did very much better, but came up with no architect and hedged its bets on a date somewhere between the baroque (i.e. 1720) and 1845.

Because this strange pair might be a rare manifestation in Britain of the revolutionary French neo-classical Grand Prix projects of 1770–1790, it was important, where angels feared, for someone to rush in; but where? C.H. Tatham had built altar-type lodges at Trentham Park twenty miles away, John Papworth had worked at Alton Towers twenty seven miles away and, in his pattern book mentioned above, illustrated a lodge with an urn chimney pot very like the urns on the Carden pair. But on the other side of Carden park was a massive neo-classical triumphal arch; and this was Cheshire, a county where Thomas Harrison executed most of his massive neo-classical designs.

There the matter had to rest, masterpieces without a master and nationally such instances proliferate. Perhaps when this book appears a reader will come up with information from family papers to prove that an entirely unexpected architect was responsible. If this book even begins to flush out such information and to stir a general interest in a neglected form, it will have served a purpose. This can only be an initial survey of a wide subject which needs ultimately to be covered by a gazetteer. The major relisting scheme of the Department of the Environment, currently taking place, will hopefully unearth many more lodges, but meanwhile the travelling involved to list buildings which most architectural studies have ignored is enormous and explains the serious omission of Scottish lodges from this book. They will provide a publication in themselves, but there will be room in the future for more than one study on separate stylistic or regional divisions of lodge building. In particular an explanation is needed for the concentration of fine lodges of several periods in limited areas such as north Somerset, Cheshire and the North Riding, or for the meagre sprinkling of lodges in Lincolnshire. Was lodge building a competitive sport?

Another justification for this study is the vulnerability of gate lodges. If they stand near major roads, any scheme of road widening puts them at risk. If they survive this then the din and vibration of traffic a few feet away makes many of them undesirable as homes and, though protected by legislation as listed buildings, they moulder empty and the hedgerow bushes invade them. Other lodges of great architectural distinction which would be

2
The 1820 main lodge to Onslow Hall near Shrewsbury. An instance of the vulnerability of a lodge even when protected by listed status.

coveted homes if they were in urban areas have been allowed to fall roofless because they have neither gas, electricity nor even water supply. Yet such excuses do not always serve. The confident triumphal arch lodge of 1815 by Benjamin Gummow to Brogyntyn outside Oswestry, Shropshire is empty and abandoned to strangling ivy. But it stands directly across the road from a 'high class' residential estate to which it is a visual asset. Two characterful single unit studios could easily, and it would be supposed profitably, be devised within its walls. Meanwhile the ivy grows over this and over the once sturdily elegant Doric lodge which Edward Haycock designed in 1820 as a main entrance to nearby Onslow Hall. This building is listed and a valuable reminder of the character of its demolished parent house. It faces north-south with sylvan views through every window but now only the capitals of its columns show above the encroaching elder.

It will seem churlish after such complaints about the lodge degenerate to find faults with the lodge regenerate, where architects have been found and money spent to convert a lodge, which was initially constructed to house a retiring pair of old servitors, into a gracious home suitable for modern needs. There are, however, inevitable losses when a lodge has been brought swinging back into the modern system.

The Gothick cubes at the entrance to Blithfield Hall, Staffordshire, are an example of a thoughtful and sensitive conversion. John Buckler's neat original boxes have had witty echoes of their original proportions set up beside them to double the living accommodation and the links between old and new are imaginative and elegant. And yet. First there were two, now there are four. The original staccato statements whose essence was isolation and simplicity now make polite jokes about themselves. Similarly it was nationally important to save Sir John Soane's experimental design in the Pellwall Lodge outside Market Drayton. Those who restored it are to be

3
One of the two south lodges to Blithfield Hall, Staffordshire, with its modern extension.

sincerely thanked, but its conversion into part of a much larger house has necessarily added a complex of moderate architecture to a quite immoderate concentration of brilliant introspective form. In a country where the single population is rising there should be a place for lodges which have quite simply been restored to their first exterior state and modernised only within.

Perhaps, since very few lodges have been built since 1939, there is something to be said for their still being part of a continuous architectural process. It is 'certainly satisfying that both the examples just quoted of the lodge regenerate show that the highly individual tradition of intense and allusive design of the park gate lodge is not dead.

The precise though cumbersome term 'park gate lodge' has been chosen to define the deliberately lower class limits of this study. The simple, single word 'lodge' is a shifting and uneasy noun with a long etymological history of serving to denominate the housing of both the upper and lower classes. It has at least fourteen different definitions in any large dictionary, some rare, some obsolete, some dubious. In its original Teutonic root it probably meant a 'shelter of foliage' and though it has travelled far since then, it has always kept a hint of the leafy and rustic about it. The particular sense of the word which is the concern of this study is that of a house, cottage or pavilion set at a park gate entrance providing living quarters for the family which had the duty of opening and shutting that gate. This is the very latest sense which the word has acquired, and it did not appear as such in a literary context until Charlotte Smith used it in *The Young Philosopher* in 1798, with Jane Austen following quickly after in 1799, though *Northanger Abbey*, its context, was not published until 1816.

The lodge had taken on its more lordly sense of hunting accommodation in a forest or other wild place much earlier, but even there the word had a dual and ill-defined meaning. It occurs in this context as early as the Paston letters of 1485, and in Malory's *Morte d'Arthur* (1485–90). In these it tended

x

to signify a substantial building used temporarily for pleasure by an aristocratic owner. But in those pinched times a house in a forest or warren was unlikely to stand empty for a long part of the year and most such lodges of brief resort were also permanently inhabited by the family of a forest ranger or warrener. The further back it is pursued, the more elusively imprecise a 'lodge's' usage. In 1386 Chaucer's cockerel, Chaunteclere, was keeping accurate time 'crowyng in his logge'. But at the same time the term was being used for the house of a master of a Cambridge college, and more humbly in castles and the colleges of both Cambridge and Oxford for that part of the building where the porter had his rooms. Yet in *Ywaine and Gawaine* of 1400 the primitive usage of a leafy arbour still survives: 'A loge of bowes sone he made'. Leap forward two hundred years to the Authorised Version of 1611 and in Isaiah (I, viii), the Daughter of Zion 'is left as a cottage in a vineyard' which sounds clear enough but also 'as a lodge in a garden of cucumbers', so the precise implication is elusive.

In Sir Philip Sidney's *Arcadia,* written only three decades earlier, a passage tells how Basilius, Prince of Arcadia, safely returned from Delphos:

> brake up his court, and retired himselfe, his wife, and
> children into a certaine Forrest hereby, which he called
> his desert, wherein (besides a house appointed for stables
> and lodgings for certain persons of mean calling, who do
> all household services) he hath built two fine lodges.

This seems very exact. A quite separate building is appointed for the lower orders; the lodges themselves are for the Prince and his immediate family. But then the social picture blurs again. Basilius, his wife and Philoclea the younger daughter inhabit one lodge 'without having any other creature living in that lodge', so apparently it was an exclusive holiday home. But his other daughter, the Princesse Pamela 'hee hath placed in the other lodge: but how think you accompanied? truly, with none other, but one Dametas, the most arrant doltish clowne that I think was ever without the priviledge of a bable'. This Dametas's wife Miso, and his daughter Mopsa also lived in the second lodge, which sounds as if it was the residence of a forest ranger as so often in fact was the case in England. It is worth noting that Sidney saw nothing unusual in the building of paired lodges.

Sir Thomas Tresham's famous Triangular Lodge at Rushton (1594–7) symbolizes on its exterior the mysteries of the Blessed Trinity and, because it features a fireplace in the topmost of its three rooms, seems designed for viewing and entertainment, yet it is always referred to in the Rushton accounts as 'The Warryner's Lodge'. Therefore it probably combined the three functions of curious park ornament, banquet house and home for a keeper and his family.   PLATE I

The park gate lodge which developed from this complex ancestry at a point to be defined in the early eighteenth century, is a distinct building type. But it is not helpful to describe it as a building type of an established form because, deriving as it did from at least a triple etymology, it could appear as either a separate building, or as identical twin pavilions, or as a gate tower pierced by an arch.

As a building type the park gate lodge may have three forms, but its architectural importance lies in its dualism. It combines a pretentious facade with a humble function. As a sociological conundrum and an aesthetic solution this is of real significance. The gate lodge offers a sequence of some two hundred and fifty years of experimental design, during which professional architects backed by rich patrons essayed the problem of housing a working class family in a small structure of style and distinction. As trumpets of an aristocratic ambience at a distant gate, these lodges are the earliest attempt to attach some of the iconography of an upper class residence to a lower class dwelling.

When the lodge began to evolve in the early eighteenth century the vernacular tradition of cottage building started to fade, and a self-conscious process of design for the detached small house began to take its place. Two separate traditions for housing two widely divided class systems were coming together. The result was that the lodge took on the element of fantasy, essentially an upper class indulgence, and became a testing ground for architectural innovation where utility fought a losing battle with symbolism and display.

It is possible to see the variety of stylistic forms in the middle class suburbs of the nineteenth and early twentieth centuries as stemming, via the builders' pattern books, from earlier experiments in park gate lodges. Certainly both lodge and suburban house often present facades completely irrelevant to the domestic arrangement of the rooms behind. The park gate lodge was an early, prominently sited, demonstration of a small house not as a *machine à habiter* but as a *machine de fantaisie*. The terraced town house of the late seventeenth and eighteenth centuries represents an entirely different building tradition, one of utility, economy and hard sense. Both traditions of how a house should be conceived survive, and recent experience of disastrous urban housing suggests that the lodge tradition — the *machine de fantaisie* — is psychologically a sounder way of housing a family unit behind gables, porches, loggias and decorative devices. This satisfies, at any class or income level, the desire to inhabit a significant image of consequence. Fantasy architecture is in fact functional because it quenches a basic thirst of the human spirit. The park gate lodge is an exploration of this and will be traced as such through all its chimera-like forms. It is the building type with a lion's head upon a goat's body, decorative, authoritative, absurd, and an unusually revealing architectural demonstration of the aesthetic games which a society chooses to play.

PLATE I The Triangular Lodge, Rushton Hall, Northamptonshire (1594-7). An Elizabethan pleasure house, a forerunner of the park gate lodge.

PLATE II The Bottle Lodge at Tixall, Staffordshire. A mysterious structure possibly of early date and pioneering function.

CHAPTER ONE

Antecedents and Origins

Leonard Knyff's book *Britannia Illustrata* was published in 1707 and contains over eighty bird's eye prospects of great English houses with their surrounding gardens, park buildings and deer parks. Though these occasionally include projected buildings as if they had been built, they are almost painfully careful in their detail. Johannes Kip's similar prospect views of the houses and parks of Gloucestershire followed *Britannia Illustrata* in 1712. There is, therefore, a large body of evidence as to the condition of estates and the fashion in gardening which prevailed in the first two decades of the eighteenth century. For park gate lodges this evidence is almost entirely negative. Prospect after prospect shows great avenues of newly planted trees reaching away from the houses into the far, but carefully recorded, distance. Occasionally these terminate in a garden pavilion or piece of ornamental ironwork. They never end in a gate with a gate lodge.

Knyff and Kip were in no way the first delineators of English country seats, but nowhere in the wide range of seventeenth century artists' impressions of these houses and demesnes, with all their twin garden pavilions, pigeon houses and arbours, is there a trace of a gate lodge.[1] If the artists' evidence were not there it would be hard to believe, as gate lodges are such a commonplace, almost an inevitable, feature of surviving parks. But their absence from the paintings and perspectives is supported by the parallel literary void and has to be accepted. Somewhere and at some time after 1712, as a result of new pressures or fashions, they began to appear.

The question which this chapter must answer is this: from what earlier building traditions were they devised — what were their origins and antecedents? Since, as has already been noted, they emerged within a limited period in the three separate forms of a pierced gatehouse tower, twin pavilions or single sentryhouse unit, three individual building traditions have to be considered to establish the source.

One feature which all three gate lodge types have in common is their decorative quality. Whatever its form, the park gate lodge is an occasion for display.

In 1282, while Edward I was still reigning, Henry de Lacy, third Earl of Lincoln, began to build a castle on the hill above the new town of Denbigh which he was settling, on the model of Edward's Caernarvon and Beaumaris, to subdue the native Welsh. In 1294 both castle and town fell briefly to a rebellious Welsh army, but when the castle was retaken, Lacy pressed on with ambitious additions to the castle. These were complete by 1311 so the gatehouse keep, probably the work of the master mason, James of St. George, who had worked at Caernarvon, dates from the earliest years of the

4 The ruined Porter's Lodge Tower at Denbigh Castle (c.1311) was an early instance of the combination of decorative and defensive features.

fourteenth century. It was a very strong three towered design. Two towers stand on each side of the deeply recessed gate, which leads into a narrow courtyard commanded by the third tower. Its strength was predictable because it was added to a castle which had recently fallen to the enemy. What was quite unpredictable was the lavish decorative detail applied to the surface of the gateway and the two fronting towers. The gate stands under an arch of five rich orders; above the arch are three elegant niches, the central one still retaining the headless statue of a seated king. Brown sandstone is inlaid into the grey limestone in a chequered pattern above the gate, and the angles of the towers are quoined in this same sharply contrasted sandstone.

None of this detail could have had any defensive purpose. It could only have been an anticipation of one of the functions of the park gate lodge: a demonstration not simply of the brutal military power at the proprietor's command, but of his aesthetic taste, his delight in pattern and design. The

5
The Porter's Lodge, New College, Oxford, begun in 1380. Religious iconography with a show of defence.

left-hand tower of the frontal pair has always been called the 'Porter's Lodge',. so at Denbigh, before 1311 and in an exclusively secular building, decorative show has become a concomitant of gate guardianship and of a lodge.

The same decorative drive is displayed in a later porter's lodge of the same century, one to a collegiate building of ecclesiastical foundation — William of Wykeham's New College, Oxford. This, begun in 1380, is a single towered gate of only superficial defensive strength. Instead the facade is dedicated to iconographic display. Though the tower is always referred to as the 'Porter's Lodge', its first floor windows actually light the main chamber of the original Warden's lodgings. Dominating the facade on the second floor are three statues in the wiry attenuated style of the period. Wykeham kneels on the right and an angel on the left presents him to the Virgin Mary in the topmost niche. The whole lodge facade is intended to suggest the austere elegance of life-style and the devout religiosity which will be found in the quadrangle beyond the gate. Here the iconographic function of the porter's lodge is established.

The increasing efficiency of siege machinery in the fifteenth century should logically have led to thicker walls and lower towers in defensive gate works. In fact the soaring and ornate gate towers of castles like Oxburgh and Herstmonceaux indicate that the desire of an owner to impress a visitor outweighed his wish to repel an attacking force. The general acceptance of a gate tower as a symbolic structure rather than one erected for defensive utility is shown by those at Queen's College, Cambridge, complete by 1448, and at Jesus College in the same university, built fifty years later. The early Tudor palaces, Greenwich, Richmond, Hampton Court and St. James's continued the tradition and so, inevitably, most of the courtyard houses of the nobility built in the sixteenth century included a high ornamental gatehouse in their design.

At Charlecote, Burton Constable, Littlecote and many other houses of Elizabeth's reign, the towered gatehouses have been designed as free standing structurally, but axially placed in a forecourt and connected by walls to the main buildings. They retain, therefore, their position on a vestigial suggestion of the fourth wall of an enclosed castle courtyard. The real test of the strength of feeling for the retention of a gate tower, in a prestigious seat of the nobility, came with the total rejection of the courtyard plan, when the new Italian palazzo form of compact house was introduced.

Longleat (c. 1572), one of the earliest of such houses, has abandoned the gatehouse completely. At Hardwick Hall, in the conservative north, Elizabeth Cavendish built a crenellated wall around the forecourt and retained an axially centred gate structure, but reduced it from a gatehouse to a gate, with triangular lodges at each side. Since these lodges are of a single storey and offered slight accommodation, they seem to have been designed for a porter rather than for the garden pleasure of the owner.

At Stanway House in Gloucestershire the gatehouse, though still close to the main building, has made its escape from central axial positioning. Built in about 1630 it was contemporary with several Oxford college entrance 'towers of the orders', featuring a similar display of columns, heraldry and mullioned windows. It has always been the main carriage entrance to the house and it afforded ample accommodation for servants who would control its gates.

Stanway was far from being the last gatehouse to be built, but by 1630 the form was beginning to look old fashioned. Twin garden pavilions at the opposed corners of a fronting garden, or a low wall with a central iron gate between ornate gate piers, were becoming the usual setting for the main facade of a house. This suggests that throughout the Stuart period little practical thought was given to the relationship between a carriage and a house. In early illustrations of country houses a carriage is almost always shown to emphasise the status of the owner, but it is usually shown as halted outside the garden forecourt and the decorative gates to the house. In wet weather, and when ladies were involved, this can never have been convenient, and a less dignified approach via a stable yard to the side, with a quick scramble into the house through the kitchen entry, must have been common. It is likely that throughout the seventeenth century carriages remained rare. Hackney coaches did not appear even in London until 1625, the first stage coach appeared in 1640 and the two-wheeled gig came out in 1670. Neither the Post-chaise nor the Landau were developed until the onset of the eighteenth century when, of course, a road system had just begun to be con-

6
The entrance gate with side lodges at Hardwick Hall, Derbyshire (1590-7).

structed on which carriages could be used safely and regularly. Consequently seventeenth century architects and garden designers failed to work out a satisfactory solution to the problem of how to approach a house on four or two wheels while wearing formal clothes. This was essentially a problem of the relationship between a house, its garden and the disposition of its garden buildings. If the early park gate lodge was often not a gatehouse but a garden building banished to an estate perimeter, and since English garden buildings

7
The Gatehouse, Stanway House, Gloucestershire. A non-axial entrance of c.1630.

were various in form and complex in history, some consideration of them is necessary.

Attempts to trace the influence of Italian fashions of garden design in England are inclined to underplay the very strong and persistent native English tradition for scattering the gardens and near environs of a great house with substantial structures of brick and stone. These are variously described as pavilions, banquet houses, garden houses, secret houses or lodges. Many purposes are ascribed to them but it would be fair to say that each must have been used according to the changing tastes of its individual owner. These English garden houses are much closer in form and probably in usage to the pavilions of French chateaux like Anet and Ancy-le-Franc than to the loggias and trellis houses of sixteenth century Italy. Clearly a cold, wet northern climate urged sound roofs, four walls and fireplaces.

If an unkind climate produced solid and lasting garden buildings, it is likely that it was the Italian Renaissance feeling for symmetry which developed them into their twinned forms of double pavilion lodges and banquet houses. Ancy-le-Franc, designed by Serlio himself and one of the earliest of French renaissance chateaux, has twin pavilions in its forecourt. Ancy was built in 1546. At Hampton Court the garden and garden buildings were exactly recorded in about 1555 by Anthonis Van Wyngaerde in a series of drawings.[2] At this date it seems to have had no twin pavilions. What it did have, connected to other buildings by a series of raised walks and walls, was a turreted, two storeyed banquet house and the Great Round Arbour, set on a mount, three storeys high, of glass and stone with a fantastic onion dome of lead. In addition there was the complex structure of the Water Gate, almost a great house in itself, and several outlying towers and wall turrets. There is little evidence of symmetry in the gardens, certainly no twin pavilions and, indeed, Hampton Court itself paid slender regard to symmetry, relying for its aesthetic impact upon a battery of towers with a domed and pinnacled roofline.

The Tudors who succeeded Henry VIII set no fashions in building and garden design and the lead given by the aristocracy under Elizabeth was generally conservative, producing the towered fantasies of Wollaton and Hardwick, or the spreading courtyard houses of Audley End and Theobalds. Wollaton did have pavilions axially placed on all its four garden walls and Robert Smythson's plan of Wollaton, which shows buildings now lost, suggests that they may have had the appearance of linked twin pavilions.[3] But banquet houses set in the centre of a formal garden, as at Thomas Cecil's Wimbledon and William Cecil's Theobalds, were usual. The Great Round Arbour at Hampton Court was a fantasy in late Perpendicular Gothic, but at Theobalds, complete by 1585, the summer house was a two storeyed exedra with twelve marble busts of Roman emperors set in the lower storey and a bath house in the floor above.

Sydney's *Arcadia,* previously quoted, makes it clear that each of Basilius's twin lodges were structures capable of housing a noble family in modest comfort while they enjoyed a rest from the formalities of state. Spenser wrote the *Faerie Queene* in the middle 1580s and gives at the end of Book 2 an impression of the usages of contemporary garden buildings. Sir Guyon, representing Protestant Temperance, entered the Bower of Bliss where the enchantress Acrasia held a young knight 'in lewd loves and wastful luxury'. Outraged by this sexual indulgence, Guyon smashed down the 'pleasant bowres and Pallace brave' and:

> Their groves he feld, their gardins did deface
> Their arbers spoyle, their Cabinets suppresse,
> Their banket houses burne, their buildings race,
> And of the fairest late, now made the fowlest place.[4]

Bowers, arbours, cabinets and banquet houses are by this penultimate decade of the sixteenth century the expected furnishing of a great pleasure garden, and there was more than one banquet house in the Bower of Bliss. Puritan suspicion may be responsible for the association of all these buildings with 'lewd loves' in Spenser, but it is interesting that Shakespeare in *Measure for Measure* has his sexual villain Angelo arrange to meet Isabella, the novice nun after whom he lusts, in a 'garden house' at night. There his sexual malpractices could be expected to pass unremarked. In an earlier play, Kyd's *The Spanish Tragedy*, Don Andrea met his lover Belimperia at night in a garden arbour for 'delight and mirthful dalliance' and was hung in the same arbour when Belimperia's brother discovered them.

The drive for privacy seems, more than any other force, to be behind the extraordinary proliferation of these garden buildings in the late sixteenth and early seventeenth centuries. A 'banket' house may originally have been a slight pavilion where sweet wines and spiced cakes were consumed as dessert while the high table was being cleared,[5] but a two storeyed building with a tower and wide bow windows is likely to have been used for all the courses of a private meal. The castle of the earlier Middle Ages may have lacked elegant form, but a battery of towers strung out along a circuit of walls must have been far more adaptable to separate living units with individual privacy than a large house like Hampton Court or Hatfield. The practice of building hunting lodges was of old standing, but the spate of garden house building in the sixteenth and seventeenth centuries must have begun as a direct response to the claustrophobia induced by a large uncorridored house teeming with retainers. Queen Elizabeth gave no architectural leads, but she was the first English monarch regularly to dine in a private room with a few chosen guests, and this must have stimulated the aristocracy to copy her practice. As houses of compact ground plan became usual, at a period when a lord still felt obliged to support his rank with an inordinate number of servants, the pressure to build pavilions for escape and privacy must have grown.

The architectural range of the pavilions was as wide as their usage must have been. At Crewe Hall in Cheshire there were substantial two storeyed houses, identical in every detail, each set at the extreme corner of the forecourt and quite separate from the columned central gateway.[6] Both overlooked formal gardens on their side elevations and seem, therefore, likely to have been used directly by the family of Sir Randulphe Crewe who built them. It was the close relationship of twin pavilions to a gate which would dictate their usage as porter's lodges; separated from a gate as at Crewe, they would be used as pleasure pavilions like the well known pair at Montacute, Somerset.

Though the great house which Sir Baptist Hicks built for himself at Chipping Campden in about 1613 has gone, its garden buildings survive

8
One of a pair of banquet houses to the vanished Campden House, Gloucestershire.

almost in their entirety, stranded forlornly in a modern orchard. The two banquet houses must be the closest surviving approximation to the kind of twin lodges which Sir Philip Sidney was describing in *Arcadia*. They face each other two hundred yards apart across what was once the south terrace of the house; identical minor masterpieces of form compressed into a relatively small compass. To the terrace they presented their principal rooms in a single storey facade topped with strapwork; but a steeply sloping site gives them, to the side and rear, three storeys of flat headed windows with round arched tracery, the decorative emphasis falling upon four twisted chimney stacks and the gabled roofline. Their nomenclature and usage has not survived. One might well have been a banquet house with entertainment rooms, even a kitchen, but would Sir Baptist have needed two banquet houses of such elaboration? Either could have housed a dowager or young married couple handsomely. The most interesting of these Campden House buildings are the twin gate lodges which led into the northern forecourt of the house.

One of these two storeyed lodges, the right hand one on entering, actually stood at an angle of the forecourt, like an ogee domed pavilion of a conventional twin set.[7] The other, linked to it by a wall of two fanciful gables and the gate arch, had no direct relationship to the house. Though less ornate than the two garden houses on the terrace, they are elegantly styled with finials to their domes and sharp cornicing. Both have every appearance of being designed to house a family. They have windows commanding both the road and the interior forecourt. If they cannot confidently be set down as the earliest park gate lodges, because of their nearness to the main house and because the deer park was on the other side of the complex, then they

9
The gate lodges of *c*.1613 to Campden House, Gloucestershire.

certainly approach very closely to the evolving building type. Their design also puts them exactly halfway between the gate tower proper and the twin pavilions, an illustration of the dual origins of such lodges.

As usual the exact date of the lodges is not known. The parent house was begun in about 1613 so they could easily be twenty years later and therefore mid-Caroline. There is every suggestion that at that time the independently sited park gate lodge was about to emerge as an established building type. What in fact happened after the trauma of the Civil War and the Restoration was the triumph of the gate pier and a virtual postponement of the evolution of the gate lodge for the next fifty years.

The change in architectural forms between 1640 and the 1660s was almost as absolute as the revolution in literary forms. The regular symmetry of the heroic couplet became the standard poetic metre as an English approximation to the admired alexandrine of France. In a parallel development, facades of an orderly subdued classicism were devised by Sir Roger Pratt and Hugh May as English versions of Dutch domestic while Sir Christopher Wren translated French baroque into an acceptable English manner.

The most immediate victim of this new feeling for foreign architectural restraint was the romantic clutter of pavilions and towers which had survived around great English houses, preserved by insular conservatism. Now

France was to be the paymaster of the English monarchy for the next eighteen years and Holland was to be integrally linked to England for the following fourteen. In both countries it was usual to demarcate the areas of garden and forecourt surrounding a house by gates, steps, ironwork and by piers without the gates. The actual gardens themselves had evolved rather than undergone a process of revolution. Much is written about the impact of foreign garden fashions upon English work over the two centuries from 1500 to 1700. In fact, however, the ideal garden created at Nottingham by the French prisoner of war, Marshal Tallard, and which featured in *The Retir'd Gard'ner,* a two volume work by London and Wise published in 1706, was no different in its essentials to Henry VIII's gardens at Hampton Court.[8] Tallard's garden comprised a garden house, a fountain and raised walks and a terrace from which to view parterres of elaborate patterns in cut turf. Only the Tudor heraldic beasts on poles were missing.

The essence of the English garden over this long period was that it was unnatural: an area near to a house where Nature was overwrought and subdued by pattern and design. What was constantly evolving and what, by the time of the later Stuarts, had made gardening a popular and expensive cult, was the range of flowers, fruit and vegetables which was becoming available, native to India, China, Africa and America. Sir Thomas Hanmer's *Garden Book* of 1659 and John Rea's *Flora Ceres and Pomona ..... or a complete Florilege* of 1665 illustrate the wide range of plants and trees which could be grown and the scientific sophistication which was being applied to their cultivation.

This had a twofold effect upon gardens. The garden buildings, temporarily banished from the forecourt, now proliferated as places for the enjoyment of the new flowers and fruit and as buildings for the care of the rarer species. There was also a move to lighten the divisions between the various sections

10
A Carolean instance of the late 17th century Franco-Dutch fashion for gatepiers at Hamstead Marshall, Berkshire.

10

of a garden so that fruiting trees, flower beds and vegetable plots could all be seen as interesting in themselves and organically related. This meant that the great formal gardens of the 'Dutch' type rarely hid away their productive sections as did the supposedly natural 'English' park typical of the next century. Canons, the Middlesex seat of the first Duke of Chandos, was one of the last and most elaborate of the old style formal gardens, and there even the beehives were made of glass for the clearest display. Macky's account of it, published in 1722, summed up the impression of the place:

> the greater pleasure of all is that the divisions of the whole are only made by ballustrades of iron and not by walls; you see the whole at once be you in what part of the garden or parterre you will.[9]

Canons has gone, but a similar vast formal garden at Hamstead Marshall, Berkshire, by Lord Craven in the 1660s, has left eight sets of gate piers carved with a riot of urns, swags and stone garlands. A Kip view of the layout shows how authoritatively they once stood in a complex yet open system of parterres, orchards and kitchen gardens.[10] An even more Roman and magnificent pair once stood in the forecourt of Sir Roger Pratt's archetypal house of the new restraint — Coleshill in Berkshire. These now guard a gate at a roadside verge in the village, evoking what was lost when the house was pulled down in 1952.

Although there appears to have been a rage at this time for piers and gates without pavilions, generalisations about English architecture in any particular period have to be made warily. The second Earl of Peterborough, a militant and conservative peer gave his seat, Drayton House, Northamptonshire, a sturdy gatehouse and a high defensive wall across the open side of its forecourt in 1676.[11] But the most prodigious exception to the new classical horizontality must be Westwood Park, Worcestershire. Here the vertical reasserted itself and the pavilion tower and spired gatehouse were revived on a scale that was not to be equalled again until the great neo-medieval castles of the Regency. A tall, narrow hunting lodge had been built there in 1598 by Sir John Packington. Between 1660 and 1670, when the generality were accepting the rules of Pratt and Wren, a second Sir John, a grandson, made the fantastic additions. To the four corners of the old lodge he added high diagonal wings topped with four steep pyramidal roofed pavilions. In the forecourt he built a gatehouse of two lodges linked by a strapwork arch supporting a cupola. Finally, he set four pavilion towers, all with steep pyramidal roofs, at the points of the star-shaped garden. In all but connecting curtain walls Westwood had the profile of a large medieval castle with a great central keep, the whole tricked out in Artisan Mannerist style of gables and canted bay windows. A fair appraisal would define it as a seventeenth century anticipation of revived medieval forms, but it was built against the tide of fashion and serves only to prove that at least two prototypes of the park gate lodge, the pavilion tower and the twin gate tower, were not forgotten forms in the time of the triumphant gate piers.

11
The forecourt piers of Coleshill House, Berkshire (c. 1660), now removed to a roadside site.

Westwood has survived with some of its towers intact to be a timely warning against generalisations on architectural fashions. A study of two of the many surviving perspective views of country estates made in the first decades of the new century, the period immediately before the park gate lodge emerged to become a standard feature of such estates, will serve to emphasise the potent contradictions of style all working together at this time. Shipton Moyne, the seat of an obscure Gloucestershire Esquire, Walter Estcourt, must have been typical of hundreds of ordinary middling country seats: a rather dismal house of Tudor Cotswold type with a small interior courtyard and a forecourt. All the decorative emphasis of the layout centred on a two towered Jacobean gatehouse standing alone and giving axial access to the main forecourt. Outside this gatehouse, on the same axial line, a small classical gateway with urns, of perhaps 1670, led directly from a rutted public lane into the outer stable court.

The whole feeling of Shipton Moyne, as captured by Kip for Robert Atkyns's *Gloucestershire* (1712), is of an estate ready for change. Three areas, the forecourt with its gatehouse and raised terrace, the four-square garden to the right of the terrace and another similar area to the left of the house, must all have once been laid out with elaborate parterres. All three are now plain grass or have overgrown fruit trees, but no less than five areas of kitchen

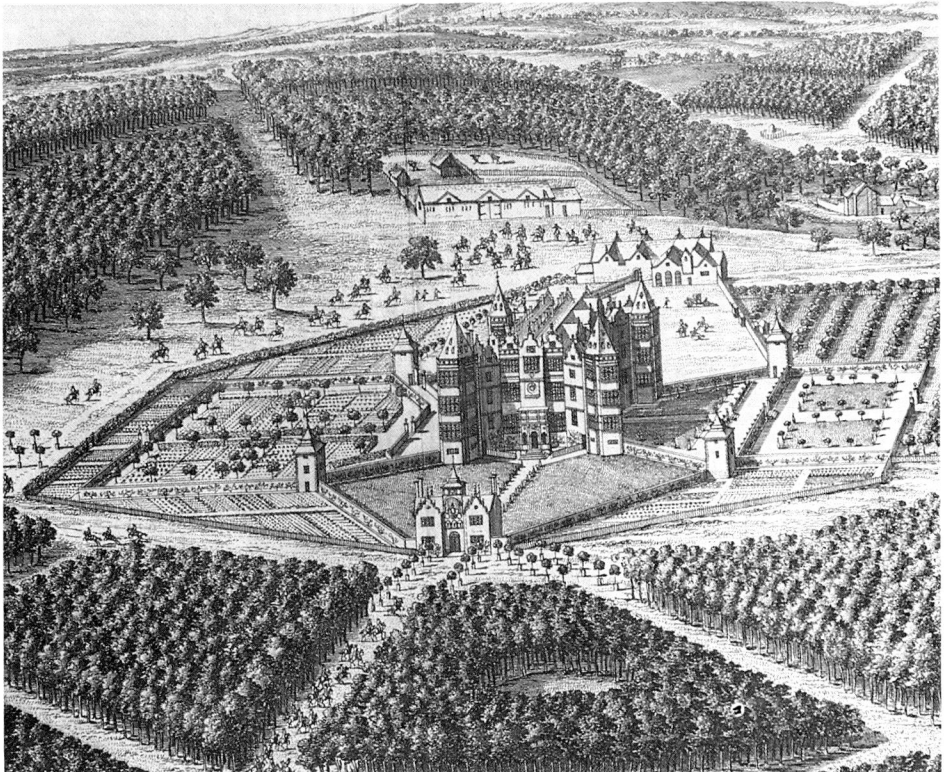

12
Knyff's engraving (1707) of Sir John Packington's seat, Westwood Park, Worcestershire, showing the additions of 1660–70.

garden are still in full production. Walter Estcourt or his wife has wearied of the expense and trouble of flower beds. The formal style has destroyed itself by its sheer complexity. In the park beyond the house several formal avenues

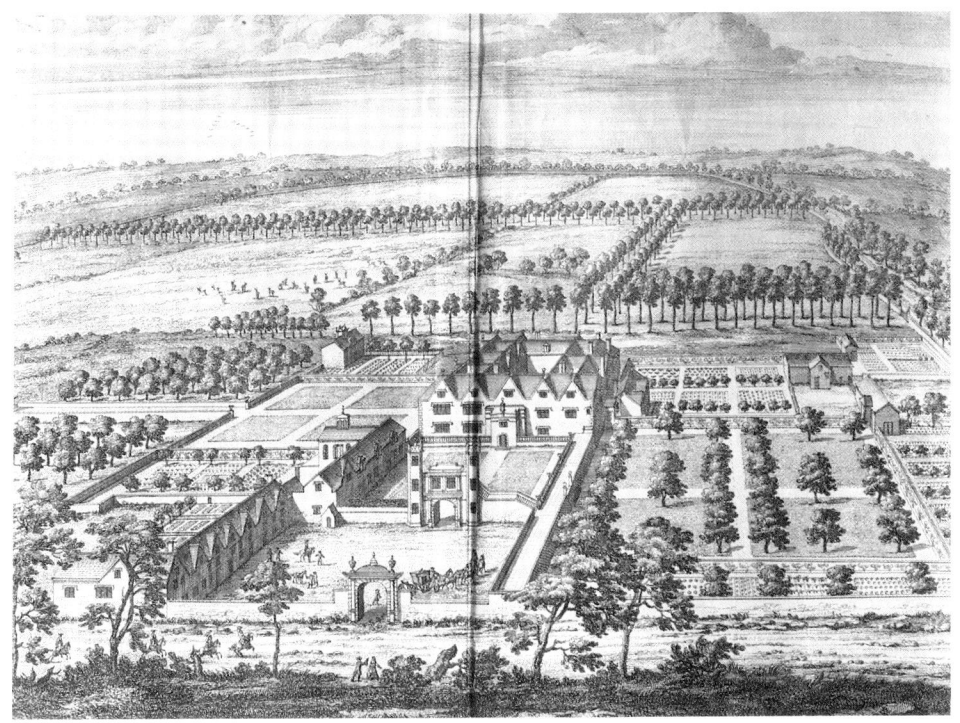

13
Kip's engraving of Shipton Moyne from Sir Robert Atkyns's *Gloucestershire* (1712)

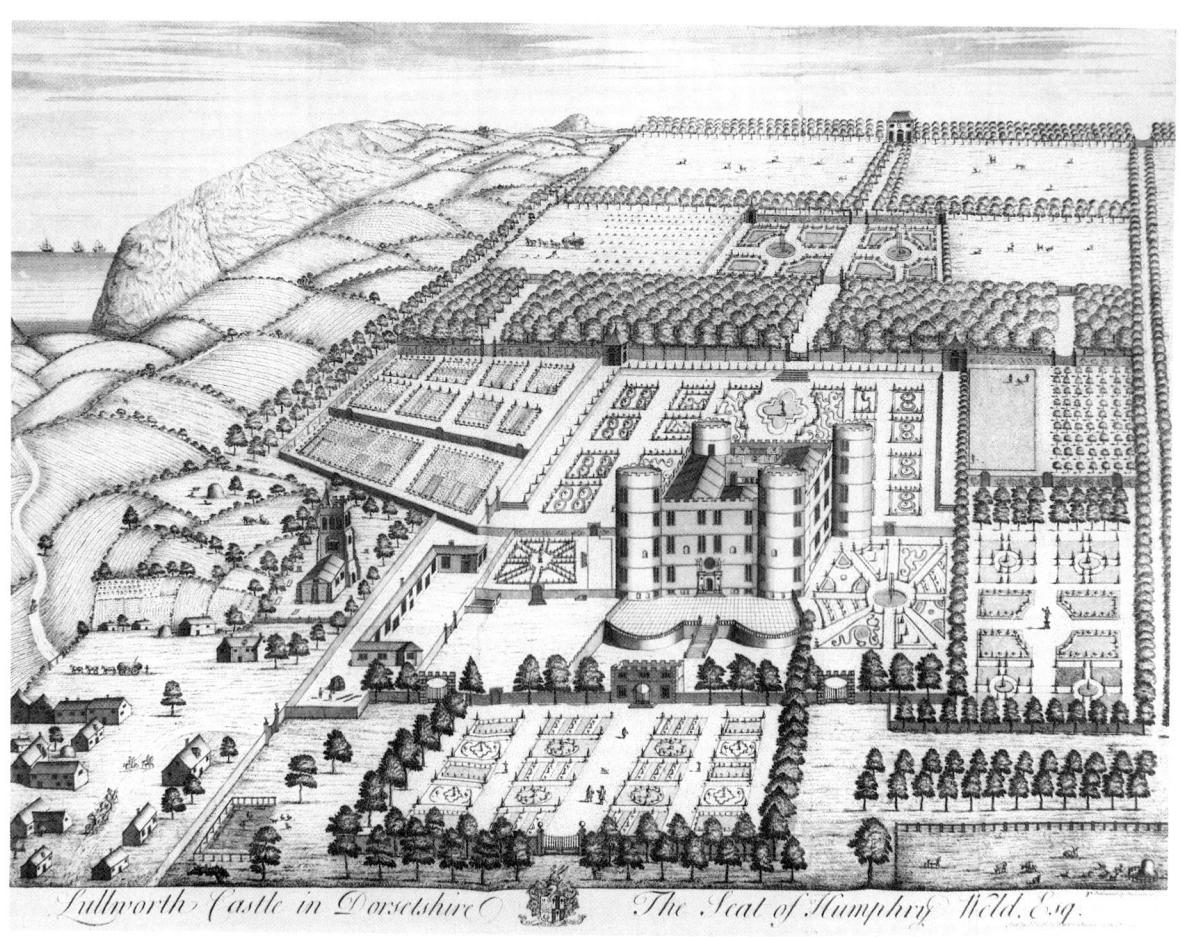

14
Lulworth Castle, Dorset. An engraving of 1721 by Mrs. Weld showing a formal garden layout in the period just before the emergence of the gate lodge as a building type. (By kind permission of John Harris).

planted in the Dutch fashion have now reached a reasonable stage of growth and assert the extent of a park area which is enclosed with palings, walls and a belt of trees. But the avenues by their very maturity stress their futility: one leads to a small gate in a wall, the others lead nowhere; their rigidity serves no purpose. The park is a wide expanse of nothing and the only access to the house, emphasised by one of Kip's standard coach-and-six, is directly from the public lane. The garden is dying, the park lies fallow of ideas waiting for use, its avenues mere symbolic devices to lead the eye outward.

The Lulworth Castle view was executed by Mrs Humphrey Weld of the resident family in 1721, and illustrates a different version of the same situation. At Shipton Moyne the park was an empty frame, at Lulworth the garden is so vast that it subsumes the park and it is pregnant with lodge type buildings. It has not produced a true park gate lodge only because it was not a true park. Shipton Moyne favoured the gatehouse; Lulworth has examples of all three progenitors of the park gate lodge: gatehouses, twin pavilions and isolated garden houses. Immediately below the terrace of the castle is an axial gatehouse, battlemented and pierced by a round arch too small for carriages. On each side of it are lesser battlemented arches. The garden to the rear of the castle has twin pavilions at its further corners — neat two storey affairs with pyramidal roofs. Then beyond a plantation is a second formal garden with two similar but single storey pavilions. Finally, at the end of the long central axis and set at the limit of the park, is a substantial three bay garden house with oval windows in its upper rooms.

The garden-park itself is very clearly demarcated by double rows of trees. The garden house stands at the end of a long avenue. Everything is there, except a park gate lodge at the end of a drive. Kip and Knyff usually make it easy to trace the carriage approach to the houses which they draw. Mrs Weld was less helpful. The stables to the left seem without access to the outside world. A carriage is unlikely to have careered through the formal garden to the east up to the battlemented gatehouse. The only apparent route would have led via the left hand battlemented gate to the stables.

What this view does firmly suggest is the need for a drive which will display the vast gardens to visitors, yet this does not seem to have been considered, hence there is no park gate lodge. The significant fact about this engraved view of Lulworth is that the gatehouse to the entrance front of the castle was pulled down in 1808, given a wider arch, and re-erected as a true park gate lodge on the Wareham road — a perfect demonstration of the move from a gatehouse type garden building to park gate lodge. But the twin pavilions to the rear and the garden house further out on the long axis could have served equally well, though they would not have supplied the approaching visitor with the appropriate castle air. Another striking thing about the Lulworth view is its formality. Everything is geometrically laid out in rectangles and squares. In a sense there is no park, only a huge garden of the Dutch fashion, with parterres and straight gated ways extending almost to infinity in the north. This formality must be the key to the absence of gate lodges. A new philosophy of nature and a new aesthetic would be needed before the park gate lodge could become a park essential. Even before Mrs Weld had limned her impressive but dated demesne in 1721, that new philosophy had been declared and Shaftesbury, the prophet of the new aesthetic, was already writing.

CHAPTER TWO

'Procul O Procul Este Profani'[1]

Writing in 1834, Talleyrand's niece, the Duchess de Dino, made an interesting and pertinent comment on the sites and surroundings of English country houses:

> English people, however, hate to be seen, and, to secure privacy, are quite willing to dispense with an extended view. It is rare that a great house in England has any prospect but that of its immediate surroundings, and you need not hope to amuse yourself by watching the movements of the passers by, the travellers, the peasants working in the fields, the villages or the surrounding country. Green lawns, the flowers round about the house, and splendid trees which block all the vistas — these are what they love and what you find almost everywhere.[2]

Her complaint was, of course, a generalisation and many exceptions to her rule, such as Aynho, Petworth or Badminton could be quoted against her. She was staying at Woburn Abbey, a reclusive house from whose stolid facades even the public road which cuts across the park is barely visible, but the general truth of her strictures is undeniable.

A large number, probably the greater part, of the houses of the English landed gentry stand on old sites, next door to the local church and half surrounded by village homes. On the majority of Kip and Knyff views a coach is shown turning almost directly off a public highway into the forecourt of the house. By the time the Duchess wrote, most of these direct approaches would have been reduced to a lowly entrance for tradespeople to the kitchen and stable area if, that is, the public road had survived a private Act of Parliament or if the village itself had not been removed bodily. The main approach to the house would probably have been resited perhaps half a mile down the road, and the drive from this new entry would have been contrived in a generous sweep to afford prospects of the park and an impressive view of the finest facade of the house. Petworth and Badminton stand as close to their villages as Versailles to its town, but both houses turn only their ragged backsides to their neighbours and reserve their impressive architecture to face the empty vistas of their parks.

Between 1710 and 1834 there had been a change in the aristocratic self concept. Where it was once natural to use the architecture of a residence to

PLATE III John Vanbrugh's Pyramid Gate to Castle Howard, North Riding (1719).

PLATE IV (a)
A section and side pier of the White Gates to Leeswood Hall, Flintshire (c. 1726).

PLATE IV (b)
A lodge at the Black Gates to Leeswood Hall. Both have been moved from their original sites.

overawe and impress, a habit of retirement and even understatement had become usual. The reasons for this shift in mood must be complex: political, sociological, philosophical and aesthetic, and only theories can be put forward to explain it. But one point can be made with some confidence. This is the period when the park gate lodge became established as a standard park feature. The lodge seems, therefore, likely to have developed as a substitute for the hidden house which it guarded, a statement of minor magnificence: if the servants are housed thus, what must be the condition of their unseen master?

Woburn is a perfect instance of this representation by proxy. The Abbey itself, before it became a twentieth century leisure centre, was wholly

15
Henry Holland's triumphal arch lodge to Woburn Abbey, Bedfordshire.

retiring. But no traveller on the A5 from London to Holyhead could fail to notice Henry Holland's triumphal arch of armorial pomp, trumpeting the power of the Dukes of Bedford from the centre of an enormous arc of blank greystone wall. Characteristically the show was all outward. Behind the triumphal arch is a lodge, but only one small spy window reveals that function to the road. To anyone leaving Woburn by that drive, however, the whole, very ordinary, Regency cottage is frankly displayed cowering behind arch and wall. The park gate lodge can be socially aggressive in function as well as defensive.

The whole idea of a park is paradoxical. It is an irony, which Jonathan Swift will have lived just long enough to enjoy, that in the name of Nature, not only were huge areas of English farmland tricked out to look like stage sets for one of Buononcini's operas, but that when they had been so devised, they were surrounded with barriers set with elegant sentry boxes to exclude the less 'natural' world outside. It is usual to blame the third Earl of Shaftesbury for the philosophical concept behind this. By identifying 'Nature' with 'Beauty' and 'Beauty' with 'Moral Good', he imposed upon the wealthy classes the pleasant duty of being aesthetic and living their lives in some symbolic association with natural scenery. Alexander Pope was the proselytizing prophet for this happily self-indulgent world view. His rhyming aphorisms made Shaftesbury's concepts easy to memorise and his ingenious suburban garden at Twickenham was a demonstration of how easily and economically an impression of concentrated 'Nature' could be devised without including anything immoderately wild. This was achieved by banishing 'unnatural' features like kitchen gardens, vineyards and stoves to a hidden corner, cutting out costly flower beds and arranging trees and bushes with casual artistry.

With the credentials of his garden and the fame of his verse Pope was then able to spend his last thirty or so years advising aristocratic friends like Bathurst, Cobham, Burlington, Leicester and Digby, with such gardeners as Bridgeman and Kent, on the planning of their infinitely expanded versions of his garden in their new parks. The importance of the actual form of Pope's Twickenham pleasance can be over-stressed. Provided that a hospitable lord was at work, Pope was ready to praise any venture where trees were the staple. Allen Bathurst's great planting at Cirencester was all in straight rides with hardly a natural curve in its layout. But it included park buildings where Pope could compose, take tea and give orders to other men's servants and the general impression was 'natural' so Pope was all enthusiasm.

The sudden concentration of writing on this theme of Nature: Shaftesbury's *Characteristicks of Men* (1711) and *The Beautiful* (1712), Addison's essays on the estate as a garden in the *Spectator* of 1712 and Pope's own 'Essay on Gardens' in *The Guardian* of September 1713, suggest that a mood was being expressed rather than a need created. Shaftesbury could apostrophise:

> 'O glorious Nature supremely fair and sovereignly good!
> all-loving and all-lovely, all divine! ... O mighty
> Nature! wise substitute of Providence'

because he had Newton's word for it that the 'Natural Order' was indeed order and was benign.[3] The extraordinary prestige of Milton's *Paradise Lost* in Protestant England lay solidly behind the park concept. Book Four established in overwhelming poetry that Paradise was not primarily a flower garden but a park of trees:

> whose hairy sides
> With thicket overgrown, grotesque and wild
> Access denied ...
> Shade above shade, a woody theatre
> Of stateliest view

and a park moreover that was walled, gated and guarded not by gamekeepers but by the Cherubim themselves. As Gabriel told Uriel:

> in at this gate none pass
> The vigilance here placed, but such as come
> Well known from Heaven

which was a perfect celestial precedent for aristocratic exclusiveness.[4]

It is not easy to decide whether this movement towards an Arcadian detachment from the normal life of the countryside was a Whig as opposed to a Tory projection. Shaftesbury was a Whig, Pope was a Tory; neither built lodges. Lord Bathurst, in whose vast park Pope wrote much of his translation of the Odyssey, was an arch Tory, even a committed Jacobite. Though his descendants have allowed a yew hedge to shield from their windows a view of one of the loveliest small towns in Europe, Bathurst deliberately rebuilt his house just off one of the main streets of Cirencester. Thus he affected that genial squire-like relationship which is often seen as typically Tory. Bathurst's great avenues through Oakley Wood seem to cry out for lodges to terminate them, but they are open-ended; his designs centre around a column to Queen Anne, the last Stuart, placed at the visual limit of the vistas from the house.

As against these signs of Toryism, Bathurst designed and built Palladian garden pavilions to house his Tory poet when the Palladian had become accepted after 1730 as the Whig party house-style.

A scattering of small Palladian buildings around grottoes and serpentine lakes seems, by its tightly knit Elysian quality, to demand protection from the humdrum world outside and might, therefore, have bred the first park gate lodges of Palladian correctness to guard its entrances in style. Yet neither Burlington's Chiswick, designed between 1715 and 1738, nor Kent's Rousham (1738–41), though both alive with Palladian ornament, sport a single contemporary lodge.[5] Sir John Summerson has estimated that 148 great houses were built or rebuilt between 1710 and 1740 and by their enjoyment of the spoils of office, an overwhelming number of these must have been built, usually with some Palladian reference, for Whigs.[6] Mathematically, rather than by innovative intention, the first park gate lodges are more likely to have guarded Whig than Tory gates, simply because they appeared in these years. In fact, the idea of two separate aristocracies existing side by side, divided by politics, life-style and aesthetic preferences is simplistic. The cultural concept of Augustanism was flattering and unifying to both parties; Pope and Swift, both Tories, were as much at home in Whig Lord Burlington's Chiswick as they were in Tory Lord Bathurst's Cirencester. The park gate lodge, it must be stressed, grew organically from the cultural pattern of the upper classes of the whole country.

Since a small house to serve a gate upon a settled carriage route into the grounds of a larger house is functionally sensible, the hunt for the earliest park gate lodge is not an easy one. Such small houses are rarely datable by records or estate maps. Large houses full of careless servants burn easily and

16
One of the main entrance lodges to Sutton Place, Surrey. A composite structure evolved over a long period.

PLATE II

often. So somewhere, in perhaps the Yorkshire wolds, in deepest Herefordshire or in a built-up suburban area of London, a gate lodge of the seventeenth or even the sixteenth century may still survive, its function forgotten and its great house levelled a century ago.

The Bottle Lodge, a diminutive stone turret, ogee domed in exactly the same style as the great Gatehouse to Tixall Hall, Staffordshire, stands improbably at the roadside a quarter of a mile from the Gatehouse. It may be as old as the Gatehouse which was built in 1575 by Sir Walter Aston, but its thin detail hints that it could just as easily be an early nineteenth century pastiche to guard a lost transriverine driveway from neighbouring Shugborough.

Two much altered and enlarged lodges on the A3 outside Guildford in Surrey could have started life even earlier, in or around 1525, as brick pavilions to the main drive from Sutton Place. Their Gothick detail is of a dateless crudity, but 1782, when a Gothick scheme was projected for Sutton Place by John Webbe, is a likelier though less satisfying date for them.[7]

Far more likely candidates as the earliest gate lodges are also in Surrey: a set of substantial brick cottages with shaped gables. They stand either side of the original main south driveway to Ham House from Ham Common. Stylistically they could easily date from 1610 when Sir Thomas Vavasour built the house. Essentially they are Jacobean garden buildings which have been adapted to serve as lodges.

Undoubtedly there are other early gate lodges to be discovered but they

17
One of the earliest of gate lodges at the Ham Common approach to Ham House, Surrey (1610).

are only likely to be found where the parent house originally stood within a utilitarian enclosed deer park. The true park gate lodge needs a pleasure park to which it can stand sentinel. There was, however, no logical reason why lodges should not have evolved before the period of Palladian-style elysiums. In the last years of the seventeenth century, notably while William of Orange was on the throne from 1688 to 1702, formal gardens of vast extent like that at Lulworth were planted, rivalling in size many of the later more informal parks.

A formal garden had far more material liable to theft and vandalism — bulbs, young specimen trees, statues and wrought ironwork — than had a Palladian park. So it is interesting to learn from J. Macky's *A Journey through England* published in 1722, that at Canons, the glittering show house of James Brydges in Middlesex, Brydges had:

> at the end of each of his chief avenues ... neat lodgings for eight old sergeants of the Army, whom he took out of Chelsea College who guarded the whole; and go their rounds at night and call the hours as the watchmen do at London to prevent disorders, and wait upon the Duke to chapel on Sundays[8]

Canons, 'this noble palace', was in its prime when Pope mocked it, the epitome of a formal layout with parterres, canals, 'an abundance of statues as big as the life, regularly disposed' and gilded vases.[9] All this lay within easy reach of London and the old sergeants' posts can have been no sinecures. Their lodges may not all have stood at entrances to the gardens but at least four must have done. The house records report that the lodge keepers at the Edgware and Stanmore gates were taking in lodgers and had to be ordered to clear these out and take no more.[10] There were two lodges at each of these gates so it sounds as if the twin pavilions of Elizabethan/Jacobean gardens were already being deployed, one at each side of a drive gate, and, if their inhabitants could take in lodgers, the pavilions seem to have been substantial.

Nothing survives of those lodges but these references indicate that a pair of lodges at the gates of a drive leading to Dyrham House in Gloucestershire

18
The Bath Lodges to Dyrham House, Gloucestershire.

from the Bath road may be survivors of a similar formal garden. The lodges stand above the house on the Cotswold brow and their drive sweeps down a deep valley which was once laid out in a flower and water garden of prodigious elaboration. The garden was made by George London for William Blaithwaite, a favoured minister of William of Orange, a monarch who was regarded, by his favoured ministers at least, as the greatest garden connoisseur in Europe. The lodges would have made a fitting entry point or finale to the gardens and it is unfortunate that Kip's engraving only shows the layout up to the statue of Neptune, from which the waters began their

19
The 1723 forecourt gateway to Boughton House, Northamptonshire.

involved descent.[11] There is a baroque feeling to the urns which crown both the gate piers and the roofs of the lodges, and the windows and doors with their recessed round-headed arches suggest an early dating. William Talman was working at Dyrham from 1698 to 1704 and he may well have designed them, though they could just as easily be later pastiche. It is intriguing to speculate that the earliest park gate lodges in England, though designed for a Whig minister, protected not a Palladian park, but a formal garden.

Several gate lodges, built in the second and early third decades of the

20
An instance of later pavilions added to a garden gateway at Ledston Hall, West Riding, resulting in a virtual prototype of the park gate lodge.

21

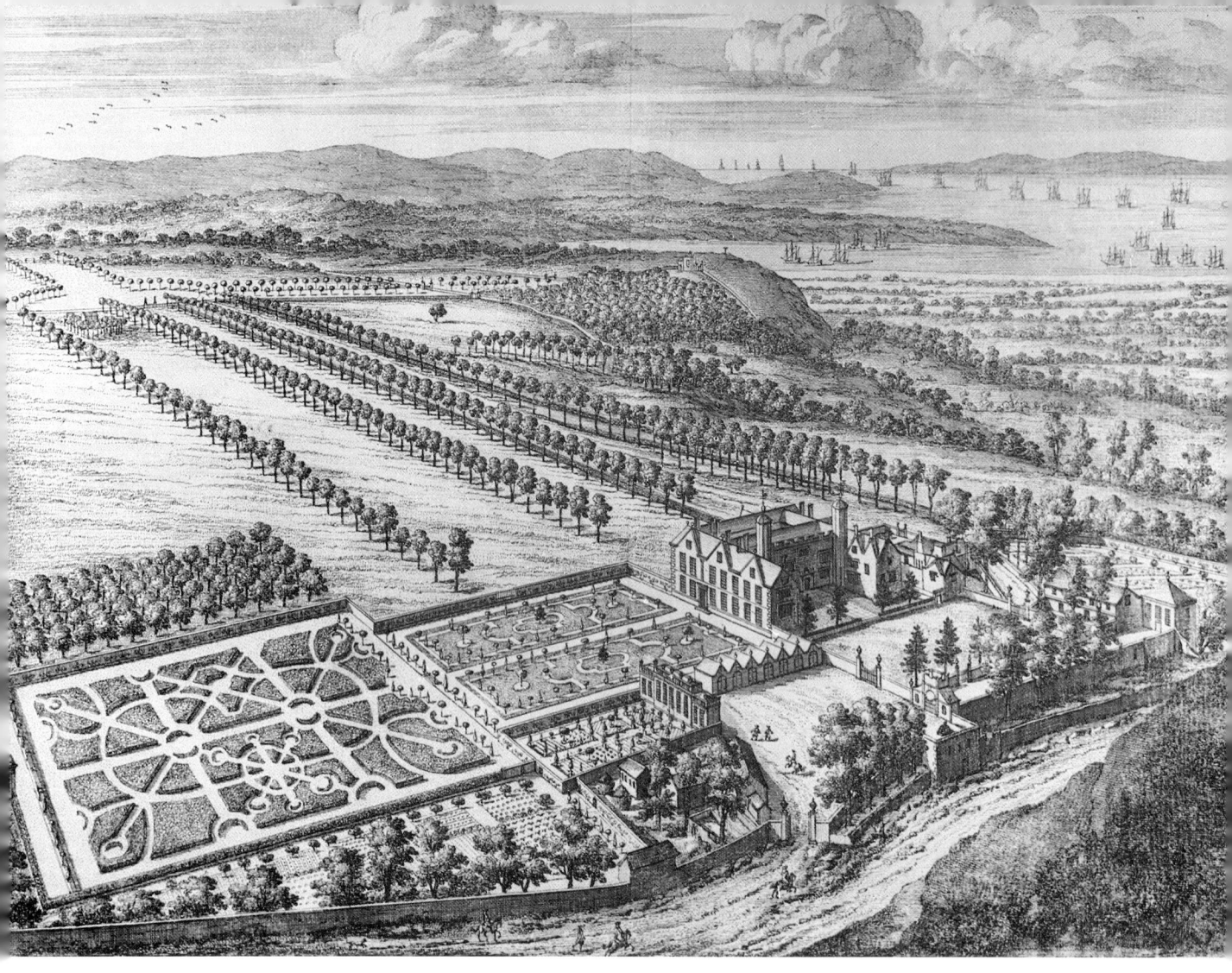

Kip's engraving of Kingsweston House from Atkyns's *Gloucestershire*.

eighteenth century, stand too near their parent houses to be labelled as park gate lodges but prove, nevertheless, that the building type was in genesis.

Two plain one storey lodges with rusticated brick quoins and parapets at The Bury, Chesham in Buckinghamshire have segmental headed windows which exactly match those of the main house. This was built in 1712 for William Lowndes, a Tory and former Secretary to the Treasury for Queen Anne, so the lodges also are probably of this date.

A severe stone arch with side rooms leading into the stable court of Boughton House, Northamptonshire appears to have been new in the autumn of 1723, but it can hardly have served as more than a penitentiary for recalcitrant stable boys.[12] There are far more impressive suggestions of the evolving building type on a terrace of the garden at Ledston Hall in Yorkshire. Here an existing classical garden gate, datable by the arms on its shield to Sir John Lewis who held Ledston in the early years of Charles II, has had substantial pavilions added diagonally to its piers. These pavilions are later in style than the gate, almost Vanbrughian in feeling. They are shown on three views of the hall by John Setterington painted in 1728, but they could easily be ten years earlier.[13] A carriage drive passes through the gate and they are not axially aligned to the hall, but they are far from the park boundaries and never provided living accommodation so their significance is in their potential, not in their actuality.

At this point of gestation and near achievement it will be useful to consider in some detail another Kip engraving, that of Kingsweston, Gloucestershire, published in 1712. The house was just about to be largely rebuilt by Vanbrugh (1712–14) and the estate restructured. As a result, a series of designs by major architects has survived to illustrate how a process was in hand which would develop a garden building into something very close to a park gate lodge.

Kip's view of Kingsweston illustrates gardens which are in marked contrast to those previously noted on his engraving of Shipton Moyne. At Shipton the owner had clearly despaired of the effort and expense needed to maintain several intricate parterres and they had reverted to grass. At Kingsweston the owner, Edward Southwell, was still, in 1712, keeping his formal gardens in spanking condition. There are two flower gardens, one before the east front and another one, more intimate, before the orangery. There is also a large garden of patterned box or turf with a kitchen garden to the side of it. Regiments of young trees lead far across the park to the south but the particular interest of this Kip view lies in the garden buildings. As usual the stables are approached directly from the public road and there is no direct indication of a drive in the park, though there are gates behind the north front which imply a carriage route through to the park. A gazebo on a high wall overlooks a second kitchen garden and the road, so a healthy interest in the outside world still prevails. An allée which leads to the gazebo is fronted by an arched and parapeted tower with two side pavilions. Sited at a park entrance, this building would have made a perfect park gate lodge of the gatehouse type. In its actual position it is hard to make out what purpose it could have served, unless an equestrian enthusiast had it made as a pavilion and viewing platform from which to supervise the grooms in the stable yard. Although a high wall surrounds the gardens, the boundaries of the park are only intermittently marked by walls and hedges.

The most unusual feature of the park lies at its far right-hand extremity near the end of a steep limestone ridge called Penpole. Here, to take advantage of a superb viewpoint overlooking the Severn and Avon with all their traffic of ships, a tall pavilion with a small side pavilion has been built on the park wall. Next to it is an ornamental gate. It is not easy to describe this structure as anything but a park gate lodge, though it stands beyond a wood on no main drive from the house. The long window in the taller of the two pavilions indicates that it was the third of Edward Southwell's viewing towers: one for passers-by, one for his horses and one for the commerce of the Indies. The gate beside it must have been put up because of a limitation in the siting of the pavilion. Though the view from the tower is fine, the vista fifty yards further to the west, outside Southwell's estate, is much finer. The gate will have permitted those taking refreshment and shelter in the pavilion to ride in a pony cart to the end of the ridge and back.

Immediately after the Kip view was published in Robert Atkyns's *Glouces-*

22
Colen Campbell's 1723 drawing for Penpole Gate, Kingsweston. (By kind permission of the City of Bristol Record Office ref. 33746).

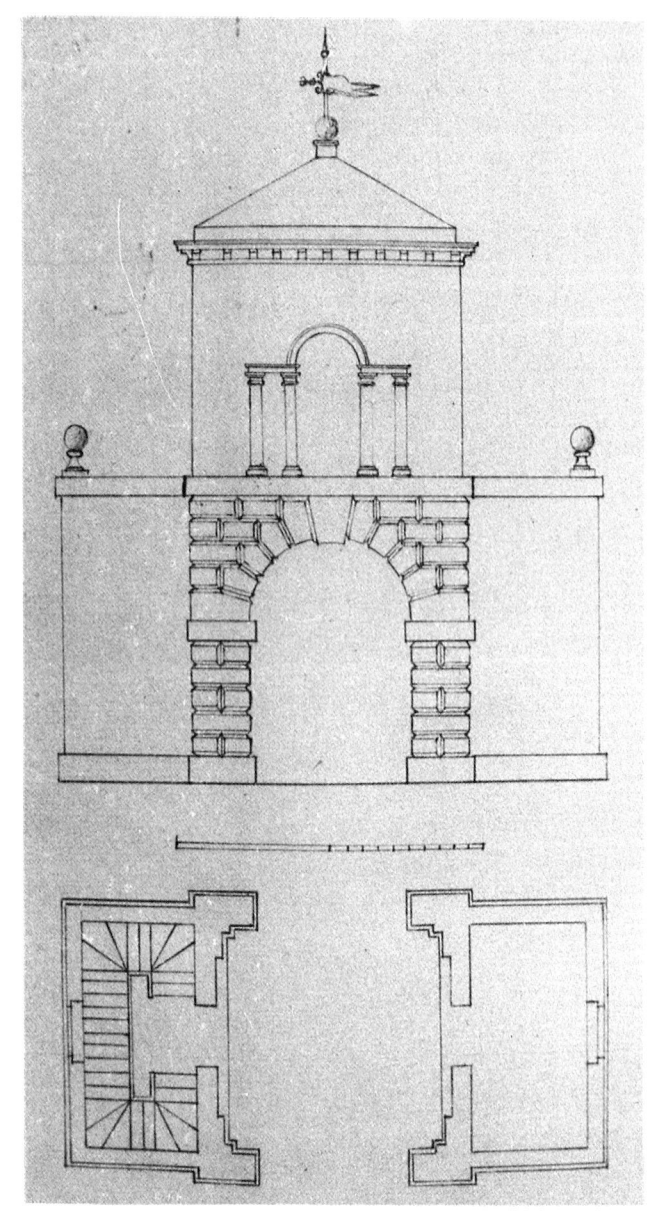

tershire everything was changed: Vanbrugh turned the unremarkable clutter of old buildings into what remains perhaps the most overwhelming and demanding house of medium size in England. The formal gardens he doubled in length, terminating them with the Echo, a dining pavilion which survives, roofless. A number of designs by Vanbrugh for other garden buildings for Kingsweston are now in the Bristol Record Office.[14] One of these, in his idiosyncratic Palladian, is for the existing loggia which replaced the gazebo to the road shown by Kip. It may or may not be significant that while the gazebo looked out to the road, the loggia looks inward to the house and park. One way or another the owner's enthusiasm for garden pavilions had survived the upheaval of Vanbrugh and this enthusiasm must have extended to at least thoughts of rebuilding the Penpole viewing pavilion in a more fashionable style.

There are two undated designs for Penpole Gate by Vanbrugh in the Elton Hall collection.[15] One, however, is not for a gatehouse as such but for a heavy two storey pavilion with side wings, the lower storey rusticated, the whole in an excitingly uncouth Palladian. The second is a gatehouse with a room over the arch and templar balconies at each side. In the Bristol Record Office is a third scheme with the handwritten inscription 'Mr. Campbels Design for Penpole Gate Rec[d] 29 May 1723'. This also is for a gatehouse: a rusticated carriage arch flanked by side wings and a viewing room above lit by a Venetian window. It is more chastely Palladian than the Vanbrugh designs and far less memorable.

Edward Southwell was apparently tempted by none of these designs and the pavilion shown on the Kip probably endured until 1771, when a simple version of the Vanbrugh-Campbell gatehouses by Robert Mylne was chosen and built.[16] It was a two storey gatehouse, its arch and side pavilions loosely based on the Campbell design, its upper storey on Vanbrugh's second sketch.[17]

These designs are of great interest. It is natural when a new building type is developing to look closely for suggestions of it in the work of the most innovative architects of the day, and in the first two decades of the eighteenth century the name of Vanbrugh comes naturally to mind along with Colen Campbell and the Earl of Burlington. Vanbrugh's Penpole designs suggest that, though he was fascinated by the permutations which could be made in the forms of small houses and garden buildings, he never felt compelled to reach out and devise a gate with living accommodation for a park perimeter. His awesomely eccentric Pyramid Gate at Castle Howard, which carries the date 1719, did not have living quarters until Daniel Garrett added wings to it in the early 1750s. Vanbrugh conceived it simply as a

PLATE III

23
The Brington Lodges at Althorp, Northamptonshire. A rustic Palladian pair by Roger Morris (1732-3).

24
Carved detail from the pediment of one of the Black Gates lodges, Leeswood Hall.

triumphal entrance gateway and it seems, therefore, not to have been a progenitor of the park gate lodge.

Colen Campbell, the author of the third Penpole design, could claim, jointly with the third Earl of Burlington, to have projected the Palladian style in England. Since his Penpole design was for a towered pavilion pierced by a carriage arch, there is an indication that the park gate lodge of that particular type grew from garden buildings in the Palladian style. Campbell may have designed such a gate lodge for Wanstead House, his innovative palace for Sir Richard Child in Essex of *c.* 1714–20, but this is speculation.

The references to the two sets of twin lodges at Canons which will have been erected by 1716 and the twin lodges at Dyrham suggest that architects designing in the dated baroque style may have been working towards a solution of the gate-guarding problem by utilising the earlier device of twin garden terrace pavilions. Certainly the two responses to the demands of lodge design ran concurrently through into the twentieth century. Unfortunately for any neatly compartmented theory of baroque twin sets and Palladian tower arches, the next two park gate lodges in chronological sequence are both in the form of twin pavilions. But those at Leeswood Hall, Flintshire, (possibly of *c.* 1726) are in flamboyantly elegant and totally impractical French baroque, while the pair to the Spencer park at Althorp (*c.* 1732–3) are of the most dour and utilitarian Palladian.

The name of Roger Morris, Colen Campbell's protégé, favoured architect of the Whig Duke of Argyll and, for all his Gothick innovations at Clearwell Castle, a sturdy Palladian, occurs predictably at this point in the evolution of the gate lodge. He was working at Althorp for the fifth Earl of Sunderland between 1732 and 1733 and by reasonable supposition the Brington Lodges are his work of this period. The Knyff view of Althorp in *Britannia Illustrata* of 1707 has a shadowy suggestion of a cottage at the point where the Brington Lodges now stand on the west drive. The present lodges are of the most basic cottage Palladian. They give a rudimentary impression of a classical pediment on their gables to the road and each has a door to the drive with a Gibbs surround of cyclopean heaviness. The dormers in the roof are later additions but each lodge in its original form had two rooms of reasonable size and would have housed a couple in comfort and a family in compression.

Not so the Leeswood lodges. These are diminutive baroque exotics with a tangled history. They have even travelled three-quarters of a mile since they were first built. Originally they stood at either end of the White Gates four hundred yards below the Hall. The White Gates are hard to describe without the use of tiresome superlatives. There are nine panels of virtuoso wrought ironwork, possibly from the forge of a local smith, Robert Davies, but of sophisticated French design, a froth of broken pediments, leaping dolphins and repoussé flowers. At each end of the gates is a tall pier on which an aloof sphinx is perched. Next to these piers the lodge pavilions were originally placed with their ornate pediments and allegorical reliefs of the Arts and War facing up the hill to the Hall. They are shown in this position on a mid-eighteenth century estate map and on a watercolour painted before the house lost its wings.[18] Local legend insists that the gates were never opened and, though they can and do open at their central panel, the drive out from the Hall always led immediately to the right of the right-hand lodge. A plain cottage stood on the other side of this entrance.

In the early nineteenth century a scenic drive was constructed to the east, and the slightly less sumptuous Black Gates were moved to this new outlet from the forecourt of the Hall. At the same time the baroque pavilions were

PLATE IV (a)

25
The Oxford Gate across the main approach to Stowe House, Buckinghamshire. The lodge is a later infilling of Kent's original design of *c.*1736.

PLATE IV (b)

26
William Kent's early Gothick lodges to Esher Place, Surrey. (1733).

taken from the White Gates and rebuilt, one on each side of the Black Gates, their rich facades of brown limestone turned now to face each other. They now house a family, extensive additions having been made at the rear. It is questionable whether they ever functioned other than as tea pavilions in their original position. The cottage across the road was far more likely to have housed the gate guardians. So, though they are, in their present site, among the most enchanting park gate lodges in Britain, they cannot with confidence be classed alongside the stolid Palladian pair at Althorp, as park gate keeper's houses of the 1730s, only as garden buildings near the entrance to a drive. They do, however, point with admirable clarity to one source from which the park gate lodge acquired its tradition of exotic ornament.

The lodges, both sets of gates and Leeswood Hall were the creation of young Sir George Wynne who made and swiftly spent a fortune from a lead mine. It is not known whom he employed as an architect; the names of Giacomo Leoni and Francis Smith of Warwick have both been suggested but stylistically neither seem very likely.[19] Wynne was a fervent Whig, and the highly un-Palladian form of the pavilions may serve as a caution against firm generalisations on the subject of political parties and their architectural house-styles.

The Brington Lodges at Althorp and probably also the Leeswood Lodges are of the early 1730s and here, at last, after uncertain attributions to Talman and Morris and unexecuted designs by Vanbrugh and Campbell, an architect emerges with a sense of purpose in his lodge design and an undoubted masterpiece of lodge building to his achievement. The architect was William Kent; the masterpiece, his Worcester Lodge to Badminton House, Gloucestershire.

The dates for all Kent's lodge designs are approximate and unsatisfactory. His triumphal arch lodge for Holkham could, for instance, have been built at any time between 1734 and 1765 and was actually put up by Matthew Brettingham, a jobbing architect who made alterations to Kent's design. The date of even the Worcester Lodge is uncertain, suggested as being 1746 on the evidence of a fireback and payments.[20] What should be borne in mind is that the first illustration of a porter's lodge in a pattern book occurs in 1740, in Batty Langley's *The City and Country Builder's and Workman's Treasury of Designs*. By 1740 then, the building type has been recognised, its function formalised. This must have been due to Kent's designing activities and influence in the 1730s because no other architect of major or minor stature had any comparable list of essays in the park gate lodge to his credit at that time.

As a design at least, the Holkham Triumphal Arch is Kent's first lodge. The first Earl of Leicester did not begin to build his house to Kent's designs until 1734 but the park was planned before this and Kent's obelisk, altered

27
William Kent's Palladian variants (*c.*1738) at Claremont, Surrey, to his Gothick lodges for neighbouring Esher Place.

31

PLATE V

inevitably by Brettingham, was in position by 1729. So it is reasonable to date the design of the Triumphal Arch to before 1730.

The quality of Kent's architecture is not easy to define. The Holkham arch has something of the brash self-confident handling of volumes present in the Worcester Lodge. Its pediment is disproportionately high above the arch and the heavy rustication of flint and brick emphasises rather than excuses the lack of relieving features on the wide surfaces. The buttresses at the sides lumber down with a deliberate Roman crudity of outline and, had the pyramids on the side arches not been excised by Brettingham, the play of forms would have been richly indigestible. On Kent's original design the areas between the gate and its pavilions and the area under the pavilion arches are shown blank, as if Kent had left it to Brettingham to fill in the domestic fenestration or leave the arch as simply a hollow park ornament.[21] He showed the same indifference to the lodging function of a park gate when he designed the Oxford Gate in about 1736 for Lord Cobham at Stowe.

The park at Stowe is initially disappointing in the search for the origins of the park gate lodge. It has a more remarkable collection of garden buildings than any other park in the country, but in the first four decades of the eighteenth century it tended to mark out its limits by eyecatchers like Stowe Castle rather than by lodges at the ends of drives. But if preconceived notions of what a lodge and even a drive should look like are set aside, Stowe does, in fact, demonstrate that movement towards park gate lodges that might be expected from a park which has been handled by so many architects, and been the subject of so much considered park design.

Its proto-lodges are the Boycott Pavilions, two miniature mansions designed about 1726 by James Gibbs and topped, until Borra gave them domes in 1758, by startling pyramids. Lord Cobham had the Boycott pair designed as grace-and-favour houses for old friends who had to be lodged in style. When they were first built the two to three hundred yard gap between them was blocked by two gates and a wall. The effect must have been bizarre, for wall and gates were later brought down and the Oxford Gate erected further down the drive to supply some sense of enclosure to the main approach. As Kent designed it, the Oxford Gate (illustrated on page 29) was merely two gate piers pierced by arches and linked by low walls to two hollow pavilions. But the right hand pavilion has since been infilled as a house for a lodge keeper with further additions to the side. Thus a sequence is laid out of the Gibbs Boycott Pavilions, Kent's Oxford Gate and the later lodge infilling: a demonstration of how a functional need for a gate keeper and his family eventually produced cramped living quarters in an elegant exterior shell.

Perhaps because he had noticed this functional inadequacy of his Holkham arch and his gate at Stowe, Kent then made the direct leap to complete park gate lodges. His solution was so satisfying functionally, and so simple architecturally, that it has never been adequately appraised as the union of common sense and genius which it represents. He had just improvised the first real house of the Gothic Revival, Esher Place, around Bishop Waynflete's red brick Tudor gatehouse, designs for which were drawn by 1733 in a high spirited Tudor Gothic with notably uncurvaceous ogees as their staple

PLATE V William Kent's Triumphal Arch to Holkham Hall, Norfolk, as modified by Matthew Brettingham.

PLATE VI Nicholas Hawksmoor's neo-medieval Carrmire Gate of 1728, on the same processional axis to Castle Howard as Vanbrugh's earlier Pyramid Gate.

PLATE VII Capability Brown's Convent Lodge. An introduction to a scenic drive through the park of Tong Castle, Shropshire (*c.* 1765).

PLATE VIII The lodge to Redbourne Hall, Lincolnshire (1783). A two-dimensional variant by Carr of his lodge to Fillingham Castle.

28 The apotheosis of the lodge as dining pavilion. William Kent's Worcester Lodge to Badminton House, Gloucestershire.

feature.²² For the gardens he designed wholly Palladian temples, but to guard the gates he proposed substantial twin gate lodges of brick which are Palladian in outline with a central pediment and lean-to wings, but have all their detail: windows, doors, even their recessed central arches, executed in the abrupt ogees of the main house. Each lodge has a cellar, two sizeable downstairs rooms and two bedrooms; nothing is cramped, a family could live comfortably in one, yet nothing is so overstated as to detract from the surprise of Esher Place itself. Kent had shown in the rigid austerity of his designs for Holkham that he understood the essential plain elegance of Palladio's houses on the Brenta better than any other English Palladian. In the Esher Place lodges he applied that restraint with amazing self-confidence to a Tudor-Palladian hybrid.

These Esher Place lodges may be dated to 1734. Then, as a confirmation of the sheer practical utility of the design, Kent was commissioned, just four years later, to produce two similar lodges for the first Duke of Newcastle at Claremont, less than half a mile away. These, of 1738, are copies of the Esher Place lodges except that their brick is yellow and the eccentric ogee shapes have been abandoned; windows, and doors are square-headed, the recessed arch below the pediment is round.²³ Thus in two leaps of invention in the middle 1730s, the archetypal Palladian lodge has been created in a fashionable area where it could be, and was, noted, approved and copied. Kent designed another pair for the second Duke of Grafton at Euston Hall, Suffolk;[24] versions by other architects will be found throughout the country: Giffard's Cross Lodge to Chillington Hall in Staffordshire is just one such example.

What must be noted about Kent's archetypal Claremont lodges is that, by their Palladian simplicity, they introduce a subdued note into park gate lodge design which was to develop alongside that other tradition of decorative display exemplified by the Leeswood pavilions. This utilitarian austerity of form was picked up soon after Kent's examples by Thomas Steel at Shillinglee Park in Sussex when he ran up, rather than designed, two ill-proportioned brick boxes on the A283 to Petworth at Fisherstreet. This pair would have provided decent accommodation for two families and they are of indubitable Kent Palladian provenance with their recessed round arches and Venetian windows. But their only possible aesthetic claim is their patterning of blue and red bricks which owes more to Bishop Waynflete or to Sussex vernacular than to William Kent.

Having set in train a whole sequence of park gate lodges which were primarily accommodation for servants, Kent went immediately on to demonstrate his virtuosity by creating a lodge which was the most aesthetic and memorable feature of its park; eclipsing easily its parent house and relegating its domestic quarters to low side pavilions.

His Worcester Lodge for the third Duke of Beaufort is the apotheosis of the gate lodge, not as park guardian, but as park focus. It is a building of great presence. It is not hard for a small structure to be perfect but a few small buildings like Thomas Archer's garden pavilion at Wrest Park or the Gothic Temple at Stowe are not merely perfect, they have a power and a completeness which commands the whole area about them. The Worcester Lodge is one of these small titans of architectural contrivance. There is nothing about its movement which is predictable. Where most classical buildings are serene, the Worcester Lodge is restless. Thunderous against an arc of broken beeches or rising in squat pyramids and high dome from the cabbage patch kitchen garden at its side, it has a baroque brashness that contradicts its Palladian calm. In some of the side aspects of its blind windows and niches it has the coarseness of a tenement, but in its combination of simple details and complex form it achieves an active geometry that puts the elephantine bulk of Badminton House to shame.

Its architectural symbolism is brutally direct: the low pyramidal pavilions house the servants, the high domed room over the arch is for the duke — a place for formal picnics or private revel under a rich display of plasterwork. The vast windows which light both sides of this room lend a paradoxical transparency to the otherwise hulking mass of the lodge.

One sadness about the Worcester Lodge is that nothing as architecturally memorable ever came after it in the whole long chain of classical gate lodge design. Perhaps Kent's suasive chat and overflowing invention had led the Duke of Beaufort into a tactical architectural success and a strategic estate error. The Worcester Lodge trumps Badminton House. It is too fine. Kent conceived it as a compressed palace rather than as a garden house. Not only did he give it the authority of its tall dome and flanking pyramids, but out at the end of the long curve of its forecourt walls he set further octagonal pavilions to counterpoise with their wide reach the height of the central feature. No other gentleman allowed his architect to over-emphasise the function of a lodge in quite this way. Thus, in one brief architectural lifespan, Kent set out for the park gate lodge the parameters within which future variations of its form would be made.

CHAPTER THREE

The Gothick Lodge as Mood Setter

> At length, the carriages emerged upon a heathy rock, and, soon after, reached the castle gates, where the deep tone of the portal bell, which was struck upon to give notice of their arrival, increased the fearful emotions, that had assailed Emily. While they waited till the servant within should come to open the gates, she anxiously surveyed the edifice: but the gloom, that overspread it, allowed her to distinguish little more than a part of its outline, with the massy walls of the ramparts, and to know that it was vast, ancient and dreary. From the parts she saw, she judged of the heavy strength and extent of the whole. The gateway before her, leading into the courts, was of gigantic size and was defended by two round towers, crowned by overhanging turrets

THIS SCENE from the most celebrated of Gothic novels, Ann Radcliffe's *The Mysteries of Udolpho*,[1] has become something of a literary cliché. What is not always noted is that, before the book was written, a visual experience very close to that which it describes must have become commonplace to a select number of the reading public. It is no slight to Mrs. Radcliffe's powers of imagination to say that she had no need to visualise a hoary stronghold in the Appenines to devise this scene. Emily could have been approaching any of a number of neo-medieval castle forecourts or, more pertinent to this chapter, embattled Gothick lodges, all of which had been built in England long before *Udolpho* came out in 1794.

Towers and gatehouse lodges of Gothick form had been built to suggest, with varying degrees of deception, the style and atmosphere of the houses within their parks from 1724 onwards. The first gothic novel, Thomas Leland's *Longsword, Earl of Salisbury*, was not published until 1762. Architecture thus anticipated literature by almost forty years in identifying and satisfying a perverse but persistent strain in the eighteenth century sensibility.

Some lodges were, in addition to their practical functions, designed to inculcate a mood of mingled awe and ancientry in the visitor passing through their gates. Jane Austen identified this psychic function while she was mocking the *Udolpho* passage in her own *Northanger Abbey*. Catherine Morland, Austen's heroine, had just read *Udolpho* with uncritical delight and been invited to stay at a house whose name 'Northanger Abbey' filled her with anticipation of medieval towers and haunted corridors. The process of her disillusionment began with the lodges as her chaise entered the park:

> ... she found herself passing through the great gates of the lodge, into the very grounds of Northanger, without having discerned even an antique chimney ... there was something in this mode of approach which she certainly had not expected. To pass between lodges of a modern appearance, to find herself with such ease in the very precincts of the abbey ... without obstacle, alarm or solemnity of any kind, struck her as odd and inconsistent[2]

The lodges, the mood setters to the house, were 'of a modern appearance', hence 'inconsistent'. A signal had been made by them, and automatically registered by Catherine, that she was not driving into crumbling antiquity and romantic tensions, only into bland domesticity and ordered ease.

What is difficult to determine from our distance in time is whether a classical lodge — a triumphal arch or a domed temple — would have been as deliberate an invocation of mood to an eighteenth century park visitor as a Gothick lodge plainly was. Palladian earls like Leicester and Burlington were, in years, much further from the Rome of Augustus than from Plantagenet England. But from at least the Elizabethan period onwards classical forms of building were becoming the accepted vernacular of the upper classes, and by the eighteenth century the age's unquestioning confidence in its own Augustan character must have made classical pretensions seem natural and Gothick gestures conscious play-acting.

There was no comparable spate of sensational historical novels set in Nero's Rome or the Athens of Pericles to balance the Gothic outpourings of the Minerva Press in the 1790s. So the literary implication is that a lodge like a Greek temple would appear modern and unexotic to the confident heirs of a classical tradition, while a pointed arch beneath a battlemented parapet would suggest melancholy and terror but also, by perverse paradox, beauty.

Burke's influential *Enquiry* of 1757 equated terror with the sublime: a detached aesthetic only possible in a country which had for many years been notably unterrified by civil shocks or religious violence.[3] But Burke's analysis of the emotional response to things darkly numinous was only a literary statement of what Vanbrugh had expressed for the Earl of Carlisle thirty-three years before in the outworks of Castle Howard. That great classical palace is so far at odds with the neo-medieval outworks of its grand approach as to suggest that the polite, conventional taste of the earl was being satisfied in the style of the house and Vanbrugh's obsession with masculine militarism in the form of the fortifications. In fact, the house was reared on the site of Carlisle's previous seat, Henderskelfe Castle, and because he retained the 'Castle' element in the title of his new home, he may have been easily persuaded both to gratify Vanbrugh's fondness for a 'castle air' and to create a permanent reminder of lost Henderskelfe by neo-medieval outworks straddling the main south approach to Castle Howard.

The sequence of building indicates that Carlisle needed some persuasion before he authorised the considerable expense of these works but that eventually he became an enthusiastic convert to the castle style. The first structure to go up, in 1719, was the Pyramid Gate which, by its position immediately across the drive, should logically have been a gate lodge. It is, however, only a triumphal arch and foil to the obelisk beyond. Its idiosyncratic design suggests that Vanbrugh was asked to produce a classical arch but contrived a perversely medieval air for it by its round-arched detailing. Only when this was complete was he allowed to add eleven convincingly dilapidated towers strung out on each side of the Gate along five-eighths of a mile of wall. These, completed by 1724, are much after the style of the town walls around Chester, Vanbrugh's birthplace. Ideally, to accord with these towers, the drive should have passed through them under a neo-medieval gatehouse, but the Pyramid Gate already occupied this position. While it was usual for a gatehouse to accommodate a porter's family, there was no such tradition of devising living quarters in a classical triumphal arch until Batty Langley's cursory outlines of such an arch room in his 1740 pattern book. But it is significant that when Vanbrugh was designing his own housing estate at Vanbrugh Fields, Greenwich in the early 1720s, he built a neo-medieval gateway with a separate house in each of the towers, a perfect design for a park gatehouse lodge but, in that position, only a piece of romantic speculative building.[4]

PLATE VI

The Earl of Carlisle must have been impressed by the air of martial antiquity which Vanbrugh's extraordinary park ornament imposed upon anyone climbing the hill to pass through it, because he had another shorter, but equally impressive, line of fortifications built at the foot of the hill by Hawksmoor in 1728. Here again a Gothick gate lodge would have been natural but yet again the form failed to evolve. The central feature, the Carrmire Gate, is a classical arch with pyramidal supporters. The two outwork towers, though trenchantly medieval in their detail and large enough to have housed families, are hollow shells, fit only for storage space, but highly effective in evoking a mood of what Mrs. Radcliffe was to call 'singular solemnity and desolation'.

What these two lines of fortification prove is that a landowner was prepared to spend a small fortune simply on the evocation of a mood at his park entry. In the process, the earliest Gothick lodge almost emerged before the earliest major house in the Gothick style. Here, as at Stowe, the lodge failed to evolve because the concept of the drive itself had not been thought through. The great width of the Castle Howard main avenue was impressive to the eye but impossible to command by a gate and a lodge without an inordinate length of supporting wall.

The earliest Gothick castle was Clearwell in the Forest of Dean, an ugly but innovative duckling designed by Roger Morris for Thomas Wyndham in about 1728. Though Morris was to build an early pair of classical lodges at

29
Clearwell Castle, Gloucestershire. The walls and gate are contemporary with the castle (*c.* 1728); the lodges are early 19th century additions.

Althorp in 1732, at Clearwell he avoided the type but, with a sense of organic fitness, gave his mock castle an embattled stable gateway and outbuildings which at least suggest the gate towers of an authentic medieval castle. These, and an outer curtain wall, carry the Wyndham arms to attest their early date, but the actual lodges and their iron gates are additions by Countess Dunraven of the early nineteenth century.

The first indisputable Gothick lodge was the Steeple Lodge to Wentworth Castle in the West Riding. This was built by Thomas Wentworth, first Earl of Strafford of the second creation, as a result of very similar pressures to those which had induced Carlisle to string out his dual fortifications.

When the second and last Lord Strafford of the prestigious Caroline first creation died in 1695, his earlier title of Lord Raby passed by collateral line to Thomas Wentworth, a soldier and Tory diplomat, but his wealth and family seat of Wentworth Woodhouse were left to a Whig relative, Thomas Watson-Wentworth. The new Lord Raby had, therefore, to support his title by acquiring a great house. This he did by buying the Stainborough estate and building on an old site a large block of Parisian baroque appearance designed by the Alsatian architect Jean de Bodt; this he renamed Wentworth Castle. Then, disturbed perhaps by the manifest brash newness of this barracks, he devised two additional buildings of antique form. The first was an ambitious mock castle for his garden which he called Stainborough Castle to preserve the old name, and the second was a mock church, the Steeple Lodge, built at the end of a direct drive to the nearest road. This last is a sizeable house, more appropriate to a steward than to a lower servant. It reproduced the three sections of a conventional village church: tower, nave and sanctuary with ogee doors, quatrefoils and pointed windows.

These two ambitious buildings, the mock castle and the mock church, worked together to produce from a short distance exactly the opposite effect

30
A gate lodge disguised as a park ornament. The Steeple Lodge to Wentworth Castle, West Riding.

to a remote Arcadian landscape. Instead of banishing a village from the skirts of his house, Wentworth spent large sums of money to create the appearance of a village of venerable antiquity without the inconvenience of its houses and inhabitants. An enormous barn directly across the drive from the Steeple Lodge completed the impression of deep-rooted rusticity.

It would be useful to establish a date for this pioneering lodge. Sir Thomas Robinson visited the estate in 1734 and reported the folly, Stainborough

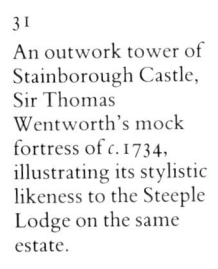

31
An outwork tower of Stainborough Castle, Sir Thomas Wentworth's mock fortress of c. 1734, illustrating its stylistic likeness to the Steeple Lodge on the same estate.

40

32
The Hawking Tower at Boughton Park, Northamptonshire.

Castle, as 'just finished'.[5] Since the mock castle outworks and the Steeple Lodge both feature quatrefoils with identical flat surrounds, it is reasonable to accept 1734 as the dating of the first Gothick Lodge.

All this architectural effort was rewarded by the revival of the title of Earl of Strafford, and the new earl was sufficiently pleased by his Steeple Lodge to build another towered lodge of very similar design at Boughton Park, his Northamptonshire estate. This is the Hawking Tower, noted with whimsical egocentricity by Horace Walpole in a letter of 28 August 1756 to the second Earl Strafford of the second creation:

> I passed Newstead and Wollaton literally in the
> dark and another place where, though quite night,
> I started at the vision of one of my own towers. I
> was sure it did not appear to me to tell me there
> was money buried under it, and I hoped it had not
> been murdered — I soon recollected that it must be
> Boughton[6]

Neither the Hawking Tower nor the Steeple Lodge resemble, in fact, any of Walpole's 'own towers', being both wholly unarchaeological in detail, but Walpole was inclined to assume credit for the whole Gothic Revival of the mid century. He would hardly have wished to record that someone had been building robustly Gothick park lodges fifteen years before he had even bought Strawberry Hill.

The next Gothick lodge was not built to further a claim to a prestigious title. It was born more naturally from the enthusiasm of Sanderson Miller, a man who had already gothicised his own house and then went on to create,

41

33
Sanderson Miller, from a contemporary portrait.

within his own grounds but on a new and commanding site, a much bolder evocation of the medieval past. The Edgehill Tower is a notable landmark, visible for many miles across the flat farmlands of Warwickshire, a compelling advertisement for the aesthetic merits of Gothic revived. It is often described as a viewing tower, a landmark set up to commemorate the point where King Charles raised his standard at the first battle of the Civil War. Its direct function is rarely noted. It was built by Miller as a park gate lodge and dining pavilion poised dramatically over the entry to a scenic drive down to Radway Grange, Miller's modest Elizabethan house on the plain below.

Miller had already mildly enlivened Radway by canted bays but his park gate lodge quite eclipsed his house. The Edgehill Tower stands in the same relationship to later Gothick lodges that the Worcester Lodge at Badminton stands to all its classical successors. In both buildings the men who conceived them appear to have taken more pleasure in their outlying dining pavilions than in their main houses. There are elements of escape, of fantasy and also of ostentation in the Edgehill Tower, but what made it a commanding architectural success, widely imitated by other park owners, was its directness.

Sanderson Miller was not an architect. He was an antiquary with bold, general notions of the buildings he wanted erected. He would rough these out in a crude outline leaving their details and technicalities to a master mason like William Hitchcox or an architect like Henry Keene. In certain circumstances, as at the Edgehill Tower, his limitations were an asset. Miller knew what he wanted for his site: a copy of Guy's tower at Warwick Castle linked by a drawbridge to a square barbican. This is exactly what he got — a simple effective profile and a grouping achieved without the distraction of correct detail. A picturesque cottage just down the road and a ruined arch now lost were all parts of the original mood setting ensemble, much as the great barn had worked with the Steeple Lodge at Wentworth Castle.[7]

The main tower is a rakish octagon of dark golden ironstone capped with

34
The Edgehill Tower, Warwickshire (1745-7). The lodge conceived as Gothick mood-setter to Sanderson Miller's Radway Grange.

a lean, boldly projecting crown of machicolation, but the most brilliant single stroke of drama in the design was the drawbridge. This, because it once hung across the driveway, was essentially part of the tower's function as a park gate lodge. The doors which led out to it and its corbelling survive to suggest the theatrical effect which must once have closed over the heads of Miller's delighted guests before their carriages plunged alarmingly down a steep drive through hanging woods, with occasional glimpses of wide vistas to the north and west. As a mood setter, few lodges can have equalled this early creation and Radway Grange itself must always have been something of an anticlimax at the end of the ride.

For this reason Miller probably often arranged such rides in reverse order with the tower-lodge as the object of the drive. The viewing and dining room at the top of the tower remains dilapidated but unaltered to evoke the mood of his antiquarian picnics. It is reached up a narrow, twining wooden staircase, steep almost as a ladder, which may account for George Lyttelton's wry response to a Miller invitation:

> Mrs. Lyttelton will like to dine at the house better
> than at the Castle, and my stomach prefers hott
> meat to cold ... so, if you please, we will dine at
> the foot of the hill and have the pleasure of looking
> up at your Castle[8]

The only decorative features in the octagonal room are some pinched Gothick mouldings and tiny shields displaying the armorial bearings of Miller's friends, their casual detail typical of Miller. Through the meagre lancets is a wide airy view of tree tops and broad counties. Room and tower survive as an exact reminder of the union of the Gothick and the Picturesque movements.

The Edgehill Tower was complete by 1747 and Miller's success was marked almost immediately when his Oxfordshire near neighbour, the third Earl of Jersey, asked him to design a Gothick lodge for his house at Middleton Stoney. Miller obliged, obviously with one of his rough sketches, and in 1749 the earl's masons put up exactly what Miller had outlined. The lodge is a satisfying gate guardian with family accommodation, a two storey octagon set alternately with roundels and quatrefoils. There are cruciform arrow slits to the porch and it presents an outer defence wall to the road with two low towers inset with blind arches. It is characteristic of Miller's work in that the lively design element of a defensive tower comes first, quite overwhelming that of a gate keeper's cottage.

This is the point at which to consider exactly what was the potential contribution of Gothick lodge design to eighteenth century architectural tradition. Classical architecture tended to produce flat facades with applied detail. Doors and porticos could vary these, but the effects were generally two-dimensional and the interiors were variants of cubes and double cubes. Crude imitations of medieval originals, like Miller's Edgehill Tower lodge, introduced a refreshing variety of profile and a strong three-dimensional feeling to exteriors. The great fan vaults of Arbury Hall's reception rooms had been tried out in miniature by Henry Keene in a small garden temple at Enville.[9] So there is evidence in the sequence of Gothick building that the liveliest experimental effects were first explored in smaller buildings such as lodges and other garden buildings. They were only developed later in the major houses. Clearwell Castle is a very early example of 1728, but it is a house ordered by classical symmetry whose Gothick detail is only skin deep and even its stables are more interesting spatially.

There was always a tendency, when a trained architect designed a Gothick building, that he would use as his basis the classical rectangles and cubes of his training and merely apply some copied Gothic detail, thereby missing the potential vitality of medieval forms. Thus, paradoxically, a barely competent designer like Miller, because of his direct dependence upon a medieval original, could produce a building which was both more archaeologically correct and more spirited in its design than Gothick work by trained architects.

Three lodges to Arbury Hall in Warwickshire illustrate this point. When Sir Roger Newdigate began his fifty year project of Gothicising the house he formed a panel of 'experts' to advise him. Sanderson Miller joined this in 1750 on the strength of his achievements at Edgehill, Middleton Stoney and several early Gothick park buildings such as the sham castle at Hagley Park, Worcestershire. Inevitably Miller suggested one of his canted bays for Arbury, but his hand is seen most clearly in two lodges: the Round Towers

35
The Round Towers to Arbury Hall, Warwickshire.

on the main drive to Nuneaton, and a simple square tower lodge at Astley. Both lodges are crude in their detail. The Round Towers in particular with 'Saxon' apertures over a Tudor arch and rough, unbattlemented parapet is more suggestive of the Dark, than of the Middle, Ages. But the two lodges

45

are confident and direct; they make an uncompromising spatial impact and they have presence. It should also be remembered that the Round Towers are the first Gothick arched lodge in Britain.

The third exit to the park at Arbury was at Griff. There the lodge is a pair of cuboid pavilions each with a parapet of sinuous Decorated Gothic character. This observed detail (St. Mary at nearby Astley, the former chancel of a

36
Henry Couchman's Griff Lodges to Arbury Hall (*c.*1776).

Decorated collegiate church, is a possible source) is more sophisticated than anything on the two Miller lodges and suggests the hand of Henry Couchman who worked at Arbury after 1776. But what is remarkable about the Griff lodges is the absolute lack of vitality in their design. They owe nothing in their essential shapes to any medieval original and are, therefore, classical cubes without appropriate classical detail — infertile hybrids.

When Miller was presented with exactly the same task, that of designing a

37
A neo-Jacobean response in lodge design by Sanderson Miller for Siston Court, Gloucestershire (*c.*1759).

gate lodge of the twin pavilion type for his Trotman relations at Siston Court near Bristol, his response was characteristic. He looked to the essential forms of Siston Court itself, which was an Elizabethan building, and designed simple Jacobethan style lodges of direct charm wholly appropriate to their house.[10] Their mood is correct for their parent house and they are real, if limited, explorations of non-classical forms.

38
A Gothick facade to an estate cottage on a drive to Downton Hall, Stanton Lacy, Shropshire.

As a result of Miller's brief, over-confident and under-informed architectural career, Gothick lodge designers and indeed designers of any Gothick park buildings had two choices. They could risk the spatial freedom of copying genuine Gothic archways and towers or they could cling nervously to the cube and the rectangle, hiding their timidity by elegant detail. In either case their work would be classifiable as 'Gothick' and not Gothic because their detail would be unscholarly and applied with the mongrel insouciance which is the charm of such work. But it is worth noting that in this eighteenth century period of Gothick lodge design, before the pattern books began to emerge and while architects were still feeling their own individual way towards solutions, there are two underlying categories: Gothick which was spatially responsive to the models on which it was improvising, like Miller's Round Towers, and Gothick which was concerned principally with applied surface decoration, like Couchman's Griff lodges. In both categories there are buildings of great appeal and interest, because in both the designers struggle with an alien medium that creates an uncertainty and a tension which breeds a living architecture.

Four Gothick lodges, all of which were conceived as habitable boxes to which surface decoration was applied, will serve to illustrate the attraction and the limitations of that category of design.

The first lies in that forlorn, appealing slope of the Clee Hills above Corve Dale in Shropshire. It is the West Lodge to Downton Hall, a parent house with superb Rococo plasterwork and not to be confused with Richard Payne Knight's nearby Downton Castle. The lodge is a plain two storey cottage with an attic room to which a Gothick facade has been applied. There has been no attempt at a stylistic treatment of the other three sides of the house so the lodge is a perfect example of superficial design. The door, the 'Venetian' window and the gable are a rising pattern of drooping ogees; there is a careful but naive display of quatrefoils, and the whole is neatly contained and cut off from the dwelling behind by a picture frame of panelled pilasters that have lost their pinnacles. It is an untouched example of that composite Jacobean-Gothick which flourished in the West Midlands in the 1760s: provincial, unscholarly, picturesque and paper thin. A classical concern for symmetry governs its composition but even the Venetian window has been gothicised.

PLATE VII   The Convent Lodge to Tong Castle is another West Midlands lodge and its date, 1765, makes it a close contemporary of Downton, but whereas the Downton lodge calmly accepts its box format and facade, the Convent Lodge struggles furiously to escape from it. The reason for this is that the latter was designed by Lancelot (Capability) Brown, an architect who was primarily a landscape gardener, and while the unknown designer of the Downton Lodge wanted only to create a light-hearted fancy at the drive side, Brown was evoking a mood in a particular area of the park and must rapidly have realised that a cube was not the best form in which to achieve this.

Tong Castle was built by Brown in a highly individual Moorish Gothick for George Durant. Durant's son, a second George, spent further sums on his father's house and park in the 1820s. Because this second George built a replica of the refectory pulpit of Shrewsbury Abbey and a Hindoo-Gothic wall and gates in front of the Convent Lodge, the lodge itself has often been attributed to him and Brown's remarkable work on the lodge has been ignored. Now time, and the workmen on the new M54, have restored the original conception. The Hindoo wall is buried in undergrowth, the pulpit lies shattered to pieces and Brown's Convent Lodge is perched seemingly alone on the scarps above the motorway.

Brown intended his lodge not simply as a gate guardian but as a park feature, an object for a picturesque excursion from the castle or an introduction to the fantasy world of the castle itself. Just behind the lodge a side drive still crosses a deep ravine in the sandstone rock by a crumbling bridge and the lodge was intended as a part of this miniature wilderness. Ideally Brown should have suggested a mysterious past by a ruined arch or tower or both, but having saddled himself with a box, he set about inscribing the surface of its sandstone masonry with historical symbols. These are delved so deeply that a spatial depth is almost achieved through surface detail. There are infilled arches to suggest lost extensions, shallow crosses, chunky diaper work and massive armorial shields that curve lavishly out from their walls. Then, as if still dissatisfied, Brown staggered the rear wall back in a perplexing stepped profile and abandoned it, despairing of the limitations within which he had trapped himself. The Convent Lodge is a perfect illustration of

48

PLATE IX The main lodge to Hartwell House, Buckinghamshire, combines an arched entrance with estate offices. A late Palladian design by Henry Keene of 1759-63.

PLATE X Clearly influenced by a design of Inigo Jones, this lodge to the vanished houses of Fonthill, Wiltshire, is probably of 18th century construction.

PLATE XI One of the twin lodges to the demolished Phyllis Court, Henley-on-Thames, Oxfordshire.

PLATE XII P.F. Robinson's Old Lodge of 1824 provides a classical prelude to its Grecian Ionic main house, Trelissick, Cornwall.

39
Classical symmetry with applied Gothic detail. James Wyatt's 1796 East Lodges to Bowden Park, Wiltshire.

the need for real medieval models in a Gothick lodge which is seriously intended to evoke a mood of the past.

James Wyatt's Gothick pair to the east of Bowden Park, Wiltshire built much later, in 1796, demonstrate an exactly opposite spirit. Despite the example across the road of a genuine sixteenth century gatehouse from Bromham House which had been re-erected as a lodge to Spye Park, Wyatt designed with cool satisfaction within the precise limits of a cube and his lodges make an oddly precious comment on the antique structure that faces them. His West Lodges for Bowden are another pair of cubes, but these are classical and the two sets present a neat essay in interchangeable styles upon identical dimensions. To be fair, Wyatt could, when required, run up a presentable gatehouse lodge as his Fletching village lodge to Sheffield Place, Sussex demonstrates. But the Bowden lodges show how, late in the century, a trained architect could still be content to confine Gothick detail within an inappropriate classical shape. Wyatt has even retained the classical gatepiers disguised as slim turrets. Lodges of this kind must have occasioned Humphry Repton's anecdote 'of a celebrated lady, who, because they looked like tea-caddies, wrote on two such lodges in large letters, GREEN and BOHEA'.[11]

If the Bowden pair can only be praised for a certain reserved elegance, the lodges to Gisburn Park in the West Riding show what life and vitality superficial Gothick detail could give to a limited geometrical structure. The Gisburn lodges are as late as those at Bowden, possibly even a few years later, but the work of an amateur, Lord Ribblesdale, the owner of the house. In basic shape they are rectangular with a pedimented gable at each end and stand one on each side of the drive gateway to the village. On these uncompromising blocks a riot of detail has been laid. This gives a superficial impression of being archaeologically correct but is in fact chronologically discordant. Sharp points and pinnacles are the basic theme. The gables and

40
The lodges to Gisburn Park, West Riding. An amateur design of c. 1800 by the owner Lord Ribblesdale.

parapets bristle with crocketed pinnacles and with a highly individual, fudged, protuberance of Lord Ribblesdale's own invention. Triple lancets of Early English feeling fill a wide window which cunningly serves, yet conceals, two floor levels. A blank symmetry of recessed arches runs down the side walls which face the drive and all the homely detail of bedroom and kitchen windows is kept discreetly out of sight of the visitors on the opposite wall. The general impression is of two pilgrims' chapels from, perhaps, Portugal, though in fact all the detail is either native English Gothic or of

Ribblesdale invention. What is interesting is to set these lodges of *c.*1800 for comparison against the Downton Lodge of about 1760. In both early and late Gothick lodge design exactly the same forces are working. There is a tight classical symmetry behind the patterning of all the Gothick detail, the facades are applied to conceal and not to express the utilitarian house behind them, and neither at Downton nor at Gisburn is there any deployment of the spatial variety which could have come from the direct copying of medieval towers or chapels.

The year 1800 in no way marks the end of this chain of applied cuboid Gothick. John Buckler's Gothick cubes to Blithfield Hall, Staffordshire of 1822–3 and his box of a lodge to Halkin Castle, Flintshire of 1824–7 are as rigidly geometrical and as uninfluenced by the 13,000 topographical sketches of real medieval buildings which he made, as any of the eighteenth century Gothick lodges. And when Thomas Rickman, the father of archaeological Gothic categories, designed a lodge for Scarisbrick Hall in Lancashire (1812–16) with John Slater, the Liverpool architect, they were content with an actual row of cottages like those in a local mill town, distinguished only by a battlemented roof. These so outraged Pugin when he was working at Scarisbrick after 1837 that he set up one of his most angular 'medieval' gestures across the drive as a lodge-protest against Rickman's devaluation of the Gothic spirit.

But all these represent only the work of the 'tame' Goths, men designing within the strait jacket of their age, caught in the conventional proportions of the classical style from which they were supposed to be escaping. To a more flexible architect like John Carr, the arched form was a natural framework for a lodge. Following Miller's lead in the Round Towers at Arbury but designing with far more elegance and stylization, he created

41
John Carr's masterly Rococo Gothick lodge to Fillingham Castle, Lincolnshire, in deplorable decay by the Ermine Street.

PLATE VIII

lodges for Fillingham Castle, Lincolnshire, and Redbourne Hall, also in Lincolnshire, of 1773. These are pastiche work in their detail but in profile and spatial feeling their twin turreted gatehouses are alive. His Ermine Lodge to Fillingham Castle has side pavilions jutting out diagonally after the ground plans of Elizabethan gatehouses at Hardwick Hall and Stonor Park Oxfordshire. These give a sense of movement as well as authority to the building which deserves better than its present condition, mouldering away with bushes in the bedroom. An identical lodge design was prepared by Carr but never used for Raby Castle, County Durham, where he was working from 1768–88[12]

The North lodges to Lulworth Castle in Dorset are an even more impressive example of what could be done when an architect was determined to impose a mood upon an entrance and not merely to set up a marker at a gate. The park at Lulworth has already been discussed in its condition of 1721 and mention made of a Jacobean garden gatehouse re-erected as a park gate lodge

52

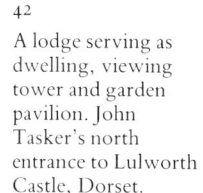

42
A lodge serving as dwelling, viewing tower and garden pavilion. John Tasker's north entrance to Lulworth Castle, Dorset.

in 1808. The north lodges were purpose-built for their site in 1785 and are much more ambitious in design. Deplorably, though in the roll call of lodges not unusually, these lodges, which must be ranked among the most ingenious small houses of their century, are half in ruins. They guard an unimportant green lane into the park and are likely to have been built half as a gate lodge and half as a place for alfresco meals and viewing parties.

The lodges are clearly visible from Lulworth Castle which was itself a glorified hunting lodge and folly in what Horace Walpole called 'King James's Gothic'. The most likely architect of the lodges was John Tasker. He designed a Gothic chapel for Milton Abbey, was working for Thomas Weld at Lulworth in 1780, and in 1786–7 the elegantly composed classical chapel for Roman Catholic worship was built in the park to his designs.[13]

The North Lodges have a quality of symbolic significance conveyed within a geometrical form. Each is triangular with a round turret at the angles. There are further towers half lost among tangled bushes but set upon walls which once curved out to receive the visitor as a castle before a castle. The lodges are built of brick covered with a finely cut silvery ashlar but the outworks are constructed in a contrasting brown carstone rubble. The round turrets and two-light Tudor windows of the lodges themselves are a deliberate utilising of the architectural forms of the main castle, like Miller's lodges at Siston. But while the castle is a gaunt overscaled toy fort, these two lodges have a metaphysical quality which is hard to express. They have an inner composure, which arises partly from their obvious trilobal hints of the Trinity, partly from the exact finish of their stonework and partly from the pathos and vulnerability of their present ruin. It is to be sincerely hoped that an interested and appreciative body such as the Landmark Trust will move to their rescue before their collapse is beyond repair.

43
Humphry Repton's planned prelude to a scenic drive immortalised by Jane Austen. The entrance lodge designed in 1794 to Blaise Castle grounds near Bristol.

The North Lodges to Lulworth have always been a remote and private pleasure for the Weld family who ordered their construction. Humphry Repton's main or Coombe Hill lodge to Blaise Castle, Bristol, built in 1801, publicised in 1803, became an immediate place of popular resort. It achieved within a few years a kind of literary immortality by being the lodge under whose arch Catherine Morland did not ride because the boorish Mr Thorpe's horses became exhausted at Keynsham. Had she achieved her aim in visiting Blaise Castle Park, Catherine would certainly have been much better pleased by the Coombe Hill lodge, which survives in excellent condition, than she was by the 'modern' lodges of Northanger.

The Coombe Hill lodge was designed by Repton explicitly to create a mood. Blaise Castle House was in what he described as 'the Grecian style of architecture'[14] but high on a hill within its park Robert Mylne, architect of the final Penpole Gate lodge at Kingsweston, had designed in 1766 the splendid sham castle which is also called Blaise Castle. As Repton remarked: 'the name of the place caused some difficulty'[15], but he decided rightly that the sham castle was a far more celebrated place of resort than the house. Thorpe had described it to Catherine as 'the oldest in the Kingdom', when it was in fact only thirty-three years old, so Repton suggested the lodge design which was actually built 'as a proper object to attract notice in the approach, which is one of the most interesting and romantic'.[16] Appropriately he began the remodelling of the estate after producing one of his Red Books, which demonstrates that the landscaping and the approach to the park was decided by February 1796, just a year after the publication of Mrs. Radcliffe's *Udolpho*.

Details from Mylne's Blaise Castle — cruciform arrow slits and heraldic shields — are used as features on Repton's gateway, just as Tasker had used the turrets and windows of Lulworth on its north lodges. The gatekeeper's tower is sturdy and four square and the arch itself lowers suitably over the entrance. Repton had a keen social conscience over the kind of housing appropriate for such a position:

> The custom of placing a gate between two square boxes, or, as it is called "a pair of lodges", has always appeared to me absurd, because it is an attempt to give consequence to that which in itself is mean; the habitation of a single labourer, or perhaps of a solitary old woman, to open the gate, is split into two houses for the sake of childish symmetry; and very often the most squalid misery is found in the person thus banished from society, who inhabits a dirty room of a few feet square.[17]

Once the visitor had absorbed the proper romantic mood from the lodge, an eighteenth century fantasy experience unfolded. The drive descends past a rustic 'Timber Lodge' built earlier for Thomas Farr, then by a Repton cottage conceived as some genre painter's dwelling for a woodman. After this the road swirls down a series of hairpin bends overhung by menacing faces of wooded cliff. Repton chose this approach because while I reserve some scenes for those who can walk to them, and who can climb steps or creep through caverns, I must endeavour to display others from the windows of a carriage with all the interest of surprize and novelty'.[18] Dark caverns are cut into the hillside, stone seats are set to command views across the gorge. Finally the drive ends at Blaise Castle, still splendid in its vandal besieged decay: a trefoil towered dining room with battlements and Gothick windows.

So fifty years after Sanderson Miller built the Edgehill Tower lodge to prepare a visitor's mood for a scenic ride down a steep hill, the Gothick lodge had become the predictable and expected preliminary to such drives in both public and private parks. The form of their towers and pointed arches had become architecturally acceptable as exotic and was well on the way to being absorbed into the standard repertory of surburban architectural practice, with all that that would imply in flexibility of house and villa design.

CHAPTER FOUR

The Lodge in the Pattern Books 1740–1830

A Lodge to a Nobleman's Park, with Sheds, or a Covered-Way, for Cattle. The Sheds may be converted into Bed-rooms, if the Gate-Porter has a Family.[1]

It is dangerous to take a building type whose first function is aesthetic display as an accurate indication of the landed classes' sensitivity to the needs of lower class housing. But Humphry Repton's remarks, quoted at the end of the last chapter, indicate that by 1803, when he wrote, the park gate keeper's lodge was in danger of becoming a social scandal as a living unit. Gandy's captions to his lodge designs of 1806, one of which is quoted above, show how little effect Repton's attack had had on his fellow architects.

This indifference to the living conditions of the tenants was not inherent in the lodge as a building type. Kent's first essays in the form at Esher Place and Claremont had provided civilised accommodation on two floors for a family. Moreover, in so far as the park gate lodge developed from the dining pavilion, as at Worcester Lodge and the Edgehill Tower, it inherited the decorative standards and comparative luxury of the gentry at play. It is in the first pattern books that a bland indifference to the lodge keeper's living conditions begins to be reflected.

The earliest appearance of a gate keeper's lodge in a pattern book has already been mentioned. Plate 22 of Batty Langley's *The City and Country Builder's, and Workman's Treasury of Designs* (1740), illustrates a 'Dorick Gate'. The two halves of the arch show two alternative 'Dorick' designs: one of plain unfluted Roman Doric, one with bands of frosted rustication. All the emphasis is decorative though the niches, one round and one round-headed, could possibly be pierced for fenestration. In the ground plans for this elevation a door is indicated to each 'Porters Lodge' but neither window, staircase nor second room. With his usual engaging self-confidence Langley has captioned all his arches as 'Gates for Enterances into Palaces etc'. This suggests that when he drew the designs in 1739 not enough gate lodges with accommodation for a family had been built for him to realise that a new and potentially profitable area of design was developing. Langley, with precedents set by Inigo Jones in mind, was envisaging his arches as symbolic ceremonial markers of Roman grandeur to be placed in the forecourts of palaces, as the Marble Arch was to be added in 1828 by John Nash to dignify Buckingham House. The Marble Arch has a doorway to its cramped interior

44 Batty Langley's 'Dorick Gate' design of 1740. (Bodleian Library).

at just the position where Langley's plan indicates a 'Porters Lodge'. A palace or great town house would be a place of such frequent resort as to demand a porter or sentry on duty throughout the day rather than a family with an occasional function of gate opening. The triumphal arch was to become a popular design for park gate lodges, so common indeed as to be classifiable as a building type in itself, but as a shell for living accommodation it is essentially unsuitable.

Although his pattern books contain no actual entrance lodges, several of Langley's designs proved so pleasing to lodge builders that they were put to use at park entrances. Plate 57 in his *Ancient Architecture Restored and Improved* (1741–2), reissued as *Gothic Architecture* in 1747, is captioned a

'Gothic Temple' and was set up as such at Bramham Park in the West Riding.[2] But at Castletown House, County Kildare, the diverting invention of its spheric triangular windows and pinnacled ogee battlements was borrowed when Lady Louisa Conolly had a lodge with a striking three sided apsidal end put up on the Leixlip approach. Plate 32 of the same collection of Langley designs, a 'Gothic Portico', suffered an even more ingenious redeployment. The Marlborough road gate lodge to Lord Bruce's Tottenham Park, Wiltshire, is in essence a plain two storey rectangular cottage, but the cresting of Plate 32 has been carried around its roof, the cross section of the

45
A 'Gothick Temple' design from Batty Langley's 1741-2 pattern book.

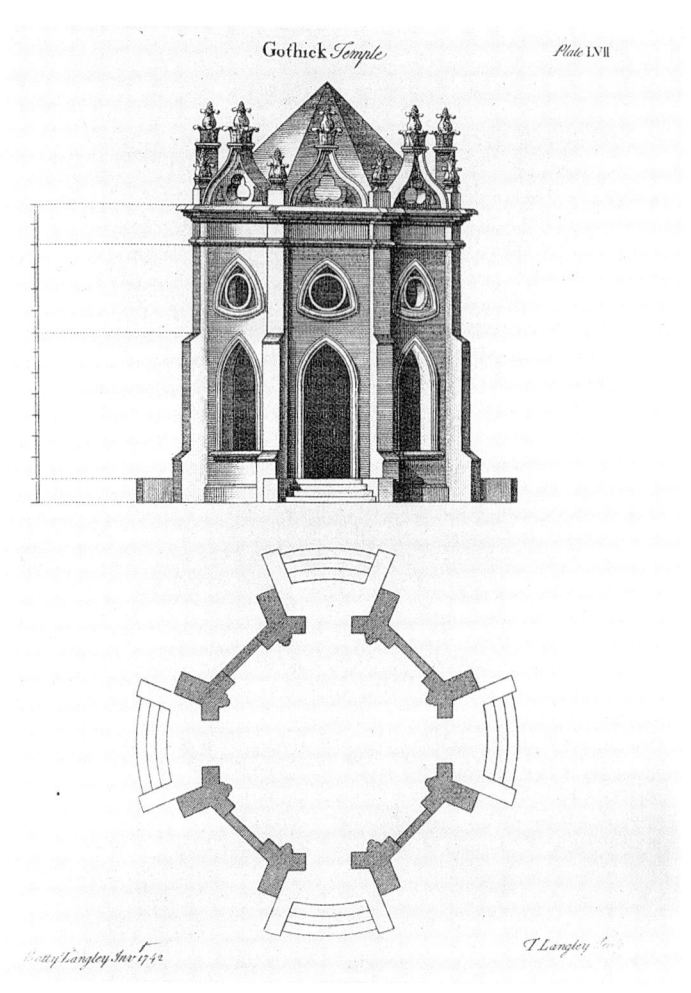

same plate's pillars has inspired the shape of its upper storey openings and the actual windows of the Portico have been copied for the ground floor.

The Castletown and Tottenham Park lodges must date from around 1750 before the springtime of Gothick invention had begun to wither in the first frosts of archaeological awareness. But the success of their happy cannibalising of the original patterns occasions regret that Langley never applied his uninhibited talents directly to the building type.

The same freedom of invention is shown in *The Country Gentleman's Pocket Companion and Builder's Assistant for Rural Decorative Architecture* of

1753 (2nd edition 1756) and *A New and Compleat System of Architecture* (1759), both by the brothers William and John Halfpenny; also in a compendium of designs by the Halfpenny brothers, Timothy Lightoler and Robert Morris, *The Modern Builder's Assistant,* mysteriously dated MDCCVLII.[3] Four of the garden buildings in the *Pocket Companion* are captioned as a 'Gothick Lodge'. One of these, however, Plate 14, a cheap £78 design, is described in the contents section as 'a Gothick Temple' which is what it obviously was: a single storey garden seat with a small room behind. The continued etymological ambivalence of the term 'lodge' at this period is further demonstrated in

46
Batty Langley's 'Temple' design adapted to a gate lodge at Castletown House, Co. Kildare.

Plate 18 of *A New and Compleat System*. This illustrates 'an octagon lodge or summerhouse' which is nothing less than a small three storey mansion in exactly the tradition of the lodges in Sidney's *Arcadia*. It has an octagonal 'Great room' lit from a deep loggia, a bedroom parlour and closet on the first floor. Beneath are a servants' hall, butler's pantry and cellars with servants' rooms in the loft above.

The last of these early Gothick designs appear in Timothy Lightoler's pattern book of 1762, *The Gentleman and Farmer's Architect*. Three of these are for 'Lodge Houses' and all are set between ornamental gates. But one is a

47
A 'Gothick Portico' design by Batty Langley.

'Farme, in the Chinese Taste', the second is a 'Lodge or Keepers House fit for a Park, Forrest etc', and the third is a 'Lodge-house adapted for any part where a Dairy is kept'. All three are shown with a plan for a farmyard and all its attendant buildings, but they all have five downstairs rooms and were intended as fashionable *fermes ornées* (illustrated pages 62–66). The third design, or something very close to it, was actually built as the Spiers Lodge in the middle of the park at Warwick Castle. This was on a very old site; there had been a house there for a warren warden as early as the fifteenth century and in 1756 it was still a utilitarian structure for a keeper with attendant stables, cart-hovel and brew-house. But it was rebuilt, probably by Lightoler who was employed at the castle between 1763 and 1769, with a triple arched Gothick loggia on its north front, to serve as an ornamental feature to improve the view from the castle's windows. Set in a thick wood immediately above a steep bank down to the river Avon, it is not easy to photograph, and its entrance facade suffered an extensive Edwardian re-fenestration, but it remains an evocative example of the 'lodge' in its earlier sense as an isolated place of resort, a *maison de plaisance* where a mistress might be kept discreetly, or misanthropic anglers resort in leafy solitude.

At last, in 1774, the first 'Plan and Elevation of a Design for an Entrance into a Gentleman's Park' appeared. It was drawn by John Carter who undertook in 1774 to make drawings for a serial publication *The Builder's Magazine* and the lodge elevation itself is dated 1 October 1775. Only an

48
The 'Portico' design freely applied by an unknown architect to a gate lodge at Tottenham Park, near Marlborough, Wiltshire.

occasional architect but a regular antiquary, Carter was devoted to recording and preserving medieval structures; so the uncompromisingly classical character of his 'Entrance' suggests that the classical had outstripped the Gothic by the 1770s as the standard form for lodges. Carter took the pediment and columns of Inigo Jones' St. Paul's, Covent Garden and set them between two plain rectangular lodges. The curiosity of his austere and noble design lies in the labelling of its plan. Each lodge has two rooms, a porter's lodge and a bedroom, the former 10 feet by 9 feet, the latter 6 feet by 9 feet, but the porter's lodge has no end wall, only a fireplace, while the large oval space under the portico, which is obviously the carriage entrance, is labelled as a 'Saloon'. Carter was notoriously eccentric but this is inexplicable.

Even after this, during decades when later comment shows that the gate lodge had become a regular park feature, there was only a scant showing of such lodge designs in the pattern books so the building type must have been establishing itself independently. This is proven by the unadventurously Palladian elegance of the next designs: six plates of 'Lodges for park or garden entrances and ornamental wooden gates' in John Miller's *The Country Gentleman's Architect* of 1787. The reserve of the book's title is borne out by the designs. The single storey examples are mere variants of Kent's 1730s design for a pair of lodges at Euston Hall, Suffolk and the two storey lodges are smaller versions of Kent's Claremont lodges. Their compositions are perhaps lighter and more elegant but the accommodation offered is less,

50
Timothy Lightoler's 1762 design for a lodge or keeper's house. (RIBA Library).

49
A 'Gothick Lodge' design of 1753 by the Halfpenny brothers. (Bodleian Library).

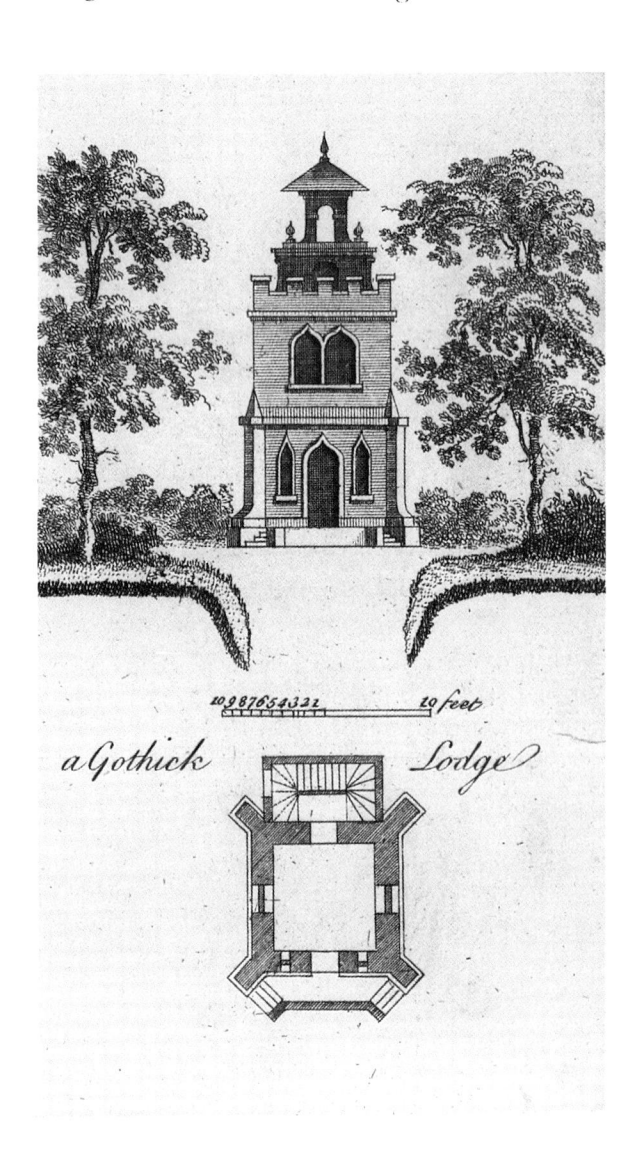

with one very large 20 foot by 18 foot chamber and one very small room downstairs. The staircases are in all cases structurally impossible as they would have only led their occupants through the roofs, so Miller's interiors must have been notional. His octagonal pair on page 26 are plain but satisfying versions of what must already, by the time of their publication, have become almost as popular a lodge form as that of the arch triumphal.

Then, without any transitional advance, the 'lodge palatial' makes its appearance in George Richardson's *New Designs in Architecture* of 1792. This, published just before the execution of Louis XVI, has a text in English and French and is an impressive, generously spaced volume. Richardson must have been in his middle fifties when he prepared the book — a collection of ostentatious but striking essays in the Adam style.[4] Richardson had accompanied James Adam on his 1760–3 Grand Tour but had to hide his drawings

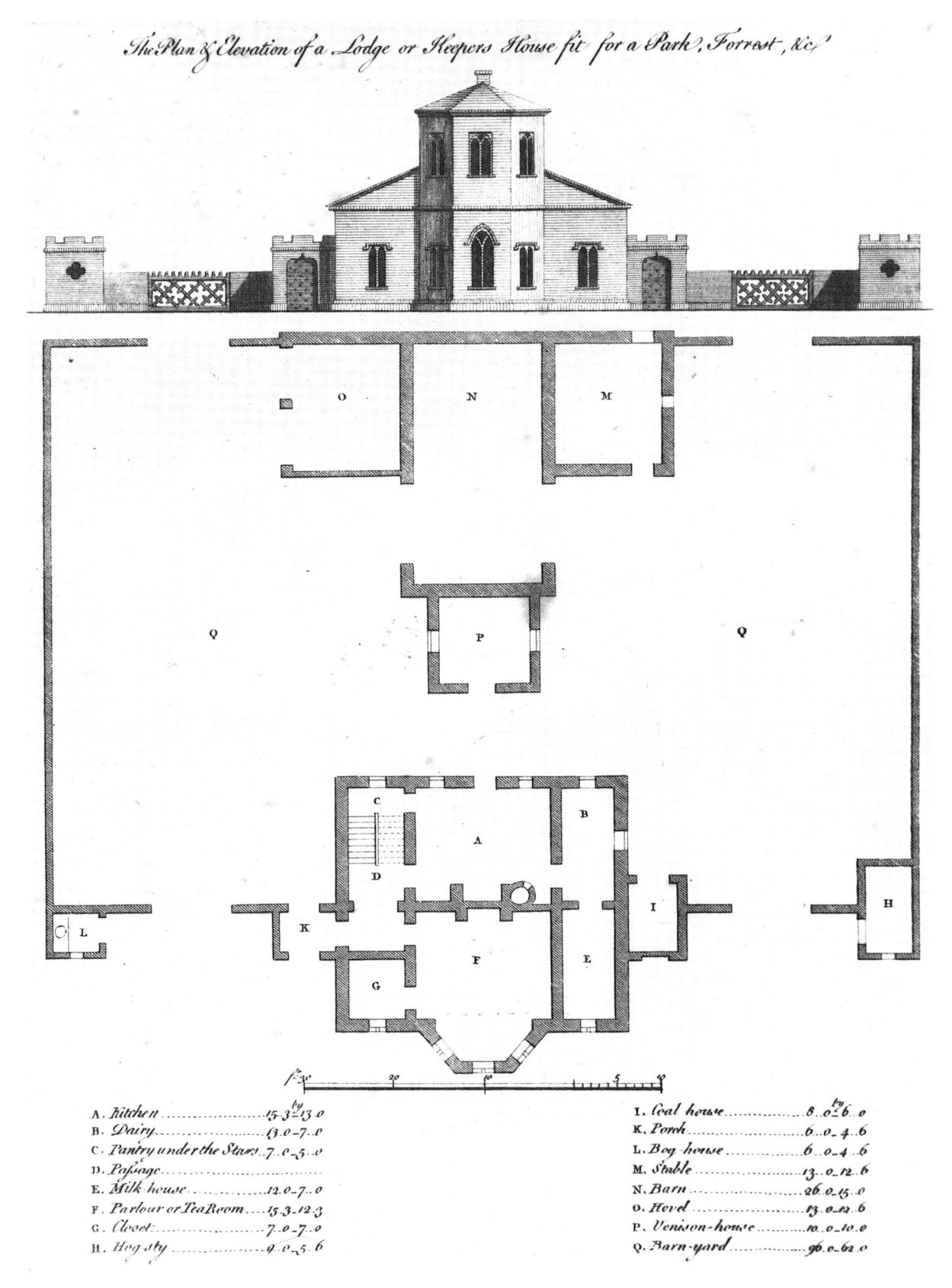

The Plan & Elevation of a Lodge or Keepers House fit for a Park, Forrest, &c.

A. Kitchen	15.3 by 13.0
B. Dairy	13.0 – 7.0
C. Pantry under the Stairs	7.0 – 5.0
D. Passage	
E. Milk house	12.0 – 7.0
F. Parlour or Tea Room	15.3 – 12.3
G. Closet	7.0 – 7.0
H. Hog Sty	9.0 – 5.6
I. Coal house	8.0 by 6.0
K. Porch	6.0 – 4.6
L. Bog house	6.0 – 4.6
M. Stable	13.0 – 12.6
N. Barn	26.0 – 15.0
O. Hovel	13.0 – 12.6
P. Venison-house	10.0 – 10.0
Q. Barn-yard	96.0 – 62.0

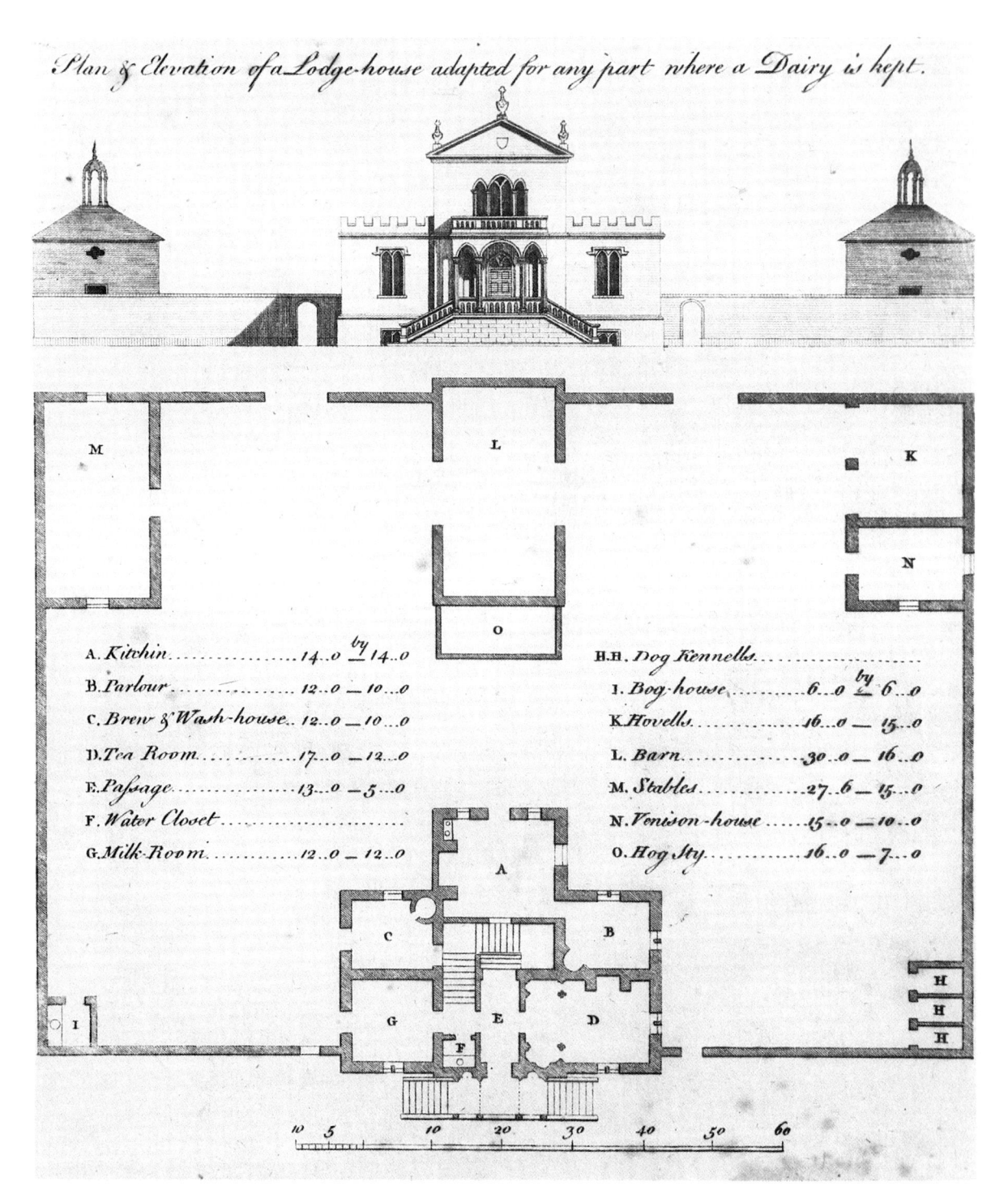

Plan & Elevation of a Lodge-house adapted for any part where a Dairy is kept.

A. Kitchin	14..0 by 14..0	H.H. Dog Kennells	
B. Parlour	12..0 — 10..0	I. Bog-house	6..0 by 6..0
C. Brew & Wash-house	12..0 — 10..0	K. Hovells	16..0 — 15..0
D. Tea Room	17..0 — 12..0	L. Barn	30..0 — 16..0
E. Passage	13..0 — 5..0	M. Stables	27..6 — 15..0
F. Water Closet		N. Venison-house	15..0 — 10..0
G. Milk-Room	12..0 — 12..0	O. Hog Sty	16..0 — 7..0

51
Timothy Lightoler's 1762 design for a dairy lodge (RIBA Library).

in case his jealous employer confiscated them. He never developed a substantial practice of his own and so turned to architectural publication. By the 1790s many more pattern books were being published as architects realised the need for advertisement, and as wealthy patrons of uncertain taste became more common through the profits of industry and trade. It was at the hyper-wealthy that Richardson must have been aiming his lodges. Four of the seven lodge designs are for 'extensive town mansions ... the plans being formed for enclosing large courts before noblemens' town houses'. Consequently on Plate 21 the lodge consists of a low single storey structure of two rooms dwarfed behind a grand Doric colonnade which would not have been shamed by Decimus Burton's Hyde Park Screen. There is an arched entrance at each end of the screen for the easy movement, into and out of the forecourt, of a large number of coaches at an evening entertainment. The park gate lodges of Richardson's collection continue in this tone of cold affluence, but at least Plate 17 would have given its occupants decent living quarters. Richardson explains this generosity in a note:

> The lodges on this plate are supposed to be situated at some considerable distance from the house; and that it might be thought convenient to have lodging rooms therein appropriated for the use of domestics and their families. One of the lodges is intended for the porter, and the other for the game-keeper.[5]

This means that the gamekeeper, who would earlier have occupied a remote woodland cottage, was now being moved, in the interests of symmetry, to one of a pair of gate lodges. The key to the right hand lodge shows a 'lodge' in the earlier but still current sense of a living room like that in Langley's 'Dorick Gate', a Gun Room, A Pantry and Store Room. In their exterior facades all Richardson's lodges have made the jump from Miller's Palladian to Adam's neo-classical, the lodges of Plate 17 bearing a marked likeness with their paterae and Doric frieze to Adam's lodges to Kedleston.

The established position of the park gate lodge by this time is demons-

52
Spiers Lodge inside the park of Warwick Castle.

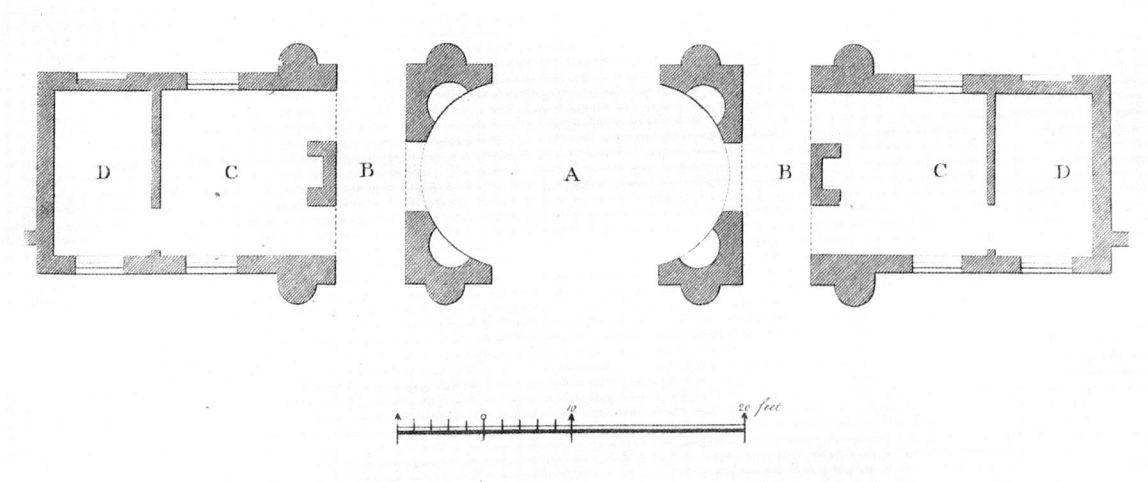

53
A triumphal arch with side lodges, designed in 1775 by John Carter. (RIBA Library).

55
Lodges and Gateway from George Richardson's *New Designs* (RIBA Library).

trated in a 1793 book, *Six Designs for improving and embellishing grounds*. This was published at his own expense by George J. Parkyns, one of the Parkyns of Bunny Hall, Nottinghamshire. It is a work of genteel good taste and claims to be based upon 'local observations made by Mr PARKYNS, in the course of a five years desultory tour, whilst he commanded a company in the Nottinghamshire regiment of militia during the last war'.[6]

The general character of Parkyns' park designs with their shrubberies, their clumped plantations and their woods planted to heighten existing rises in the land is conventionally Reptonian. Parkyns' fondness for 'the highest order of neatness and propriety'[7] in the upkeep of his parks marks him as one of the older generation of landscape designers whom Payne Knight and

66

Uvedale Price were vigorously attacking in the very year he published his book.

The book takes six seats with natural advantages and demonstrates by

54
A screen from George Richardson's *New Designs in Architecture* 1792. (RIBA Library).

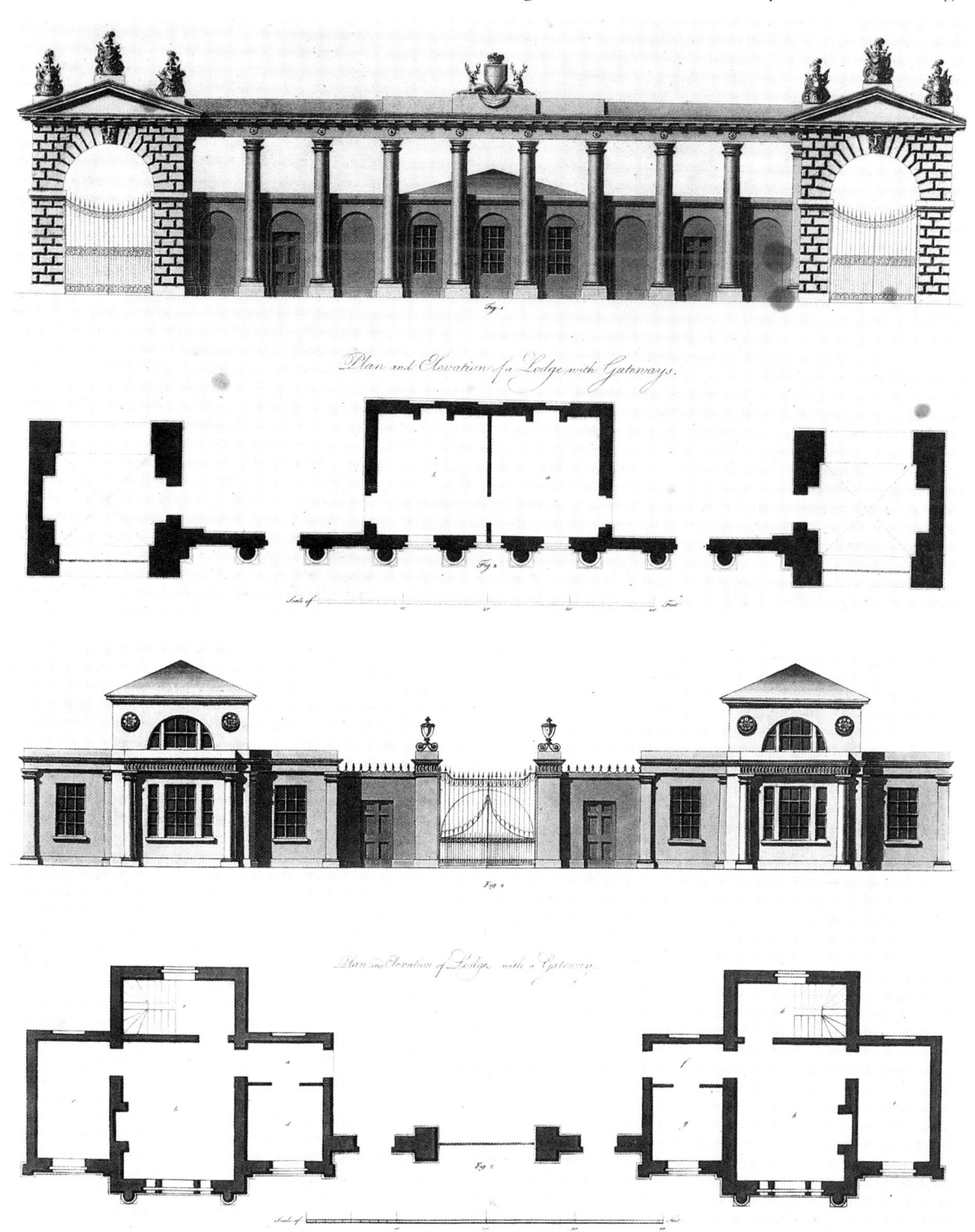

means of a map and notes how each park could be developed advantageously. Parkyns' maps are at least as fine as, and probably more detailed, than those in Repton's Red Books. His fifth scheme is for Belmont in Herefordshire, at that time the seat of Dr. John Matthews. This raises some doubts over the assertion that the scheme was devised during Parkyns' 'desultory tour' with the militia between 1773 and 1778. Belmont was burnt down in 1785 and had been rebuilt by James Wyatt in 1788–90. In 1794 Repton had just finished laying out the grounds for Dr. Matthews. This makes it likely that Parkyns prepared his plan after the house was burnt and then rebuilt, and when a new layout for the park was being contemplated, probably around 1790. Repton's scheme being preferred, Parkyns published his Belmont plan in 1793 rather than wholly waste his time.

Parkyns approved of the position of the house close to a lane 'by which the coach-road is spared the injury it would otherwise sustain from the heavy-loaded carriage, and kept in the highest order with the least possible expense'.[8] But for pleasure and display he devised two drives or, as he called them, 'carriage roads' for the park. One was a winding circular scenic way passing almost all the park features such as the Root-House, the Banqueting Room, the Temple of Harmony and the Temple of the Doric Order. The second drive was designed expressly as the entrance to be used to impress visitors:

> To shew the grounds to advantage, it is introduced from the turnpike, and winds past a lodge at the farthest point, down the side of an hill. On the right, relieved by a waving plantation, and on the left by a wood, is the hollow, through whose shade a rivulet gurgles its plaintive stream, which the road crosses over a neat bridge of one arch, and, rising the lawn ornamented with clumps of trees, it passes through a small shrubbery to the mansion.[9]

All the park buildings are thus reserved for the circular scenic drive, the only feature on the entrance drive is the lodge, so Parkyns is depending upon a small valley and a rising view across the Wye to impress the visitor. The lodge and the actual entrance are to sound the key note. His description emphasises this: the lodge is to be 'a Gothic building adjoining the turnpike road'. Significantly he remarks: 'edifices of this nature are so frequent and so varied, that taste cannot err in the choice'[10] and the house itself is classical. The lodge together with 'neat iron gates divide the coach from the turnpike road; this, together with the shrubberies and plantations, kept in the highest order of neatness and propriety, must impart a cheerfulness which it is presumed will accompany the stranger during his tour through the grounds'.[11]

The fact that Parkyns' lodge was to be the only Gothic feature in a park with several classical structures and a classical house is interesting. In *An*

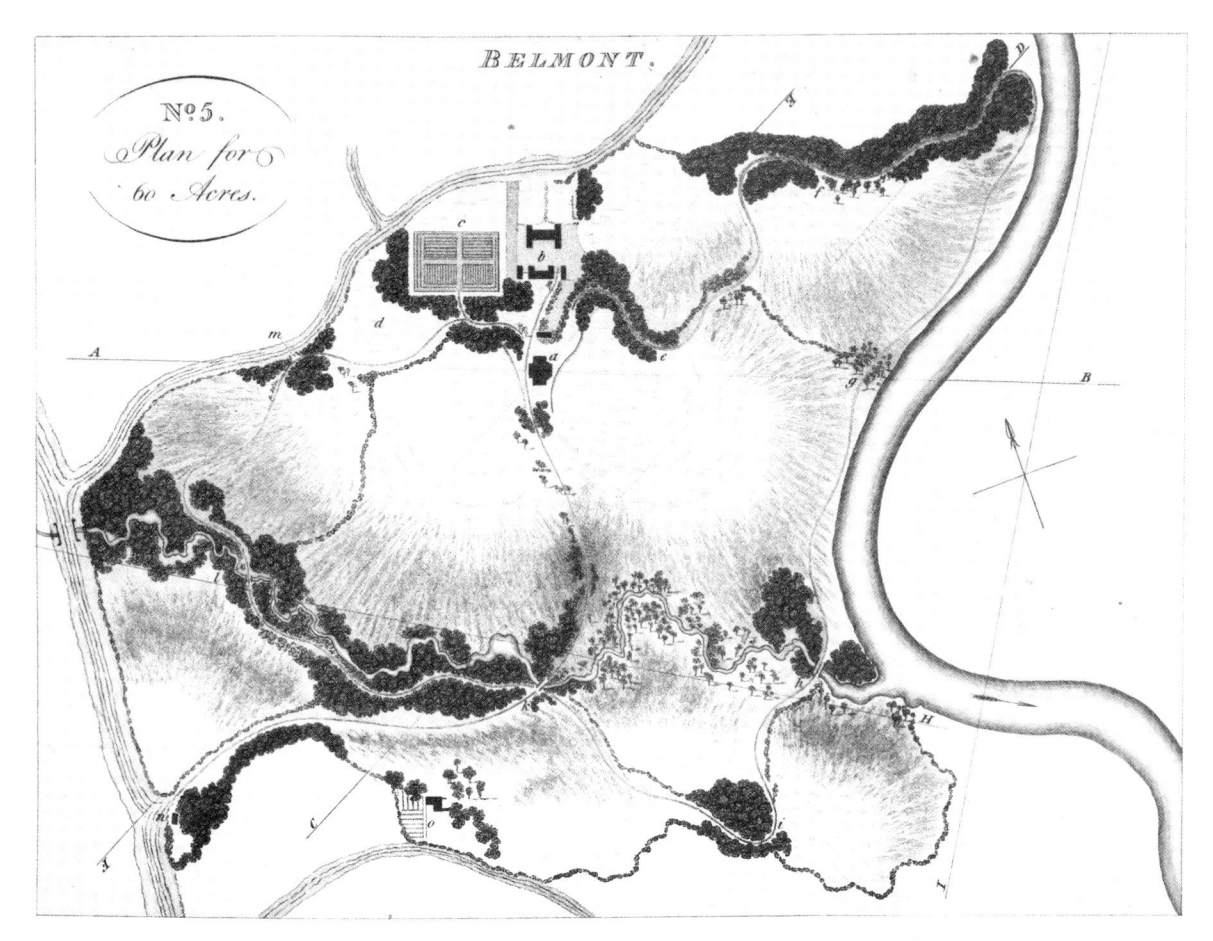

Essay on Rural Architecture of 1803, Richard Elsam sounds as casual as Parkyns about the range of lodge styles available to park owners. Elsam's note to Plate 29, a neo-classical lodge topped by an urn, states that 'so many excellent designs have been submitted to the public upon this subject, it seems difficult to devise any form which hath not been some time or other executed, but justness and simplicity of character I have always remarked, succeed the best among the purest examples.'[12]

Certainly there are lodge designs in many of the pattern books of this period but hardly in such quantity as to support Elsam's statement. It is possible that they may have been 'submitted to the public' in the annual Royal Academy exhibitions.

Some of the pattern books come from distinguished hands. Sir John Soane produced a youthful *Plans, Elevations and Sections of Buildings,* published in 1788, which illustrates, with ground plans and elevations, a pair of diagonally set lodge pavilions for the gates of Tendring Hall, Norfolk (Plate 22), a similar pair for Langley Park in the same county (Plate 23) and a far more ambitious 'Design made before the situation was determined' (i.e. not built) for a triumphal arch with two attached lodges (Plate 24) for the same house. Soane actually built a much more modest version of this design for Langley's owner, Sir Thomas Beauchamp Proctor.[13] However, most pattern books were the consolation of failed designers like Richardson, who died in pover-

56
George Parkyns' proposed improvements to the park at Belmont, Herefordshire, illustrated on a map of 1793. (RIBA Library).

ty, Elsam, notorious for litigation and expense, or Parkyns the park designer who seems never to have actually designed a park. Successful and competent architects are unlikely to have resorted to the schemes of failed co-professionals and the various lodge types must have evolved organically over the years in response to the general requests of patrons.

The role of the landscape designers in the evolution of the lodge is oddly indeterminate. The man who might have been expected to play a major part in the genesis of the lodge was Capability Brown, the most successful designer of park Arcadias. Some of his park schemes, notably that for Blenheim, mark lodges at major drive exits, but comparatively few of these were executed. This suggests that they were quite apart from the contracts which he always drew up with proprietors before he embarked on his improvements, and that Brown himself must have seen them as of secondary importance. His pair for the Ditchley Gate of Blenheim which would have terminated the grand but impractical main drive into the park across Vanbrugh's bridge, were Kentian boxes like those for Euston Hall attached to

57
The lodges of a theorist. A plate from Joseph Gandy's *Designs* of 1805. (Bodleian Library).

Kentian gatepiers.[14] For Packington in Warwickshire he devised a much grander balustraded pair on each side of a pedimented archway; these were for a grand axial driveway, not for a meandering drive designed to display the beauties of the park's planting.[15] They were not built. Lodges from his hand which were actually erected like the Convent Lodge at Tong and the High Lodge at Blenheim are park features, objects for an excursion, rather than mere neat houses for gate openers. Repton had, as has been noted, very strong views on lodge design and often attached them to his schemes for improvements, but he always saw himself as landscape designer first and only architect as a poor second. He often passed on architectural openings which came his way to partners like William Wilkins, John Nash or his son John Adey Repton, but he was at least completely lodge conscious and sensitive to the mood a lodge was to evoke: a Tudor lodge for a Tudor rose garden, an embattled gateway to a folly-crowned wild park, a picturesque *cottage orné* to a bosky landscape.[16]

Sensitive is the last word that would ever be applied to Joseph Gandy's pattern book lodge designs. Relatively unsuccessful in his lifetime, Gandy has of late achieved a reputation as the English equivalent of the French monumental symbolist architects Boullée and Ledoux.[17] His lodge designs in *Designs for Cottages, Cottage Farms, and other Rural Buildings including Entrance Gates and Lodges* (1805) and *The Rural Architect* (1806) are strikingly delineated in sepia washes. Harshly geometrical cubes, cones and obelisks with virtually no relieving detail, they anticipate the most doctrinaire effects of 1930s modernism. None of them were ever built and it is hard to understand why Gandy thought that there was any mood among landed proprietors of these war years for such outrageously revolutionary designs. At £150 for the pair illustrated on Plate 41 of his *Designs for Cottages,* they had not even the attraction of economy. The epigraph to this chapter outlined Gandy's insolent indifference to the living standards of a lodge keeper's family. The Egyptian obelisk lodges of Plate 42 in *The Rural Architect* feature an upper bedroom 'the ascent to which is by a step-ladder,' while the conical pair in his second book would, if they had ever been built, have provided only a few square feet in which the lodge keeper could have stood upright. Gandy proposed to have them 'thatched down to the ground; this would have a singular and not unpleasing effect'.

The lodges in Edward Gyfford's *Designs for Small Picturesque Cottages* (1807) are conventionally classical pavilions or columned screens but they exhibit the same contempt for the comfort of the lodge keeper. Plates 15 and 16 have a single storey box, 10 feet by 10 feet, on each side of the brutally overscaled colonnades, while Plate 17, a lodge 'intended as an entrance to two paddocks' has one room only. Gyfford appropriately drew a depressed looking mother with her child quitting this elegant slum. This was, of course, a period when stylish elegance was to the fore, and if horses' heads were commonly held in check by bearing-reins and men's chins kept rigid in stiff towering collars, it might not have seemed outrageous to confine a working class couple in two small rooms with a drive between them provided that those rooms expressed a taut economy of design. Such lodges are

58 J.B. Papworth's interchangeable design of 1818 for a 'Steward's Cottage' or 'Lodge'. (RIBA Library).

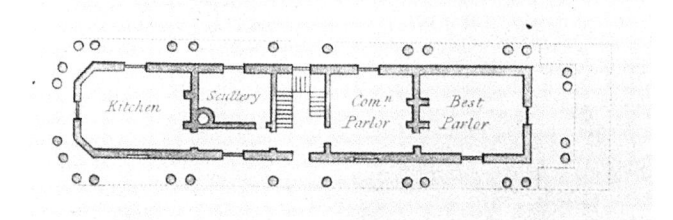

not limited to the pattern books. Thomas Harrison's neat Doric sentry boxes at the north entrance to Chirk Castle, Denbighshire, were inhabited, it has to be supposed cheerfully, for well over a century, and lodge pairs of similar dimensions are not uncommon.[18] To an old couple or a widow with a child they may have seemed preferable to the miseries of a workhouse. On the other hand a 'Steward's Cottage' like the charming specimen illustrated in John Papworth's *Rural Residences* would, Papworth suggested, 'be suitable to a small lodge or as a decorative cottage in a park' though 'intended for the residence of the under-steward to a nobleman's estate'.[19] Many of these generously scaled and attractive houses were built at park entrances even though they were not primarily entrance lodges. As Papworth pointed out, the lodge formed in the visitor's mind an impression of the park owner's character and there may well have been a correlation, now unfortunately unverifiable, between the stiffness of the proprietor's collar and the formal neatness of his gate lodges.

The first pattern book to be entirely devoted to lodge designs came out in 1811 with a second edition in 1823 suggesting its popularity. This was T.D.W. Dearn's *Designs for Lodges and Entrances*. It has 20 plates of a generally conventional and lacklustre styling, some Gothic, some classical. Its one unforgettable design, never executed, was for a vast and ingenious

59
The gate lodge as a tenement block for estate workers. A design of 1811 by Thomas Dearn. (RIBA Library).

medieval gatehouse-style lodge for Bayham Abbey on the Kent-Sussex border.[20] This was to have been the apotheosis of the lodge as tenement with accommodation in the two flanking wings for no less than four families,

60
The moral lodge. A single bedroom design from Thomas Dearn's 1811 collection. (RIBA Library).

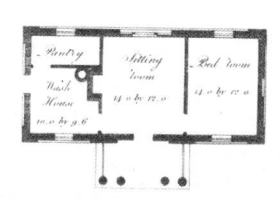

73

each provided with a separate stair turret to mount up to their single, but strictly private, bedroom in the tower over the arch.

Dearn was nothing if not morally alert. His trim lodge on Plate 6 has a four columned Doric portico fronting four rooms: a pantry, a wash house, a sitting room and a bedroom. To this he adds the following cautiously prurient note:

> To more than one lodging room, in a building of this sort, many persons object. An Entrance Lodge is usually intended, either for an old man, an old woman, or both, or for a mother and daughter; in short, for any thing but a family. A group of small children, though occasionally picturesque in a situation like this, is not, on the whole, desirable. That neatness and air of comfort, which should mark the approach to a gentleman's residence, would, by such an assemblage, be too frequently destroyed; and by giving more than one room, where there are no children, an opportunity is afforded for a much more serious objection.[21]

So here, more than a century later, is another suggestion of the lodge as a potential nest of rustic impropriety. Dearn is anticipating the kind of looseness which had resulted in the old sergeants from Chelsea Hospital being given severe warnings by the Duke of Chandos's steward for letting out the spare room in their lodges to undesirables. Dearn's comment is further

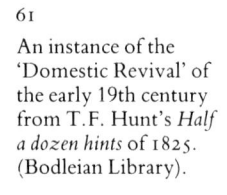

61
An instance of the 'Domestic Revival' of the early 19th century from T.F. Hunt's *Half a dozen hints* of 1825. (Bodleian Library).

evidence that many gate lodges at this period were built small expressly to avoid the untidiness of a family with children living at the park entrance.

This mood of meagre morality and cramped lodge design was, however, just about to change. The long reign of the park as Arcadia was ending and a

62
An early Italianate lodge design by T.F. Hunt of 1827. (Bodleian Library).

new mood for the Gardenesque was ripening. The new park layouts required a different style of gate lodge and this the pattern books were prompt to express and supply. T.F. Hunt's book *Half a dozen Hints on Picturesque Domestic Architecture* (1825, 2nd edition 1826) analyses the change in mood adroitly in its 'Address':

> In these Designs the Old English Domestic Style
> has been preferred to every other as admitting of
> greater variety of form and outline, and as being
> better suited to the scenery of this Country, than a
> Greek Temple or Italian Villa.

Only Plates 1, 7 and 9 are labelled as actual gate lodges, but there is no essential difference in style between these and Hunt's gentleman's sporting lodges or fishing pavilions. All achieve their 'variety of form and outline' by gables, bow and dormer windows, jettied storeys, richly fretted bargeboards and towering 'Tudor' chimney stacks. In this Tudorbethan style, lodge design finds the courage to explore the spatial variety that eighteenth century Gothick tended to shirk. The idealised cottage proved more liberating than the tower or the gatehouse.

Hunt's second book *Archittetura Campestre* (1827) followed quickly upon the success of his first and was not, despite his earlier insular protestations, above including designs in the then fashionable Italianate. He shaped this in his third plate to combine a lodge with a viewing tower of the campanile style which Prince Albert's Osborne was to make so popular. Hunt's theme remained, however, as strongly native and Gardenesque in his second book as in his first:

> Since the introduction of the present chaste system of landscape gardening, Gate-Lodges and other small domestic structures, have become objects of greater interest than when pyramids, grottos, and hermitages,
> 'With all the mournful family of yews',
> were the only embellishments which attracted notice. Pure and simple architecture has superseded the artificial absurdities; and of the gloomy trees, Pope has already told us —
> 'The thriving plants, ignoble broomsticks made,
> Now sweep the alleys they were born to shade'.
> A better taste is established and encouraged; everything must be suitable to its required purposes: useless masses no longer disfigure the beautiful scenery of our parks and lawns; nor ought we to
> 'Turn arcs of triumph to a garden gate'.[22]

The century long reign of Gothic and classical fantasy was near its end. In its place a new feeling for an essentially native rusticity in cottage form was emerging. Cottages that would house their occupants in a style appropriate to a new generation of landowners, who felt bound to make gestures at least to social responsibility.

CHAPTER FIVE

The Arc of Triumph as a Garden Gate

As A FEATURE of Elizabethan and Jacobean forecourts, the detached arch precedes the classical arched lodge by more than a hundred years. Of the three distinct proto-forms of the park gate lodge — the single side pavilion, the twin pavilions and the gatehouse tower — the latter was always the most emphatic piece of architectural punctuation for an entrance to a house or a demesne. Stanway, Westwood and Drayton House prove that the arched gatehouse of medieval form was too potent a symbol of wealth and ancestry ever wholly to be rejected but as it came, with lodges like the Edgehill Tower, to be also a symbol of self-conscious romanticism, the classical triumphal arch took its place by natural evolution as the more appropriate and discreetly prestigious form of entry marker to the park of a gentleman with a classical house, or at least a classical education. At continental towns like Trier, Saintes or Orange, Roman triumphal arches of diverse design had survived to impress the informed traveller; and at Rome the final object of most grand tourists, the arches of the Emperors themselves, Constantine and Vespasian, stood in the Forum, half sunken in debris, but still symbols richly evoking a lost order.

As lodges came to be accepted as standard park furniture, it became usual, though by no means an absolute rule, for a lodge controlling the most important drive to be in the arched triumphal form and for the twin pavilion type lodges to be placed at drives of lesser importance. If a drive out towards open country or a sporting area was marked at all, a single small house of some slight stylistic pretension was sufficient.

A park gate lodge in the form of a triumphal arch has already been described as essentially unsuited to its function. Such it is. There is also something not only impractical, but inherently absurd in the notion of fitting a living room and a bedroom into a vaunting symbol of Roman militarism, then placing the whole at the entrance, not to a city's forum, but to an Arcadian landscape. Only an insular, fundamentally unmilitary, yet vainglorious nobility would have attempted this naïve device so often.

This is not to denigrate the aesthetic importance of the form. Like park gate lodges in general they have been underpraised, perhaps because they are scattered widely and disconnectedly across a whole countryside. Though they are often hidden up leafy back lanes or crudely exposed by recent road widening they are the most numerous and inventive group of these structures in Europe and should be assessed as such.

The inventiveness of their form is occasioned by their dysfunctionalism.

In one sense they were not a building type which could evolve. Because they sprang from perfected antique prototypes they were merely reflective unless their designers were obliged to modify their form in order to combine their original function with the secondary one of living accommodation. It was a task which William Kent deliberately shirked in his design for the Holkham Triumphal Arch, leaving blank spaces in which Brettingham had later to insert fenestration.[1]

From the beginning of the eighteenth century it remained an open option for landowners to erect a simple triumphal arch without concession to living accommodation. Hawksmoor's Woodstock entrance to Blenheim Palace of 1723 is an instance of this with just a small door inside the right hand pier to a porter's room and a crude aperture or two on the side walls of the arch to make a minimal distraction from the Roman image of the structure.[2] The arches in Langley's 1740 pattern book follow this model and for at least the next century and a half there were to be some estate owners content to erect a triumphal arch without a lodge. Yet in most such cases: the fine Ionic arch to Highhead Castle at Ivegill in Cumberland, the Doric Nelson memorial arch to Duncombe Park in the North Riding and William Everard's fusion of the

63
The Lion Gate. A triumphal arch isolated from its later lodge at Ince Blundell Hall, Lancashire.

baroque and the neo-classical in the Lion Gate to Ince Blundell Hall, Lancashire, custom or functional need has demanded the later addition of a detached gatekeeper's cottage in a discordant style.[3]

For this reason the architects of most triumphal arches have applied their wits to a design which would combine the two functions of making outward show and of providing accommodation for an estate worker's family, or even two such families, within a structure which was originally conceived as a framework to hold statuary, and an inscription commemorating a successful campaign. The essential interest and tension within such designs was the probability that the more adequately a family was housed, the feebler the evocation of Roman grandeur became.

Three main alternatives were open to the architects and their arched lodges will be considered under these three separate types. The first was to include the lodge keeper's living quarters within the actual piers and superstructure of the arch. The second was to avoid the basic problem: to build a two-dimensional arch with side screens linking it to lodges which were really structures apart, attached merely stylistically to the central feature. The third alternative, a compromise in compression, was to provide for a lodge keeper by two pavilions built immediately one on each side of the triumphal arch, thus creating a single composition of three functionally separate units.

Although the first alternative was the most demanding of the three it was obviously the most appealing, being visually closest to the Roman originals; and when handled with skill it was the most satisfying, combining as it did, war and peace within one frame.

Hawksmoor's Woodstock Gate is, at the outset, a frank admission of the difficulty of such a union. Its appearance is all Roman, though a highly original variant with a narrow attic storey. For the porter it provided little beyond a dark box that would have held a wide-backed porter's chair or perhaps a narrow bed for a needy pensioner. A later attempt at the form was far more ingenious in its use of internal space. This was the Corinthian Arch at Stowe, the design of an aristocratic amateur, Thomas Pitt, Lord Camelford, a friend of Horace Walpole. The Corinthian Arch is a key feature of the park. Most of the earlier structures which litter the grounds had been inward

64
Two houses are ingeniously concealed within the piers of the Corinthian Arch of 1767 at Stowe, Buckinghamshire.

in their intention, markers to an Elysian field or symbols to an earlier proprietor, Lord Cobham's frustrated political idealism.[4] The unsatisfactory nature of the Boycott pavilions and Kent's Oxford Gate on the main approach avenue to the park has already been considered. Now, with the Corinthian Arch, Lord Temple was attempting a structure which would both centre the vista from his south front and unite his park to the outside world in general and Buckingham town in particular. The old Oxford Gate avenue continued to be the main drive to the house, but the ceremonial avenue from Buckingham across three miles of farmland terminates at this new Corinthian arch perched on a rise of ground and framing a surprise view of lake, park and house. Nothing in the sides of the arch which face the house or the ceremonial avenue betrays the fact that accommodation on three storeys is concealed within each of the piers. To the approaching visitor all is truly triumphalist; four great Corinthian pilasters support an entablature with balustrading and flanking swagged panels. There is not a window or a chimney in sight to distract the eye from the view which it frames. The apartments hidden in the piers are still occupied by estate workers, one family enjoying exclusively the sunrise, the other the sunset, so Thomas Pitt's solution has endured the test of time.

Inexplicably, no other lodges of this type seem to have followed the Stowe arch in its device of concealing windows and doors in the side walls. Perhaps the paradox of domesticity in triumphalism was found pleasing. Humphry Repton's original solemn design engraved for 'The Theory', for the main lodge to Harewood House in the West Riding, had concealed all domestic

65
The triumphal arch to Harewood House, West Riding.

detail but it was rejected for an uninspired Roman Doric archway executed by the mason John Muschamp in 1803.[5] This openly sets round-headed windows on both main facades to light the lodge within. The south lodge to

66
A ponderous exercise in the Greek Revival at Carden Hall, Cheshire.

Carden Hall in Cheshire does the same but achieves a much richer three-dimensional effect by recessing the very tall ground floor windows of the lodge back between Ionic columns that carry a section of the entablature projecting forwards. The unknown architect has thus injected an almost baroque movement into an otherwise neo-classical lodge. If the same hand designed the pavilions of the north lodge to the same park then a notable episode in lodge building has gone sadly unrecorded.

North Cheshire and south Lancashire may seem to feature disproportionately in this episode of lodge design but it was an area where a rapid burst of industrial development took place towards the end of the eighteenth century, and where the Napoleonic wars had created boom conditions. As a result there were new men with new money to spend on houses and parks. In addition, Thomas Harrison was living at Lancaster in the 1780s and moved to Chester in 1793. Consequently his enthusiasm for neo-classicism would be felt in both counties, supported as it would be, in a region which valued technical expertise, by his prestige as the engineer of the Lune Bridge (1783–8) and of the world's largest single span arch — the Grosvenor Bridge at Chester of 1827–33.

Three lodges of the integrated arch type remain to be considered together because they give the lie to the suggestion that such arched structures are reflective of a prototype and not an evolving form. They are Henry Holland's Gatehouse to Berrington Hall, Herefordshire (1778–81), an amazingly late essay in the same style by Professor Reilly for Greenbank, Chester, of 1923, and the most stylistically modern of them all, which must, however, be dated to 1819–20 — the South Lodge to Tabley House, again from Cheshire.

All three quite frankly place the triumphal arch in a context which was modern for their times, ultra modern in the case of the Tabley Lodge.

67
Henry Holland's Gatehouse of 1778-81 to the gardens at Berrington Hall, Herefordshire.

68
A late revival of the triumphal arch as a chauffeur's cottage to Greenbank, Chester (1923).

Holland's arch for Berrington marks the junction between park and garden. Its classical detail is minimal — a keystone and a scrap of balustrading, elegant sash windows are cut directly into the smooth ashlar, the effect is monumental yet discreet. Reilly's gatehouse to Greenbank in the Chester suburbs is a thoughtful 1920s improvisation in the neo-Regency style. It

82

served as a chauffeur's house to Greenbank whose more ornate doorway Reilly also designed. Reilly was as indifferent as Holland to the classical detail which the form might seem to demand. The two-bay recessed section over the central arch cuts unpredictably up into the pediment to give a dimensional depth to the composition, only the running dog frieze and the consoles each side of the ground floor windows reassert the period of the main house, 1812–25.

Though it was actually built in the same period as the main house at Greenbank, the South Lodge to Tabley House eschews even those minor concessions to period style. It is noteworthy as a demonstration of how close certain buildings of the late Regency came to the International Modernism of the 1920s and 1930s. Apart from the plain arched recesses for the lower windows which pick up the outline of the central arch, there is absolutely no hint of decorative detail. The lodge relies totally on the depth of its archway

69
The South Lodge of Tábley House, Cheshire. The ultimate refinement of the arched form (*c.*1819-20).

and the basic form of hipped roof and twin chimneys to command the bridge and drive in front of it. George Moneypenny worked at the house in 1819–20 reinstating the east wing after fire damage, and his experience as a gaol builder at Winchester and Leicester suggests that he may have designed this intensely uncompromising building which, though Soaneian in its simplicity, has none of Soane's invention and perversity. It concludes the tally of such integrated arch lodges appropriately, as here everything has been stripped away leaving the basic form.

Before moving to the second of the three alternative forms of such lodges it is worth considering why the triumphal arch was so rarely applied in the one section of the outbuildings of a great house, the stable block, where an

PLATE IX

arched entrance naturally occurred. There are a few instances of triumphal arches in such sites. The shortest way into Hartwell House, Buckinghamshire from the main road runs through a deep arch under a grandiose seven bay stable block probably designed by Henry Keene between 1759 and 1763. The approach is both impressive and convenient, but what sufficed for Louis XVIII of France in the last years before his restoration rarely served for the English nobility whose houses were so often built close to public ways and could easily have been entered by a route such as that at Hartwell. John Morris, a stonemason of Lewes, constructed an outstandingly practical and satisfying main entrance to Glynde Place, Sussex through such a stable arch for Richard Trevor, Bishop of Durham in 1753–6. Like the Tabley South Lodge this is a minor masterpiece of functional restraint, a plain pedimented brick arch below a wooden cupola with flint-faced stable ranges on either side. But though the flints on the western side are knapped and squared for a perfect textural finish, like Arts and Crafts work of a century later, the Bishop must have felt the whole composition to be insufficiently grand and in 1759 John Cheere was paid £48.5s for heraldic wyverns to lend artificial dignity to the piers beyond the arch. This implies that the whole point of lodges in general and of triumphal arches in particular, was that they should convey splendid excess not practical convenience.

If this was so then the second alternative type of arch triumphal was perfectly adapted to generous display. In this the arch is treated as a two-dimensional feature linked by side walls to two side lodges, thus separating structurally the functions of display and housing. As with the integrated arch the first instance of such a solution is an early one.

A ghost of such a scheme, datable to 1729–30, survives overlaid by nineteenth century additions in the East Gate to Studley Royal in the West Riding.

Colen Campbell had been advising the park owner, John Aislabie, on the design of the stables to the main house but when Campbell was taken ill in 1729 his assistant Roger Morris took over the work, subject to sharp rebuke from his tetchy and, in fact, dying superior. There is no direct evidence to connect the East Gate with Campbell and Morris. It is a handsome early Palladian design: a central arched carriage entrance flanked by straight-headed pedestrian openings; the whole is enlivened with vermiculated rustication and topped by ball finials. At a superficial glance the two lodges at the end of the side walls are of nineteenth century date, but each on its outward face retains an earlier doorway whose dramatically overstated pediments and quoining are more Vanbrughian than Burlingtonian. These doors must originally have served side pavilions which have been built into the present lodges. The stables to the house have the same combination of Palladian and Vanbrughian detail and it is a fair supposition that a triumphal arch gate lodge to Campbell and Morris's joint design had been built at Studley Royal as early as 1730, though its original form is lost. The supposition is the more tempting in view of Campbell's supposed authorship of the Kingsweston Penpole Gate design of 1723, Morris's near approach to lodges at Clearwell in 1728 and his final achievement of the classical pair, with similar overdramatised doorway surrounds, at Althorp in 1732. What is particularly interesting is that the four designs cover all three possible lodge types: the arch, the tower and the pavilions, so if any architects are to be credited with the development of the park gate lodge these two men seem

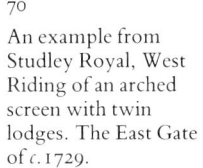

70
An example from Studley Royal, West Riding of an arched screen with twin lodges. The East Gate of *c.*1729.

71
Robert Adam, in the entrance screen to Syon House, Middlesex, emphasised the decorative possibilities of the arch and not the social requirements of the lodge keeper.

85

entitled to share the achievement.

Aesthetically, the Studley arrangement of arch, side walls and flanking lodges is impressive in its breadth but in danger, without firm points of emphasis and articulation, of straggling. Significantly, two of the essays in this particularly expansive deployment of a triumphal arch were both for dukes. The first, by Robert Adam, designed in the 1760s and erected in 1773, was the Isleworth entrance screen and lodges to Syon House, Middlesex for the first Duke of Northumberland. The second was Stephen Wright's spectacular Apleyhead Lodge to Clumber Park, Nottinghamshire, seat of the second Duke of Newcastle, which was complete by 1778.

Adam's lodge is confidently innovative in overall design, an arch flanked on each side by five bay screens of columns and minimal pavilions. Its detail is a rare *plein air* demonstration of the delicate feminine detail which Adam customarily lavished on his interiors. A frieze of garlanded bucrania, ill-suited by its fine modelling to withstand the weather, unites the lodges to the screen whose capitals are of an idiosyncratic sub-Corinthian. The arch itself has pilasters up which Vitruvian scrolls climb like elegant vines to a flourish of swags and paterae. The whole is intended as an outward advertisement to the interiors of the house, a proclamation rather than a defence. If anything in the composition could be criticised it would be the abrupt angles which the arch makes as it rises above the screen. Adam himself can hardly be blamed for the archaic boldness of the Percy lion which surmounts the entablature.

Wright's Apleyhead Lodge is as sparing in detail as the Syon screen is

72
Stephen Wright's ambitious Apleyhead Lodge to Clumber Park, Nottinghamshire.

73
John Nash's pedestrian version of the triumphal arch at Attingham Hall, Shropshire (*c.* 1807).

lavish, but as both a composition and a social unit it excels Adam's Syon design. The severe central arch is enriched by balustrading and linked easily to its three bay screens by sweeping curved panels. The twin lodges themselves are of great length, curving outwards to enclose the visitor approaching from Nottingham, but punctuated sparingly by two niches and one pedimented window in an arched recess. The end facades are a blind but complex enrichment of concave and flat section disks and an arch which echoes the carriage arch. Almost all the fenestration of its generous living accommodation faces the park.

Wright's lodge occupies a plot of land broad enough for an interchange on a motorway, but no subsequent arched lodge of this type is quite as satisfying. John Nash's Atcham Lodge, the Shrewsbury approach to Attingham Hall, Shropshire, of about 1807 is a disappointing prelude to the same architect's rich yet stylish arches to his Regent's Park terraces. It has a certain frowning grandeur as in a Roman aqueduct, but the detail is dull and the outline has the same angularity as the Syon arch. The lodges themselves are infilled versions of the pedestrian arches offering no individual statement of design.

Two further lodges of this type are much more successful but both of them, James Wyatt's Chippenham Lodge to Dodington Park, Gloucestershire and his nephew Lewis Wyatt's Knutsford Lodge to Tatton Park, Cheshire, cheat. They pull back from the daunting task of uniting one arch, two screen walls and two lodges by cutting, in the former case, the left hand, and, in the latter, the right hand, lodge. Only thirteen years separate the two lodges and uncle and nephew often worked closely together but the difference in discipline and control is complete.

For his Barbados millionaire Christopher Codrington, James Wyatt made all the emphasis inwards to the park.[6] The only austerity is in the five bay screens. The triumphal arch itself is conventionally tripartite but blank panels above the side arches bind the composition together. All the detail is shallow and undemanding to allow the eye to rest on the lodge which is virtually a house for the middling gentry, ample enough for a Codrington dowager though never so used. Although this must be one of the largest lodges in Britain its design is of a rambling inconsequence, as if the older Wyatt had been simultaneously engaged in another project: a stage set perhaps for Kean's *Romeo and Juliet* from which a balcony has escaped to be pressed within an elephantine and quite unrelated recessed round arch. Below the balcony is an Adamesque tympanum. A winged dragon sits over the carriage arch as if brooding over a monstrous clutch of reptile eggs, an appropriate symbol for this complex which signals very clearly that eclecticism has begun to run riot and that patrons of great wealth, but little discernment, are beginning to demand their money's worth.

74
Grecian austerity in the Knutsford Lodge (1811) to Tatton Park, Cheshire.

No vestige of this decay in taste appears in Lewis Wyatt's lodges for Wilbraham Egerton at Tatton Park. These were built between 1807 and 1813. The temple type lodge at the north west exit of the park will be reserved for the next chapter, but that and the main lodge to the park, the triumphal arch to Knutsford, are both of powerful neo-classical severity. The arched lodge, of 1811, is extraordinarily successful. It is not gigantic in its dimensions but the excellence of its proportions gives the two Greek Doric columns and the central pediment a significance out of all measure to their function. This is a real arch for triumphs; through such a portal a Prussian army could march in triumph after Waterloo. Placed in a capital city it would become a landmark for tourists, placed in a shrubbery outside Knutsford, it goes unremarked, though a reminder of the petty pomps of Yeomanry, Trades and Benefits Societies, Fire Brigades and Mayoralty with which the gentry of the period were accustomed to celebrate their comings of age and their wedding days.

Lewis Wyatt avoided rather than solved the problem of the lodge unit here by placing the one storey building humbly behind a heavy screen wall. This is the one weakness in his design and a highly significant one. There is a whole series of drawings in the RIBA Drawings Collection from this period, 1813-18, by William Edwards, a Welsh bridge builder.[7] All are attempts to overwhelm utilitarian lodges with grandiose arches or screens. It was a device which seemed briefly to obsess a generation of the upper classes reared through almost fifteen years of European war. Their lodge designs are those of an aristocracy which has found itself in control now of a world empire and they are an expression of the consequent neurosis of grandeur. The triumphal arch is essentially an imperial device and they were built as the symbols of the aristocracy of an empire rather than of an island kingdom. Hence the Hyde Park Screen (1825) and the Constitution Arch (erected 1846) were superimposed upon the superior residential area of a merchant city. The giant Ionic columns of the Carden arch look fairly absurd in the bucolic nowhere of rural Cheshire but the Empress Elizabeth of Austria stayed at the hall and hunted through its portal, so the triumphal entrance was a well-aimed gesture of state to balance the homely huddle of Elizabethan Carden Hall.

The last alternative version of the arched lodge was that of the triple unit: the arch with twin pavilions built immediately on to its side walls. It had the apparent virtue of unifying the three blocks dedicated to two separate functions. It was to prove the most intractable and unsatisfactory of the three forms. The neo-classical style evokes the antique past so effectively when deployed on the central arched unit that it tends to dissociate itself awkwardly from the homely living units which shoulder it at each side. As a result the most successful design of this type is stylistically and perhaps chronologically the earliest.

The Bishops Fonthill gateway lodge to Fonthill Splendens, the short-lived Wiltshire palace of Alderman Beckford, is so completely Palladian in appearance that it has been attributed to Inigo Jones himself.[8] In style and scale it is close to its lost house and must date somewhere between 1757 and 1770 and be the work of Hoare, the City builder who designed and built Splendens in a lavish but dated manner for a brash millionaire and political malcontent. If Splendens, destroyed 1807, has lingered as an architectural memory, this lodge is largely responsible. Its scale is only realised when a human figure stands against the vast urns and supporting scrolls that flank its approach from the village. The lodge succeeds as a unit of three diverse sections

PLATE X

75
A detail illustrative of the massive scale of the Fonthill gateway.

because it is astylar and not, therefore, aggressively antique. Instead a pattern of rich alternative vermiculated rustication binds the arch and its flanking pavilions together. The effect is urbane and friendly rather than Roman and stiff. Urns crown its pediment not stylised lions or scaly wyverns. The balustrading on the lodge units eases the transition to the perpendicular rise of the arch itself and Hoare has introduced a subtle asymmetry of detail of scroll and balustrading below the pavilions themselves. The whole gateway

76
Robert Adam's Roman Doric North Lodge to Kedleston Hall, Derbyshire. (1761-2).

lodge suggests a triumph of wealth not of war and succeeds by this relative integrity.

Robert Adam's North Lodge to Kedleston Hall, Derbyshire (1761–2), the main Derby approach to the house, may be earlier in date than the Fonthill lodge but it is already falling into the ensnaring theatricalities of the neo-classical. Its very simplicity is its undoing. Two giant columns of the Roman Doric order support a frieze of triglyphs and a pediment with heraldry. In

77
Adam at second-hand. James Wyatt's entrance gateway (1778) to Bryanston House, Dorset.

contrast the Fonthill pediment has no escutcheon. It is lined simply with modillions and has a grotesque Mannerist head on the keystone below it grinning away any suggestion of pomposity. At Kedleston Adam realised that he had to effect a transition from the perpendicular of the arch to the horizontal of the side pavilions. If he had followed historical precedent he could have used Palladian design and topped the pavilions with a half pediment, as Palladio had done at San Giorgio Maggiore and just as Kent did at Esher. Instead, over-conscious perhaps of his role as an innovating neo-classicist, Adam compromised with a sloping tiled roof. The effect against the classical chill of the central arch is domestic and weak. The triple unit lumbers in proportions; yet it seems to have pleased because James Wyatt put up almost an exact copy of it in 1778 at Bryanston in Dorset with no attempt to correct the flaws in Adam's design.

Most later attempts at this triple unit type of archway were as angular and uneasy as Adam's version but Sir John Soane provided an elegantly simple solution to the problem in his gateway at Tyringham, Buckinghamshire.[9] His design makes a virtue of the angularity by stripping the arch itself of all classical detail and flattening the entablature. The resultant composition is a theme of right angles, and the side pavilions are further tied into the arched section by a string course with a triple moulding, set at a point where the capitals of the arch would have been based if Soane had allowed his arch any such old-fashioned detail. The only references to a classical past are a niche in a recess and two inset Doric columns. Understandably this lodge has been much admired since the Bauhaus became a force in British architecture.

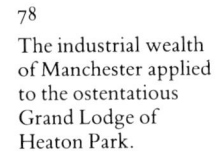

78
The industrial wealth of Manchester applied to the ostentatious Grand Lodge of Heaton Park.

Whether such an arched lodge can correctly be styled as triumphal is questionable, but it is certainly forward looking and economical.

The Tyringham gateway was built between 1793 and 1800 and Lewis Wyatt's Grand Lodge to Heaton Park, just outside Manchester, built sometime between 1806 and 1824, uses Soane's trick with the string course effectively, to unite the three units. Otherwise, as the title of the lodge suggests, he had the neo-classical appetites of north-western industrialists to satisfy and his arch is a tremendous composition with four attached columns of Tuscan Doric and rustication to the level of the string course. It is an impressive though wholly inhuman facade which predicts that later such structures would be more aptly deployed in public institutions and in an environment of mechanised industry.

79
Philip Hardwick's Propylaeum for Euston Station. Built 1836-40, demolished 1962. (Royal Commission on Historical Monuments (England))

It was right that the ultimate and most majestic demonstration of the triumphal arch in this tripartite form should be made, not at a park entrance, but as Philip Hardwick's Propylaeum of 1836-40 for Euston Station. Surrounded by a tangle of lesser buildings it continued to awe by its scale and its simplicity. Only its pavilion lodges survive in the reshaped Euston that went up when the Greek Doric arch was demolished in 1962, but the comment of *The Civil Engineer and Architects' Journal* of 1837 can serve as a fitting obituary to Hardwick's achievement and as a summary of the aims behind this whole outstandingly theatrical genre of lodges:

> We here behold the full majesty and severity of the order exhibited upon a scale that renders it truly imposing. Till now, we had nothing that could convey an adequate impression of the majesty of a Doric portico ... We have the effect not only of magnitude as well as of forms, but that also arising from breadth of light and shade, heightened by that of great depth, and the contrast of perspective.[10]

CHAPTER SIX

The Long Reign of the Classical Box 1740–1800

BESIDE THE Oxford road on the approach to West Wycombe village in Buckinghamshire stands a curious pair of buildings that symbolise in their shape, and more exactly in their disposition, the record of the classical lodge in the latter two thirds of the eighteenth century. They stand one on each side of what was once the main drive to Sir Francis Dashwood's seat, West Wycombe Park, and at first glance seem a matching pair of lodges in umber and cream liveried stucco with neat pyramidal roofs. The left hand building of the two is in fact a lodge, Kitty's Lodge, purpose-built and one of the oldest surviving, clearly marked on Jolivet's 1752 map of the estate;[1] but

80
Kitty's Lodge and Daphne's Temple, West Wycombe Park, Buckinghamshire. The rear elevation of the garden building has been given an architectural treatment to link it with the lodge opposite.

the building on the right of the entrance with its blind facade raked at an uneasy diagonal to the drive only pretends to be a lodge, out of architectural good manners. It is the butt end of a garden temple, DAPHNI DICATUM NYMPHA PROBATA SINCERA MANE, as its inscription whimsically declares, and it too is shown on the 1752 map. Its handsome Ionic loggia, probably, like Kitty's Lodge, to the design of John Donowell, architect of West Wycombe house,[2] faces directly away from the drive towards the lake and the house, an integral feature of an Arcadian scene in which Kitty's Lodge, its apparent twin, plays no part at all nor is there any reason on its architectural merits why it ever should. Kitty's Lodge has never been anything more than a neat two storey box. Sir Francis Dashwood lavished imagination and money upon the many garden buildings of his park but upon his park gate lodge he did not spend the money for a single column.

It would be dishonest to pretend that in the 1740s and 1750s there was not a hiatus in the development of the lodge. After the decorative flair of Leeswood, the compact brilliance of the Worcester Lodge, Edgehill's high Gothic Tower and Kent's civilised Palladian houses there is undoubtedly a falling off. Though disappointing, this was inevitable as lodges lost their first function as dining pavilions for the gentry and adapted to their basic role as stylish tenements for under-servants. But what the West Wycombe pair exemplify and what, in view of the ancestry of the lodge as a garden building, is not easy to explain, is the near total absence of classical columns from lodges of the pavilion type for the next few decades. There were, of course, columns enough on lodges of triumphal arch type — superior lodges for only the most stately entrances. But again it would be dishonest to

81
John Vardy's design for lodges to Hackwood Park, Hampshire of 1761. (By kind permission of Rt. Hon. Viscount Camrose).

pretend that there were many of these before the 1760s. Even Kent's Holkham Arch, probably designed by 1730, may not have been built by Brettingham until 1765. This uncertainty of dates, like the parallel uncertainty of architects, clouds the whole history of the development of the park gate lodge.

What does emerge when a large cross-section of English lodges is considered is that, though columns were commonplace on Palladian main houses and garden temples, the early classical lodge was generally astylar. The classical column was the mark of gods and gentry. It should also be remembered that these decades of the 1740s and 1750s were the period when Isaac Ware, Sir Robert Taylor, Henry Keene and James Paine were practising that modified astylar form of Palladian which is sometimes described as an English Rococo. This, while occasionally expressing itself in interiors of recognisably continental Rococo as at Chesterfield House, inclined on its exteriors to avoid classical orders and use instead canted bays and a superficial patterning of carved swags and panels. The astylar trend in lodges of this period may, therefore, be part of this reserved Rococo. Certainly until neo-classical forms became fashionable the lodge was conceived as a box, often a very stylish box of delicately contrived decorative form, but a box for all that. This chapter then is not a study of small houses but of fine boxes, which may explain why an eighteenth century lodge is automatically recognisable as a lodge and not as a small house of the period.

John Vardy's lodges, executed but demolished, for the fifth Duke of Bolton at Hackwood Park, Hampshire of 1761, are perfect illustrations of the superior inferiority of early lodges: each one of these is only twelve feet square with no columns to suggest gentry status, but a carefully considered miniature in its exterior decoration, the walls alive with a chequer board of flint rustication and a double recession of pilasters which carry ball finials. They are a pleasure to the eye but not a vaunting one, dolls houses for adults. In just one detail these Vardy lodges are atypical: they have no recessed round arch, and the recessed round arch containing a window or a door is almost a standard feature of the eighteenth century box-lodge.[3]

With these limitations it would be idle to list many variants of the type. The mould from which they seem to pour had been cast by 1746 in Kent's design for lodges at Euston Hall, Suffolk. Thereafter each architect effected his own characteristic variants within the inevitable limitations: Adam his infinitely smooth ashlar, linear definition and consciously innovative frieze

82
A refined and innovative Adam-style design. The South Lodge to Kedleston Hall, Derbyshire.

of paterae in Kedleston's South Lodge of 1761–2, John Carr, a very standard pair, brick with stone dressings, triglyph frieze and pyramidal roofs at Tabley, also begun in 1761. Then ten years later William Chambers predictably exercised the form in its ultimate heavy authority in the Higher Lodges to Milton Abbey, Dorset. These stand like gestures of classical atonement for the Gothick facades which Lord Milton had forced Chambers to perpetrate in the valley below. Everything is outsize — the depth of the recessed arches which cavern in on three sides, the projection of the dentil cornice which

83
The Higher Lodges to Milton Abbey, Dorset, (1771-6) are quintessentially masculine Palladian designs by William Chambers.

thrusts out to assert the pediment and the bulk of the gatepiers to which each lodge is linked. It is a *mea culpa* in stone.

What perhaps neither Adam nor Chambers were quite justified in doing was to set the windows for two storeys in a recess which could only logically contain one. For that reason the title of the most perfect classical boxes in

84
One of the East Lodges to the demolished Thornton-le-Street Hall, North Riding. A visually successful confinement of two storeys within a single classical unit.

Britain must, only half jokingly, be awarded to another lodge pair: the East Lodges to Thorton-le-Street Hall in the North Riding. The house itself has gone, and if it was of a calibre to equal its lodges, then it was a lost masterpiece. Without exaggeration these are the box carried to perfection. Only the side to the road is pedimented, but this avoids the toy quality of the pyramidal roof and lends a certain slight movement to the basic four-square repose of the form. One whole round-arched recess is occupied by a Venetian window with floral swags in its frieze. This suggests the dignity of a much larger house yet avoids the crowding effect of Chambers's windows for two storeys. The upper storey is, however, conveyed with exactly the right demure charm by a round window over the door on the side wall to the drive. The swags in the frieze above the door recall the eye automatically to those on each side of the Venetian window and a strong, plain string course

85
The essence of Robert Adam's social indifference is demonstrated in this minimal structure of the Stag Lodge to Saltram House, Devon.

and delicate eaves frieze with paterae are further uniting features, these last being a subtly contrasted masculine and feminine note.

The frustration, common enough where lodges are concerned, of not knowing the architect is, in this case, serious and extreme. The lodges are quintessentially Adam in style, yet rather of his essence than individually from his drawing board. How far Adam was involved in the social dimensions of his usual lodge keepers' rooms it is not easy to say, but the meagre chambers behind the delicate scroll work of the Syon screen and the contemptible boxes which he supplied for Mistley Hall, Essex, and the Stag Lodge to Saltram House, Devon, are a far cry from the urbane and civilised proportions of Thornton-le-Street. There is an arched lodge on the other side of the same park and at Forcett Park, twenty miles away in the same Riding, James Paine may have designed in 1762 the fine triumphal arch and lodges of one bay with Venetian windows of Adam type.[4] Paine, a highly sophisticated architect with a chiefly northern practice, was one of those practitioners of the subdued English Rococo, previously mentioned, who seized eagerly upon Adam's delicate, feminine classical detail when he first demonstrated it. It was exactly the style of elegant finesse to which they were inclined, but authentically antique and with no French associations to damn it.

The Thornton-le-Street lodges are then probably Paine's work and a choice example of English classical design of about 1770. If not masterworks they are the ultimate expression of a limited form. As such in Japan they would have been declared a national treasure and surrounded by raked gravel and a viewing park set up across the road. In Yorkshire they are lived in and pleasantly unregarded. At least they have escaped the fate of what was once a very similar lodge pair to Painshill, Surrey where the indignities of lean-to porch, gabled extension and crudely projecting windows have been heaped

86
An instance of insensitive later treatment suffered by an originally elegant lodge pair at Painshill, Surrey.

PLATE XI

upon the just recognisable central box. Another pair to Phyllis Court on the Marlow road into Henley-on-Thames has been more fortunate, though their detail is coarser than the Thornton Lodges[5] and there is an interesting variant, more overtly Adam of *c*.1775, by Robert Mitchell set alongside and according excellently with the 1681 gatepiers, all Carolean swags and heraldic beasts, to Ramsbury Manor in Wiltshire.[6]

The only other alternative to the box-feminine with thinly recessed arches was the box-masculine with all its detailing robust and coarsely projecting. The Skelton lodges to Newby Hall in the West Riding are a richly mature example of this last, effecting by detail everything which Sir William Chambers achieved by scale. They stand on a rusticated base; at all four corners the quoining projects dramatically from the ashlar, the central window is heavi-

100

87
Originally attributed to Robert Adam, the Skelton Lodges to Newby Hall, West Riding, suggest by their robust modelling the designing hand of William Belwood (c.1780).

ly pedimented and set between Doric columns with alternate vermiculated rustication like sections of a drought-cracked lake bed. Finally the roof projects a clear two feet, has its corners emphasised by stone balls and its top crowned by an uncompromising square chimney pot. These expressions of masculine identity in gate lodge form stand beside no less than four fat gatepiers of further alternate rustication with trophies of battle axes and ferocious beast finials. Predictably all this was designed by a Yorkshireman, William Belwood, trained, quite unpredictably, by Robert Adam.[7]

If an architect's identity is often clearly expressed in a lodge then the three identical gate lodges to Weston Park, Staffordshire are something of a puzzle. James Paine was working there between 1765 and 1770 and two of the park buildings: the temple of Diana and the Roman Bridge, feature in his *Plans*,[8] but nothing could be further from the polish of the Thornton boxes than the Weston lodges, or further from standard lodge design of the period. They are recognisable 'normal' double fronted houses with hipped roofs; only their central features: a coarsely detailed recessed arch under a pediment with a projecting porch under another, faintly absurd, toy pediment, suggest the uniform of a lodge. If they are Paine's work they are crudely direct in his pre-Adam style, which their dating contradicts. Paine must also have been designing to the dictates of a proprietor, Sir Henry Bridgeman, with generous notions of how his servants should be housed.

The name of John Carr of York, another contemporary architect with a wide northern practice, was never suggested as the author of the Thornton-le-Street lodges because he had such a strong feeling for the contrasting textures of his materials and there is none of this in the smooth ashlar and sensitive linearity of Thornton. The west lodges to Norton Place, Bishop Norton, Lincolnshire, show that Carr had tired of the box with recessed arch

88
The identical late 18th century lodges to Weston Park, Staffordshire, are early examples of a social concern usually associated with the 19th century.

formula which he had been using at Tabley House in 1761 and was beginning to design his way towards his crowning achievement in lodge building, the North Lodge to Wentworth Woodhouse, but that was not built until 1793. What, in essence, was Carr's innovation at Norton, was to put the lodges themselves between the gatepiers where the iron railings might be expected to stand. There are four tall, heavily rusticated piers, each urn-topped, and between these, flat-roofed and punctuated by a single window in a Gibbs surround, the lodges appear as if supported on robust crutches.

Carr's single lodge at the original main entrance to Wentworth Woodhouse from the B6091 is a far more subtle composition but equally reliant upon rusticated piers. The gatepiers, themselves a fine set, stand quite separately at right angles to the lodge and it is interesting that by the end of the century one lodge was considered sufficiently stately to guard the main way into the enormous palace of the Rockinghams. The lodge is indeed a small villa and one of the most satisfying small houses ever built in England. The ground floor has three bays and the first floor one. The three sash windows are set between plain piers topped by ball finials, but what disturbs this simple rhythm and makes the facade memorable are two rusticated piers of much darker stone. The eye sees these as an intrusion into both the textures and the logic of the ground floor, and this is exactly what they are. Carr has superimposed a Kentian pavilion of two storeys with a recessed arch upon a quite distinctly composed, single storey three bay house with a flat roof. There are, therefore, the elements of two houses in one, co-existing yet going their own ways. The dark stone cornice line of the single storey house cuts straight across the recessed arch of the other, becoming temporarily a string course to demarcate the upper and lower floors then continues as a cornice again, thus binding the two compositions. Lacking a visible door the lodge has a withdrawn and faintly guarded air, correct for its function.

The poetry of its proportions apart, this Wentworth Lodge is a firm escape from the box. But it is curious that the reign of the box should have endured so long when the garden buildings from which lodges sprang are so often octagonal in form, and the octagon would have offered an easy escape from the tedium of the cuboid. The form was used but infrequently. The East Lodge to Holkham by Matthew Brettingham is an early instance, probably of the mid 1750s,[9] a crudely proportioned affair of stock brick with little pedimented extrusions on alternate faces. It immediately suggests that one reason why octagons were rarely used for ordinary human habitation would be the difficulty of fitting in the furniture. Paine built neat east and west lodges to Cowick Hall, West Riding between 1752 and 1760. There are octagonal lodges in Miller's pattern book of 1787 but John Carr's Mausoleum Lodge on the drive to the Rockingham Mausoleum at Wentworth Woodhouse is much later, 1791. This is as much a confusion of upper and lower storeys as his North Lodge was a clarification. One upstairs window pretends to be a fanlight to the door and another absurdly tall round-headed window cuts across two floors. Each of the eight sides has to be given a feature which suggests how comparatively expensive the form must have been to build. It has, nevertheless, an undeniable geometric fascination.

It was in this last decade of the century that, if war had not been virtually continuous, a whole outbreak of geometrical exploration and symbolic perversity might have been expected in lodge buildings. The park lodge was

89
The North Lodge to Wentworth Woodhouse (1793) marks the summit of John Carr's small house design.

the building where a rich eccentric tended to try out the architectural experiments he might hesitate to unleash upon his own house. Du Fourny's dictum: 'L'architecture doit se régénerer par la geometrie' was not issued until 1793 but long before that, in the 1770s and 1780s, the award winning projects at the French academy had included a dazzling series of designs by visionaries like E.L. Boullée, J. Gondouin and C.N. Ledoux for buildings in the shape of pure spheres, half-spheres, truncated cones and all varieties of geometrical solids.[10] The neo-classical movement was in natural harmony with this feeling for purity of solid shape and volumetric clarity, and this is likely to have been another force besides social responsibility working to terminate the reign of the box by the introduction of more diverting and perhaps practical solids.

One early instance of an English reflection of this French movement dates from 1778–88. It is the twin lodges by Samuel Wyatt which are all that survive of his Hooton Hall in Cheshire designed for Sir William Stanley.

90
Matthew Brettingham's East Lodge to Holkham Hall, Norfolk.

Cheshire was, of course, a heartland of neo-classicism and a county where the industrial wealth of the newly rich might be expected to finance innovative rather than traditional architectural forms. The Hooton lodges in their present condition, with all their windows blocked by cement, give an impression of total volumetric solidity. They are domed Greek crosses, the slight transeptal projections being towards the road, the squat pediments

91
An early reflection (1778) of French neo-classicism. Samuel Wyatt's lodges to Hooton Hall, Cheshire.

facing the drive. The windows are cut directly into the stonework and a semi-circle of Ionic columns links the two lodges. Wreaths and swags on alternate faces and a 1914–1918 War Memorial which has been set between them combine to give an air of deep funerary gloom as in some Boullée project in *architecture parlante* to commemorate *Des Poètes sans Gloire* or the Dead of a Hundred Wars.

John Adey Repton's Tern Lodge to Attingham Hall, Shropshire may stand as a last instance of the gate lodge's absolute escape from the prison of the box while still remaining just recognisably classical in its form but astylar. Attingham is, of course, an early neo-classical house by George Steuart for the first Lord Berwick but Repton's volumetric octagon was commissioned by the second Lord Berwick immediately after the park had

92
The Tern Lodge, Attingham Hall, Shropshire by J.A. Repton.

105

been disencumbered of a public road in 1802.[11] Though very small the lodge is so exceptionally pure in its lines and insistent upon the solids of which it is composed that it can stand comparison with the grand simplicities of the French Grand Prix projects. The octagon is the centre of the geometry but rectangles project boldly from alternate faces, as in Brettingham's much earlier lodge, and each rectangle emphasises by crisp linear treatment the triangle of its pediment and the three-headed arches or recesses of its sides. These are picked up again in the round-headed windows of the remaining four sides. Only the plainest of keystones and string coursing are allowed to pattern the ashlar and divert attention from essential form. Set in the subtlety of great trees the directness of the lodge is remarkably effective. It stands on the A6 and on either side of it, four miles in one direction and six in the other, is an octagonal toll house of similar dimensions but grossly inferior styling. If Repton's lodge is later then his reference to these must be deliberate and the Tern Lodge may, therefore, be a genuine English attempt at *architecture parlante* — an essay in Boullée's theory that function must be suggested by form rather than decoration, a park gate lodge being in essence a private toll house on a private turnpike.

CHAPTER SEVEN

The Columned Temple at the Park Gate

De Greeks ver Godes!

THE GREAT temple lodges of the Greek Revival stand in Glasgow, Liverpool, Newcastle, Bristol, Kensal Green, Brompton and Peckham Rye. Without exception they are generously scaled, finely proportioned and of an awesome monumentality; and there, as the bounds of this study demand, they must be left. None of them are park gate lodges; they all lead into cemeteries.[1]

The epigraph which heads this chapter was recorded with unkindly phonetic accuracy from the conversation of the painter-translator John Henry Fuseli by his student Benjamin Haydon.[2] It encapsulates that mixture of reverence and eccentricity which dogged the development of the Greek Revival in Britain. The columned temples of Paestum and Athens, suitably modified, should have provided the ideal model for a park lodge: the columns on the front elevation for perfect expressions of culture, harmony and state, with a rectangle behind them into which a normal house of two storeys could be fitted without contrivance. Such park gate lodge temples were built but they are remarkably few in number, generally modest in scale and often more homely than scholarly in their detail. As the preceding chapter concluded, there was a general reluctance in the eighteenth century to apply to lodges the stylar detail commonly used to enrich and diversify the design and spatial texture of main houses.

The earliest garden temple with a portico of correct Greek Doric columns, six in all, fluted and without bases, was built at Hagley, Worcestershire, by James Stuart in 1758 only three years after his return from Athens and before even the first volume of his and Nicholas Revett's *Antiquities of Athens* was brought out in 1762.[3] But this temple and Stuart's Greek garden buildings for Shugborough were premature sports of Greek revivalism. The correct fluted Doric was not applied to a new house until the first decade of the next century,[4] so while a lodge with Greek Doric columns and of eighteenth century date would not have been impossible it is not surprising that none is recorded.

To a casual eye there is a lodge pair from Basildon House, Berkshire, to the Oxford road which look to have been put up in the first enthusiasm of this early period and are very fair copies of the Tower of the Winds as delineated in Stuart and Revett's volume. But lodges are not always what they seem. John Carr built a single storey octagonal pair here in 1776. They did not

93
The Oxford Lodges to Basildon Park, Berkshire, represent a neo-classicising by J.B. Papworth (1842) of simpler early structures by John Carr.

achieve their modish Athenian form until 1839–44 when J.B. Papworth, who was working at the house, dressed them up with an additional storey. So there appear to be no Greek Revival lodges of the eighteenth century.

What is harder to explain is the rarity of templar type lodges with columns of a Roman order in this 1758–1800 period. Pediments of the Doric, Ionic and Corinthian orders in their less refined Roman form are common on main houses of this Adam or Roman phase of neo-classicism, but they are infrequent on lodges.

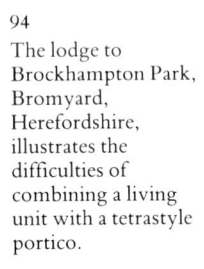

94
The lodge to Brockhampton Park, Bromyard, Herefordshire, illustrates the difficulties of combining a living unit with a tetrastyle portico.

A lodge with a tetrastyle portico in Tuscan Doric at Brockhampton Park near Bromyard, Herefordshire, suggests some of the difficulties inherent in such a design when it is carried out on a small scale. Because the columns are thin the portico looks weak as well as plain. The essence of Doric is that it should be sturdy; but these columns have been kept meagre to allow more light to reach two sash windows, one on each side of the door beneath the pediment. Yet the windows look almost as incongruously modern in this temple facade as they would if they were set into a church. The architect, probably George Byfield who was working here in 1799 for J. Barnarby,[5] should have given the windows a more substantial surround. Finally, because the columns are not of a giant order, the upstairs rooms are cramped by the roofline and, since dormers would look absurd, can be lit only from the pediment by a small circular window or from the rear.

Solutions to these difficulties must be found in all templar type lodges. The far more impressive Kennel Lodge to Wynnstay Park, Denbighshire, probably by James Wyatt and also with a tetrastyle Tuscan Doric portico, ruthlessly sacrifices convenience to appearance, setting grim but appropriate blind niches on each side of the door and having no window to weaken the pediment.[6] Significantly perhaps, Wyatt avoided the design in his later neo-classical lodges.

P.F. Robinson's Old Lodge of 1824 to Trelissick House, Cornwall and Charles Barry's Helmsley Lodge to Duncombe Park, North Riding of 1843 both use slender Tuscan Doric columns in their porticoes, but keep their front elevations blind apart from the doors and compensate their inhabitants by a substantial cross wing at the rear. William Hakewill's Rostherne Lodge

PLATE XII

95
This genre painting of 1785 by William Briggs illustrates the now demolished Cambridge Lodge to Audley End House, Essex. It gives a rare insight into the social unit likely to occupy a small 18th century lodge. (By kind permission of the Hon. R.H.C. Neville).

96
The Rostherne Lodge. A piece of full-blooded Greek Revival by James Hakewill for Tatton Park, Cheshire (1833).

PLATE XIII

of 1833, on the other side of Tatton Park to Lewis Wyatt's neo-classical triumphal arch lodge, is one of the most ambitious of templar lodges. Not only does it have the rare distinction of a hexastyle portico to the drive with authentic fluted Doric columns, but two more columns are set at the rear to give an apparent glimpse of another full pediment which does not actually exist. The front portico is windowless and the two sash windows on the side elevation preserve the formality of the design. What is lacking for templar dignity is a plinth to give it command. Thomas Hope was right in pressing for such a base to be included in William Wilkins's design for the chapel of Downing College, Cambridge; a Greek temple needs to look down.[7]

Hard as Hakewill has tried at Tatton, the amateurish nature of these park templar lodges appears when his hexastyle is compared with the tetrastyle cemetery lodges which Charles Underwood built (1837–40) for Arnos Vale Cemetery in Bristol. Though two columns shorter, there is a strength and height to the Bristol porticoes which brings out the masculine quality of the Greek Doric, and the treatment of the side elevations, instead of being merely tactful like Hakewill's lodge, deliberately demands attention with heavy straight entablatures into which are sunk the two first floor windows. Both lodges are raised upon three steps and being placed relatively close to each other achieve an overwhelming effect of doom and gloom.

The development of Greek Doric porticoes at cemetery entrances is, therefore, an instance of Boullée's theory of *architecture parlante* being put into practice. The geometrical authority of a temple portico, which suggests nothing but harmony and light when set on a rock in Greece, looks like an entrance to the Underworld when built in a sooty suburb. Carefully considered proportions only work upon the eye when they are absolutely visible.

The logical place to look for a perfect park lodge in templar style would be a park where an architect has been employed who had experience building

97 The Doric Lodge at Wentworth Woodhouse, West Riding, here attributed to J.P. Pritchett and Charles Watson (c.1818).

Greek Revival porticoes on public buildings. Wentworth Woodhouse has, in its Doric Lodge, perhaps the finest Greek Revival park lodge in the country. Though only tetrastyle, its fluted columns are even taller than those at Arnos Vale and appear consequently more elegant and aspiring. The monumentality of the composition is strengthened by three blind elements: the rectangular panel over the door and two round-headed niches in the recessed flanking pavilions. Pilasters are, as Thomas Hope urged, only used as antae.[8] The whole confident building not only commands a great sweep of valley, which results in the portico being viewed for the first time from below like the Athenian temples, but it is within sight of a second and complementary Greek experience, the round Ionic temple which is perched even higher up on a long bastion wall of the inner gardens.

This great lodge has been attributed to John Carr of York without a scrap of factual evidence or stylistic support, but simply because he designed other buildings in the park. Carr continued into old age to design imaginatively in the style of his youth. The Doric Lodge is almost certainly the work of the partnership of James Pigott Pritchett and Charles Watson. Pritchett was architect and surveyor to Earl Fitzwilliam for fifty years and in partnership with Watson from 1813 to 1831. In 1807–10 Watson had built a tetrastyle Greek Doric portico to Wakefield Court House and Pritchett built a Greek Revival Library and Newsroom in the same town in 1820–1. The elegance and restraint of the side elevations of the lodge indicate an early rather than a later date, 1818 perhaps. If the same partnership designed the Ionic temple (Pritchett's library has both Ionic columns and pilasters) on the bastion wall, then they were responsible for a Greek composition that can hardly be rivalled outside Edinburgh.

Yet this notable lodge inspired no local imitations on the same scale. Perhaps landowners were reluctant to have a version of the Wakefield Court

98 Greek sentry boxes to Chirk Castle, Denbighshire.

House at their park entrance; and the fashion for Doric entrances to cemeteries, which began with the opening of Liverpool's Low Hill General in 1825,[9] would have given the naked Greek Doric, sprouting baseless, directly from a plinth, unhappy connotations. Major architects of the Greek Revival like the second William Wilkins (1778–1839) and Thomas Harrison (1744–1829) collected notably few domestic commissions. Most of Harrison's houses were small and built around Chester. If he designed the neat Tuscan Doric sentry boxes on the north drive to Chirk Castle, Denbighshire, when he was working there around 1820, then they are a genteel and disappointing work from the designer of the great propylaeum to Chester Castle (1811–13).[10] William Wilkins produced the ultimate Greek country house in the Grange, Hampshire, a building which contrives to marry grandeur with restraint and which, in its downland valley, is one of the very rare houses to which the word numinous can be applied without pretentiousness. But its lodge is an unrewarding cottage in the conventional Picturesque and most of Wilkins's other large houses are in Tudor Gothic.[11]

The style was never generally popular in England for large houses and the gap of more than forty years between the first Greek garden temples and the first Greek Revival house of any size has never been adequately explained.

One reason for this delay may be literary. In the early 1760s the works of two German writers began to appear in a number of English translations. The first were the *Idyls* or *Rural Poems* of Salomon Gessner.[12] The second

PLATE XIII The lodges to Arnos Vale Cemetery, Bristol, by Charles Underwood (1837-40).

PLATE XIV A contemporary print illustrating John Nash's ambitious spatial experiment for the Hanover Gate to Regent's Park, London (*c.* 1827).

PLATE XV Autumnal symmetry at Shugborough Park, Staffordshire. Samuel Wyatt's Milford Lodges of 1803-6.

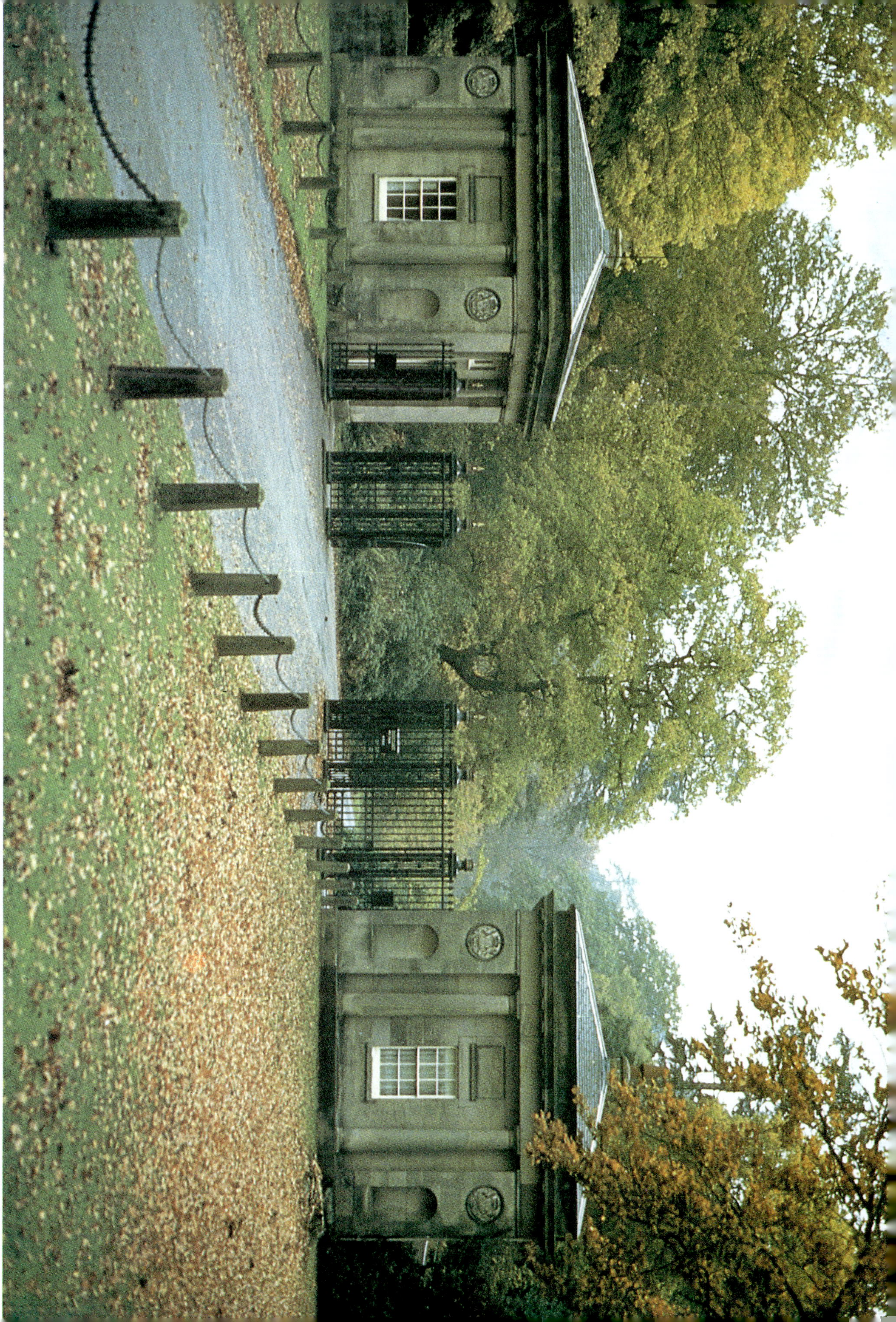

PLATE XVI An almost lost lodge at the south west entrance to Ammerdown Park, Somerset.

were J.J. Winckelmann's uninhibited raptures on Greek art. The moral shepherds of Gessner and the intoxicating enthusiasm of Winckelmann should have launched an immediate Greek fashion. Gessner and Winckelmann were widely reviewed in the periodicals and the implications of their style and arguments were vigorously debated. But at the same time that these writers, the first Swiss and the second Prussian, were bringing things Greek to the attention of the public, they were also associating Greek art with suspect politics and suspect morality.

Gessner's eclogues, or *Idyls* as he termed them, were written in an innovative style, half prose, half poetry, which in its avoidance of cliché and periphrasis anticipated in some measure the style of Wordsworth's *Lyrical Ballads* of 1798. The English of the translations was widely accepted as a conscious return to primitive simplicity: a literary equivalent of a Greek Doric pillar. The shepherds and shepherdesses not only trembled on the edge of free love but lived in a golden age and in a classless society, the egalitarian nature of which Gessner stressed repeatedly. The implications of his ideal world were revolutionary, as the French, who discovered Gessner some years before the British, were to realise.

Winckelmann was even more of an embarrassment to the Greek cause. In Fuseli's unidiomatic but zestful translations it was clear to any reader that the god-like beauty and nudity of male Greek statues was the inspiration behind Winckelmann's claims for the superiority of Greek art over any other.

Readers of the *London Chronicle,* among accounts of judicial cases, sales by auction and new methods of treating the gout, learned from Winckelmann's letters that 'the young Spartans were obliged, every ten days, to appear stark naked in the presence of the Ephori', that 'the flower of youth danced naked at Athens on the public theatres' and that 'the youth, who needed no other veil than the public chastity and purity of manners, performed quite naked their various exercises'.[13] In the third letter Winckelmann discoursed for twelve lines on the superiority of the Greek sculptors' technique for carving marble testicles on statues of ephebes. Even his famous apostrophe to the Apollo Belvedere falls in its conclusion into manifest emotional involvement: 'such organs human nature knows not, such attitudes no mortal: an Eternal Spring like that of Elysium, blends the grandeur of man with the charm of youth, and rosy beauty wantons all down the godlike system ... my breast dilates to adore that which dwells with the spirit of prophecy'.[14]

Such writing might titillate the prurient and arouse interest; whether it would arouse imitation was another matter. In an early satire written in 1784, William Blake expresses a weary contempt for the neo-classical bore, Etruscan Column the Antiquarian, who enters the mock Symposium 'and after an abundance of Enquiries to no purpose, sat himself down and described something that nobody listen'd to'.[15] This may well represent a general response to the finer points of antiquarian research. In the event English Hellenophiles were content to collect vases and marble fragments for the next forty years, before architecture on a large scale to evoke this nude and socially seditious nation was assayed.

All this goes a certain way towards explaining why the general body of park gate lodges which can be described as stylar and neo-classical are designed rather to suggest a Greek awareness than to convey an overwhelming and numinous Greek presence. For a time it was fashionable to hint at Hellenism but to subdue it to modern convenience and an image of elegance. The interest in this episode lies in the ingenuity of the architects' attempts to modify rather than to achieve an alien style.

They had four basic devices around which to improvise variations. They could surround an octagonal or circular building with columns. They could take the old Kentian standby of the recessed arch, level its head and insert columns. They could reduce a pediment to a small central feature supported by a few engaged columns and flanked by wings; or they could modify domed buildings to suggest an antique altar.

99
A subtle non-templar variant of the Greek Revival. William Wilkins' West Lodge to Stoke Edith, Herefordshire (1792).

Both the first and the last of these four variants were Roman inspired and in no way Greek. The circular temple at Delphi was not known at this time while the circular temples at Rome and Tivoli were famous. Domed lodges were likely to present structural problems to provincial masons and bricklayers therefore they are not common. When they were assayed these were of particular interest. The first William Wilkins, father of the second and more famous Wilkins, designed an early domed lodge in 1792 for Stoke Edith in Herefordshire.[16] This is remarkable for its reliance upon structural ingenuity rather than superficial decoration. The dome is copper, the walls, perhaps to match the main seventeenth century house, are brick with stone string courses. It is a measure of the success of this lodge and of a later domed pair to Carden Hall in Cheshire that their exact shape eludes description because they are in constant movement. From the dome, pinned centrally by a stout round chimney stack, the Stoke Edith lodge expands into an octagon in theory but into a sixteen sided ground plan in fact because there is a bold projection on all four sides, that facing the road having Tuscan columns *in antis*. Apart from these columns there is no actual classical detail so the building is pure and satisfying in form. The Carden pair, known

100
The Honey Pots,
Carden Hall,
Cheshire.

locally as the Honey Pots and now dangerously decayed, are even more interesting but architecturally they are a mystery. Carden Hall, an Elizabethan structure, was burnt in 1912 and these two and the noble arched lodge to the south are the survivors of the park furniture, along with an ice-house. Their domes are deeply coved and topped, not with chimney pots, but with terracotta urns which make them far more suggestive of pagan altars. Being concave sided they solve the transition from dome to base more fluently than the Stoke Edith lodge, and the round-headed niches in their canted corners pick up the rhythm of the round-headed windows. The bases are rusticated; the upper walls are of smooth ashlar.

It is important to establish an architect or at least a date for these fascinat-

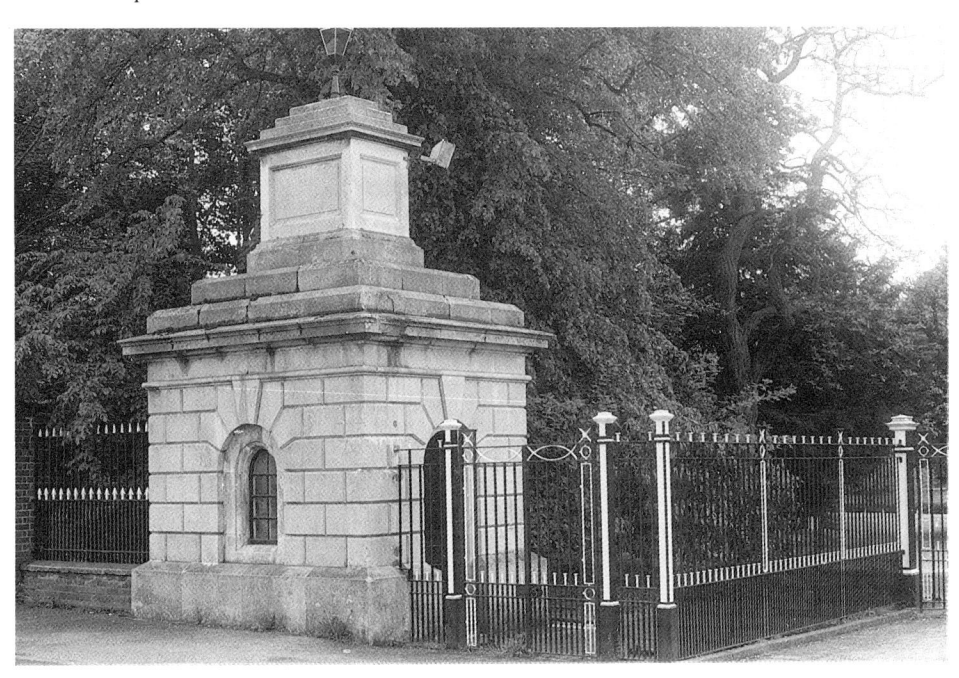

101
The lodge as a classical altar. The Mausoleum entrance to Trentham Park, Staffordshire, designed in 1807-8 by C.H. Tatham.

ing lodges, but even to label them as neo-classical depends upon an appeal to their spirit rather than to their form or to any precise detail. Their movement is baroque but the attenuated shape of their windows is similar to local examples of the William IV period. One of the Leches of Carden is known to have spent considerable money on his estate in the early nineteenth century and so may have had the lodges built then.

They could be from the drawing board of C.H. Tatham whose *Etchings of Ancient Ornamental Architecture* of 1799–1800 influenced Thomas Hope.[17] He was actually building the aggressively altar-shaped Mausoleum Lodges at Trentham Park, Staffordshire, only twenty miles away, in 1807–8 for the second Marquess of Stafford, and built or designed several other park entrances.[18]

Tatham's Mausoleum pair stand opposite and act as a deliberate echo of his brutally oppressive mausoleum for the Leveson-Gower family. The busy road which now separates the lodges from the mausoleum damages the tripartite composition. Tatham intended it as an English essay in that mingling of Piranesian effects and Boullée ideas which was fashionable at the Academie de France in Rome when Tatham was resident in that city in the 1790s. Like the two domed lodges which have just been considered, the Trentham lodges are neo-classical by their deliberate exploration of antique forms rather than by actual detail.

After these confident spatial ventures the circular and octagonal lodges of

102
James Wyatt's Bath Lodge to Dodington Park, Gloucestershire (*c.*1802).

the Wyatt family seem superficial, even bungling, in their effects. James Wyatt's circular lodge to Dodington Park, Gloucestershire, (*c*.1802) is in danger of becoming a cliché of the architectural text books, but when

103
An octagon with a loggia. The Mere Lodge to Tatton Park by Lewis Wyatt (1807-13)

compared with his nephew Lewis's octagonal Mere Lodge (1807–13) at Tatton, Cheshire, its relative authority can be appreciated. Neither lodge solves the incongruity of the central chimney, both carry their Tuscan Doric columns only to first floor level, but the broad entablature with which the

104
The loggia as an ombrello. The Smithy Lodge, Heaton Park, by Lewis Wyatt.

older Wyatt tops his columns produces a stronger design. The less said about the fenestration of the two lodges the better for their architects' reputations.

117

Round-headed windows in an octagon and square-headed openings in a circular building make little visual sense.

Lewis Wyatt tried his hand at another octagon when he designed the Smithy Lodge for Heaton Park, Manchester. His Grand Lodge, a triumphal arch, stands at the opposite corner of the same park and a comparison of the two is revealing. The arched lodge may have been dark to live in but in form it is assured, based upon ancient precedent and modern examples. In contrast his Smithy Lodge is a disaster. The columns, Tuscan again, rise this time above the two storeys and their entablature is topped with a dentil cornice before the wholly unclassical octagonal roof and weak central chimney. The windows and the door are cut into, rather than placed upon, the elevation. What results is a gaunt and stilted ombrello which goes some way to explain the popularity of the thatched cottage with Regency architects. At least with those they could soften and diversify the contours of their roofs and relate their buildings more easily to the land on which they sat. Lewis Wyatt would have found a circular temple with its columns carried quite gracefully

105
One of an ornately Roman lodge pair at Ottershaw Park, Surrey (*c.*1800) by James Wyatt.

PLATE XIV

up to the roof if he had studied Nicholas Revett's Island Temple at West Wycombe, though that only attempts one interior storey.[19] The body of English architecture has nothing like the number of domed structures that are found in Germany or Italy to serve as precedents in handling the shape.

John Nash's octagonal lodge at the Hanover Gate to Regent's Park is, like the Carden and Stoke Edith lodges, dextrous in its handling of an unusual ground plan, but all three lodges avoid the problems set by a major display of columns. The Hanover Lodge, like the Carden lodges, is more baroque than neo-classical, a pointer to the increasing readiness of Regency architects to embrace eclecticism rather than to be confined within one style and its scholarly rules. The extensions which project from alternate sides of the Hanover Lodge rise only to the string course below the first floor and contain decorative, not structural, details. The large double volutes which lead them back to the cornice give a curvaceous swagger to the whole design but, with the statues now inset into all four extensions, they create the effect of stage scenery, not the honest structures openly displayed of the Stoke Edith design.

Surprisingly in a collection of facades as diverse and inventive as the Regent's Park terraces, this lodge at the Hanover Gate is the only one on which Nash spent much ingenuity of design. After the dazzling arched preludes to Cumberland Terrace, the neighbouring Gloucester Gate lodge is deliberately low-keyed and astylar. The lodges which Nash did design supremely well at Regent's Park, with quite atypical economy and restraint, were the four identical miniature ones which punctuate the passage of the

106
A compact Greek Doric design for a gate opener to Regent's Park. By John Nash, 1823-5.

Marylebone Road across Park Square. But these have projecting pediments with attached columns and so belong to a later section to be studied after those lodges which feature the more passive design of a recess with columns *in antis*.

This last was the variant in which the Wyatt brothers, James and Samuel, achieved their finest neo-classical lodges. Perhaps this was predictable. The templar form with full portico and pediment confined individual expression within a stereotype. The circular form with surrounding columns was not easy to adapt as a house, as James Wyatt had discovered at Dodington. But the third variant — that of taking a rectangle or cube and enlivening its elevations with recesses and columns, was only a civilised step forwards from the well-tried classical box.

Almost as if working in competition with each other on a set theme and at roughly the same time, Samuel Wyatt built a pair of these lodges at the Milford entrance to Shugborough, Staffordshire, (1803–6),[20] while James Wyatt built a pair for Ottershaw Park, Surrey. Comparisons may be odious but in this case they are irresistible. Samuel's lodges are of limited perfection, crisply detailed and complete, of far more architectural merit than the

PLATE XV

shambling facades of the house in the park beyond. James's lodges are blousy and full blown, Roman villas for all their small compass. Both would pass John Betjeman's test for a Grade One building — does it justify a fourteen mile bicycle ride with the wind against you?

In dimensions and overall design the two lodge sets are almost identical: cubes with plain entablatures and pyramidal roofs, and a recess on three walls containing two Tuscan Doric columns *in antis* which flank the fenestration of two floors. The Ottershaw lodges have suffered some alterations and appear to have been conceived from the first as superior lodgings. They consist of two cubes, the one stepped back from the other and set diagonally, linking only at one corner. This results in a far richer front to the drive than to the road. The lodges are stuccoed and the panels above the ground floor sash window, which is kept blind at Shugborough, contain at Ottershaw Coade stone reliefs of the Arts and Sciences, highly coloured. The ironwork of the gates stresses this decorative mood with baskets of fruit perched high on the piers. At Shugborough Samuel Wyatt relied for effect upon fine ashlar and the spatial depth of a round-headed niche below a Viscount's coronet in a Coade stone circlet.[21] These lodges have depth but no movement; if a single example needed to be chosen to express the essence of English classical architecture then the Shugborough pair would serve admirably. They stand well back from the road with fine woods behind them. The Ottershaw pair must be hunted out down the unadopted roads of a well-heeled suburb behind Ottershaw church, but when found they present a wholly unex-

107
Great Exhibition-style ironwork to Queen's Gate Lodge, Hyde Park.

pected vision of two villas of the Roman prime caught between the thin Surrey birches and the shrubby gardens of commuter land.

The last variant, that with a small pediment supported by columns *in antis*, admits, because the pediment extrudes, of more movement and spatial feeling. Those by Nash in Park Square which have been previously mentioned, are early examples of 1823–5, compact and pure, relieved only by the fluting of their columns and by the pylons of ironwork set against the stucco of their three exposed corners. They have pediments on two sides because of their position on a crossroads. In Hyde Park the Queen's Gate Lodge of 1847 has only one public face but four columns to support its pediment, two Doric and two with strange alternate rustication: the dolls' house of a child who has learnt too many tricks. At Park Square the ironwork set off the lodge; at Queen's Gate a great wave of iron bars, twisted and hammered into a display of technical virtuosity appropriate to the Great Exhibition, impends beside the lodge, obliterating it visually.

Two further examples of the variant need to be mentioned, one at Ammerdown Park in north Somerset because the slight beauty of its stonework is in imminent danger, the other at Wrelton in the North Riding because it carries the type with bravura to the absolute limit of its potential development to become almost a small mansion.

PLATE XVI

The Ammerdown lodge, or lodges, for there is a pair, are the epitome of this lodge type. James Wyatt designed the house in 1788 then, in his usual slapdash style, left it to Joseph Towsey, a Blandford builder, to supervise.

108
Columnar excess in the North Riding at Wrelton.

Because the two Ionic columns which support the pediment are close copies in their deeply carved capitals and delicately modelled feet of the Stuart and Revett illustration of the Ionic order used at the Erectheion,[22] it would be interesting to attribute them to Wyatt himelf as a pioneering instance of the Greek deployment. The Soaneian finials to the gatepiers and the dense soft patterning of the ironwork tell another story, however, and whoever designed them, the lodges must have been put up around 1830. Set back from a

121

lane on the north west corner of the park, they can be easily missed as a wave of greenery has settled upon both buildings, higher and far more threatening than the wave of iron by the Queen's Gate Lodge. There is neither electricity, water nor mains drainage and unless a lover of the primitive life rescues them the lodges must go.

No such fate threatens the Wrelton lodge. This is so large and so habitable that it has been divided into a semi-detached. Its architectural significance was increased by the destruction in 1900 of a house, Silverton Park, at the other end of the country in Devon.[23] Silverton marked a high point of the stylar. English houses are often grudging in their use of columns but Silverton was a forest of them, a double row on the main elevation and lesser thickets of them reaching back at the sides. The Wrelton lodge has only one storey yet it too is a pillared prodigy of lean elegant Ionics. It has pediments on three elevations each with four detached columns as supporters. Antae are used as buttresses to extend the facade to the drive and emphasise the double projection of this front.

It is tempting to conclude a chapter on the columned temple with Wrelton, but behind its columns even Wrelton has a basic structure of finely toned austerity, and it is this feeling for the bare bones of the structure of a house which makes the neo-classical so appealing to architectural modernists. Laugier's theorising about the primitive origins of the Greek style was never forgotten,[24] and some late neo-classical buildings of the 1830s call across one hundred years of decorative detail and Victorian excess to advanced designs of the 1930s which speak with exactly the same voice. Sir John Soane's designing career is a perfect record of this tendency to move from

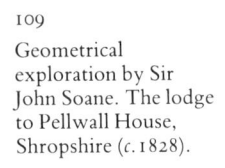

109
Geometrical exploration by Sir John Soane. The lodge to Pellwall House, Shropshire (*c*. 1828).

122

classical form to pure form. It was when he was creating a lodge around 1828, unrestricted by the conventions inseparable from the design of a large house, that he finally broke through into the pure geometry of the Market Drayton Lodge of Pellwall House, Shropshire. This building is an uninhibited exercise in triangular forms carried through with only a hint of neo-classical survival in a vestigial triglyph frieze. If it were not by a roadside in unfashionable country it would have become a place of pilgrimage for the devotees of modernism, an English Ronchamps, unhonoured because the Victorians ignored its possibilities and chose to design derivatively.

110
A curvilinear crescendo to the vanished Cothelstone House, Somerset, by C.H. Masters (1818).

Cothelstone House in Somerset has been pulled down, but it has left a lodge on a side lane up the Quantock slope which exploits the curve as opposed to the straight line in a way quite uncharacteristic of the period. Even the pediment over its door is bowed out and the entablature above has been stepped back three times in a bent pyramid to emphasise the sinuosity. Apart from this central feature and a niche with apron above, the lodge relies like the Stoke Edith lodge on its basic form for its effect: a Greek cross with rounded bays instead of squared arms. It undulates beside its lost green drive like some seaside villa of the Art Deco. Indeed, C.H. Masters who designed Cothelstone in 1818, did build in a residential suburb in a spa town — Lyncombe in Bath, though he also designed the Sydney Hotel which ends the heavy vista of Pulteney Street in the same town with meticulous formality.

If the Cothelstone lodge exploits the curve then Thomas Trubshaw's north west lodge to Heath House at Tean in Staffordshire does exactly the same for the square and rectangle. The lodge (1830–1) by its ground plan seems to demand a columned frontispiece: instead Trubshaw has allowed it only the most meagre pilasters. All the play of its elevations depends upon a series of recesses which give spatial depth and an elusive delicacy to what began as an uncompromising and unadorned square.

Finally, for a return to the veritable Laugier roots of neo-classicism, a visit

111
Thomas Trubshaw's north west lodge to Heath House, Tean, Staffordshire (1830-1).

112
A cottage for the Pythoness of Delphi. The Hope Dale Lodge to Millichope Park, Shropshire, by Edward Haycock (1840).

should be paid to the most basic of all Attic versions. Edward Haycock built Millichope Park, Shropshire in 1835–40 for a neo-classical zealot, the Rev. R.N. Pemberton. The house and the garden temples are conventionally stylar, but for the stables Haycock was obviously asked to economise and to signify a move from gentry to servant quarters while still retaining a Greek feeling. As a result the stables and their attendant cottages are more interesting than the house: bare form emphasised by incised patterns. On the north drive from the park up into remote Hope Dale a small lodge has been given the same treatment. The pediment is suggested only by a thin wooden gable end. There are no columns, yet Haycock has achieved a feeling of mystery and templar dignity simply by recessing the front door deeply within a porch and incising a rectangular panel into the side walls to double their basic form. It is a cottage for the Pythoness of Delphi. The pheasants in the pens behind make their rural noises and there is a curious familiarity about this composition until another lodge is recalled. Millichope is at the very end of a classical lodge evolution but it has come back with its simple pediment to just that point where it began with Roger Morris's first cautious pair in 1732 at Althorp.

CHAPTER EIGHT

A Carriage Drive to the Castle Perilous

THE LAST CHAPTER on the Gothick ended in a burst of neat symmetry with lodges like Blithfield, Halkyn Castle and Scarisbrick. It is easy to pick up the superficial impression that the medievalism of the Regency and William IV periods was generally governed by this feeling for tame balance: window against Perpendicular window, white glazing bars and a five-centred arch in the middle, all enclosed in a firm rectangular frame. This may be true of Regency vicarages and of Thomas Rickman's reedy and mechanical churches[1] but it is anything but an accurate generalisation about the Regency Gothic lodge.

In the earlier eighteenth century Gothick period a very limited set of motifs: large quatrefoils and cruciform arrow-slits, tended to be applied to the walls of lodges in symmetrical patterns that were basically classical in spirit. An influential architect like James Wyatt was still designing lodges in this trite yet charming manner when he was young. His West Lodge to Sheffield Place, Sussex, built in 1776, is an entirely unconvincing gate arch with houses symmetrically disposed at each side. The quatrefoil rose windows and the heraldic shields are token medievalisms and the cornice beneath the battlemented parapet is of the type that was being applied to Gothick drawing rooms and libraries in the 1750s.[2]

PLATE XVII

In 1780–90, however, Wyatt returned to Sheffield Place to work again and from that period his East Lodge must date. This second lodge has been conceived in a quite different spirit, that of the Picturesque. In detail it marks no notable advance on the West Lodge, though it is less coyly mannered, but in outline it is dramatic and completely asymmetrical: a bold three storey tower and turret with a thin Tudor arch over the drive. Wyatt is already anticipating in the 1780s the spirit — confident, sprightly yet unconvincing — of the Regency Gothic lodge. In one park and in ten years he has moved from 'Gothick' to 'Gothic'.

Regency architects did not all at one time abandon the style of the elegant Gothick toy, but they were more appreciative of the irregular outline of real medieval castles and often their repertoire of details was much wider, even archaeologically correct. They were not usually concerned, as their Victorian successors were, with using their culled scraps and fragments correctly. The overall aim of a Regency lodge of this type was to be picturesque, to suggest the outline of the castle waiting further on down the drive if there was one and, if there was not, to be a cheerful substitute for what was missing.

Thomas Love Peacock's *Nightmare Abbey*[3] catches their mood. Written to mock the 'atrabilarious' its house stands on a narrow strip of land between the sea and the fens with a wing of ruins next to a comfortable modern residence. Here morbid young men pose at night on gloomy battlements and tumble through windows into the moat when 'ghosts' have frightened them. The Abbey is the sensational prop for a civilised romp. Regency Gothic lodges, like their main houses, tend to sensational style, not authenticity. It was only towards the end of the period, in the late 1820s, that patrons began to demand an antiquarian correctness of detail and that architects like Thomas Hopper and Edward Blore emerged ready to supply this.[4]

The West Lodge to Bryn Kynallt is an ideal instance of the carefree picturesque manner of the Regency, set a few yards off the main street of Chirk, half a mile out of Shropshire, and just into Wales. To begin with, it is flagrantly asymmetrical: an octagonal two storey tower tacked on to a single storey rectangular block. It is picturesque and demands attention but it is an obvious toy. Heraldic shields are carved into the tower walls and Latin mottoes of progressive Tory flavour: *'Pro Rege et Lege'* and *'Per Aris et Focis'*, all in crooked Gothic script. There is a bedroom in the top of the tower but its window faces away from the drive to preserve the illusion of battlements. In the single storey block which holds the living room is an engaging three-light bow window hanging over the drive like a ticket office, perfect for an alert but sedentary gatekeeper. It is an easy unit for a family to live in, it has playful charm, and all has been achieved for a modest sum without the building of a Fonthill or an Arbury. '*MDCCCXIII Inchoatum*' its inscription reads, '*MDCCCXIV Perfectum*', and would, for the sake of good scholarship, that all lodges were as exactly labelled.

113
A lively late Gothick exercise of 1813-14 at Bryn Kynallt, Denbighshire.

The Bryn Kynallt lodge is just shrugging off, stylistically, the 'k' in 'Gothick' by the rough boldness of its details, as in the dripstones and in its avoidance of the feminine ogee curve. The North Lodge to Newark Park, high in the Cotswold beechwoods south-east of Wooton-under-Edge, is another example of this half-way stage of design. In its conception it is Gothick, a symmetrical cube with every window and door an ogee, but every detail has been deliberately coarsened: the window surrounds are wide

114
Pastry work Gothick at the North Lodge to Newark Park, Gloucestershire.

and flat without any elegance of moulding and the quoining is bold enough for a house four times its size. The Clutterbuck arms over the door prove that the lodge is of the very early 1790s and it must be by a very local architect, obliged by lack of expertise to follow the patterns of the Halfpenny brothers (1753–9) yet obviously resenting their toy delicacy.

The North Lodges to Alscot Park, Warwickshire, appear to be perfect examples of that style which the Newark lodge builder was reluctantly imitating. The lodge keepers' houses are paper thin in all their detail: the

PLATE XVII The West Lodge to Sheffield Place, Sussex (1776-7) in its prime, from a contemporary painting. (By kind permission of Mrs Morrice Jennings).

PLATE XVIII The Lower Lodge of Caerhays Castle, Cornwall. A private entrance to a bathing beach, John Nash's design of c. 1808.

PLATE XIX A view from within the park of the Tennysonian towers of the Lullington Gatehouse to Orchardleigh Park, Somerset (c.1816).

PLATE XX One of a pair of matching chantry-chapel lodges at Rushton Hall, Northamptonshire (*c.* 1820).

115
False Gothick work.
The lodges to Alscot
Park, Warwickshire,
by Richard Hulls
(1813).

ogee windows snake sinuously within the pointed recesses and the incised quatrefoils have no archaeological subtlety, the symmetry of the pair is absolute. Everything suggests the Gothick of the 1760s. In fact these lodges are an indication of how stylistically sophisticated in their eclecticism Regency architects were becoming. They are of 1813 and their architect, Richard Hulls, built them deliberately to this retardaire design to accord with the parent house which John Philips had built in Gothick style between 1750 and 1764. They are as much pastiche as a 1930s neo-Georgian post office.

When not held back by such refined environmental sensibilities, the real Regency Gothic mood was for the rough and tumble of towers and battlements. They are a visual commonplace of the English countryside. Some must be the military gestures of an aristocracy sitting comfortably at home growing wealthy while their country waged a long world war. Others are billboards of false ancestry set up by nouveau riche profiteers from that war. There is so much light-hearted castellation that it is necessary to remember the lodges of the last chapter to preserve a balanced account of Regency society. Would the Doric and Ionic lodges of neo-classicism have been seen by contemporaries as 'modern' architecture and the Gothic lodges as mere playthings? How natural would a thatched *cottage orné* appear to a contemporary? Had the greedy eclecticism of the time confused critical opinion so far that a standard form no longer survived?

The Marquess of Cholmondeley designed his own Cholmondeley Castle in 1801–4 and so presumably his own West Lodge. It is a serious square tower of two storeys, windowed widely enough to be an obvious living unit but otherwise martial and plain with none of the token medieval gestures which the Gothick would have made. For Caerhays Castle, Cornwall in about 1808 John Nash designed two lodges. The Upper Lodge is in the

116
A tower lodge by the Marquess of Cholmondeley for his castle in Cheshire (1801-4).

PLATE XVIII

Cholmondeley mood. Its outline is firm but the fenestration is unashamedly modern with four wide sash windows to the road. Then in compensation Nash added the picturesque element of an archway across the drive and a stern round tower which could only be used as a tool shed or for coal. At the Lower Lodge on the seafront the impact of the design is quite different, the pretence is almost absolute. To the road there are only arrow-slits. Massive battlemented walls fit for a siege run out on either side, yet for all the martial show there is not an architectural detail which an intelligent child of ten could not have drawn. Nash has made not the slightest effort to inform

117
The Upper Lodge to Caerhays Castle, Cornwall, by John Nash (c. 1808).

himself on medieval military forms.

Two more castle type lodges, both built in 1810 and within a few miles of each other, impress the point that at this time it was the spirit of a lodge's conception rather than its stylistic detail which decided its impact. The

118
The toy fortifications of Midford Castle, Somerset, repeated in the later lodge of 1810.

designer's concepts decide that the one is 'Gothick', the other 'Gothic'.

The Gothick lodge is to Midford Castle, Somerset, the Gothic lodge is the Combe Lodge to Ashton Court, Bristol. Both lodges use quatrefoils symmetrically placed as decoration for vacant spaces and the octagonal turrets and actual finish of the battlements in each lodge are so close as to suggest the same team of masons. There are two-light square-headed windows with

119
Generous accommodation contrived within an entrance appropriate to a medieval abbey. The Combe Lodge to Ashton Court, Bristol (c.1810).

drip-stones in both and the two central arches are five-centred Tudor.

With all this they are achievements apart. The Midford lodge, like the Alscot pair, is consciously retardaire, contrived to accord with the saucy Ace of Spades planned Gothick castle which it serves.[5] If it were shrunk it would make a fine mould for a Staffordshire mantlepiece ornament. The Combe Lodge is not simply much larger, it makes a deliberate gesture. Only one element in its detail is new: the pointed two-light windows with quatrefoil heads, the remainder is the recipe as before. But with these windows, six of them to the road, it achieves a melancholy consequence. The Midford lodge

120
An ingenious fly-over lodge in Regency Gothic carrying the west drive to Mostyn Hall, Flintshire, across a minor road.

is a mere prelude, the Combe Lodge is an architectural event; by sheer bulk and by multiplicity of turrets the architect has built a gatehouse fit for a large monastery. If it is the work of Henry Wood, who designed the loutish Lower Lodge closer to the city in 1802, then he had made the same leap in design which James Wyatt had made earlier at Sheffield Place.[6]

Size alone was not enough. That a feeling for profile and spatial depth were needed to compensate for thin detail is proven by Sir Jeffry Wyatville's tedious square tower lodge to Lypiatt Park, Gloucestershire, (1809) and by Nash's weary 1807 lodge to Shirburn Castle, Oxfordshire, where the hasty architect has taken three elements: an arch, a square tower and a square cottage all of exactly the same height, and cobbled them together without articulation.[7] The result now stands in decay beside the B4009, a proof that

132

good lodge design of any style and at any period requires a thoughtful and carefully dramatised concentration of units and surface decoration.

The unknown architects who built at about this time the Drybridge Lodge to Mostyn Hall, Flintshire, and the Clopton Bridge Toll House at Stratford-upon-Avon, both relied upon the drama of their sites to carry off the simple authority of towers with Tudor fenestration. The side elevation of the Drybridge Lodge rises over a tunnel into which the road plunges under a grinning stone head as the drive from Mostyn Hall passes overhead under yet another arch which links the two lodges. The sharply edged string coursing and the slender window bars contrast with the massive dark solidity of the tunnel arch in a scenario which is more engineering than architecture. The Clopton Bridge Toll House achieves a similar drama by imposing its stock polygon upon the multiple arches of the bridge.

Thomas Telford might have been expected to aim at this same drama by simple contrast of forms in his Mythe Bridge Lodge at Tewkesbury,

121
Thomas Telford's toll-house (1823-6) on the Mythe Bridge at Tewkesbury, Gloucestershire.

Gloucestershire, where his single span carried the road from the west over the Severn.[8] Rather unexpectedly his toll lodge is not only Gothic with a bay porch under a pedimented roofline, but it sports no less than six pinnacle pillars, two of them rising high above the eaves and all of them structurally meaningless. Here, as in the classical pedimented lock lodges on his Gloucester and Berkeley canal,[9] is an instance of how the park gate lodge with its tradition of decorative display influenced the architecture of the industrial revolution.

Almost all the changing lodge styles contrive to produce at least one design so outstanding as to be unfunctional in that it completely exceeds aesthetically the house which it serves. This series of towered Gothic lodges, often playful in their conception, flowered into such a lodge in the Lullington Gatehouse to Orchardleigh Park, Somerset of 1816. Nearby Farleigh House had, between 1806 and 1813, added a blockish Gothic gatehouse of

PLATE XIX

122

The forecourt of the great Lullington Gatehouse to Orchardleigh Park, Somerset (c.1816).

giant size to its park furniture and the Lullington Gatehouse may have been conceived in a spirit of competition by Sir Thomas Champneys whom Lord Hylton called 'a lesser Beckford'.[10] The Gatehouse must have originally been his inspiration and it is the conception of the lodge rather than the style which is so dramatic. The high Somerset hedges are interrupted by two modest and unlinked towers. Through the wide ungated gap between these opens up an entire castle courtyard, a full seventy yards across. It is set with trees growing from rough grass. All round are high walls with a powdery feeling of ruined age. Across the grass stands what many a first visitor must have taken for Orchardleigh House itself. In fact it is only the lodge, or rather the lodges, for on each side of a pinnacled gate tower is a three storey tower with a jaunty stair turret angled out over the court to complete a symmetrical composition. Stylistically the building is Regency Perpendicular with no exact beauty or novelty of detail, but as a whole the complex is Arthurian — 'four grey walls and four grey towers, overlook a space of flowers and the silent isle imbowers the Lady of Shalott.' Even the 'silent isle' is there a little further on into the park with a church in the trees. Again and again at this period one is struck by the way in which the architecture precedes the literature: Orchardleigh before Shalott, the Edgehill Tower twenty years before *Otranto*. It is an absorbing essay in the growth of concepts, the material before the ideal. No architect's name can be attached to this enchanting circuit and it is just that it should be so. The notion of the place was enough to lift a commonplace compromise style to its apotheosis.

It was after Lullington that the, in many ways fateful, grip of antiquarian correctness began to close in upon lodge design vitiating imagination and encouraging careful copying of older structures. There is already an element of this in the deeply recessed and thoroughly convincing Early English doorways which face each other in the two chantry chapel-like East Lodges on either side of the main drive into Rushton Hall, Northamptonshire. But the bizarre incongruity of the surrounding detail: quatrefoil circlets, a trefoiled cornice and absurd crocketted pinnacles reduces the lodges to the likeable and avoids the formidable.

PLATE XX

The first sign of consistent correctness came when Samuel Rush Meyrick failed to purchase Goodrich Castle, Herefordshire, in 1827. He bought the hill across the valley and commissioned Edward Blore to build as a fitting

123
Gothick phasing into Gothic. Edward Blore's scholarly adaptation of a German gatehouse for Goodrich Court, Herefordshire (1823-31).

showcase for his superb collection of armour and antiquities 'a building of stone of the very best masonry, and of the architecture of Edward I'.[11] This Blore did, along with village buildings in the same style and the Monmouth Gate, the main lodge to the new Goodrich Court.[12] Blore intended to cap one of the towers of the Court with spires but this was never done, and the whole Camelot-like complex which Wordsworth had described as 'an impertinent structure' was demolished in 1956.[13] But the Monmouth Gate was given its cap of spires and spirelet and this survives, not like the Lullington Gatehouse on some leafy lane, but on the very brink of the roaring four lane highway which links the M40 with Merthyr Tydfil.

Rush Meyrick was not only an antiquarian fanatic but a sincere believer in the social merits of the feudal system and an Olde England of beef and ale, hence his medieval style inn and social buildings for Goodrich village. Love Peacock, who had handed out some rough satire on the melancholy Goths in *Nightmare Abbey* in 1819, gave Rush Meyrick a much milder and more thoughtful treatment when in 1831 he brought him into his dialogue novel

Crotchet Castle as Mr. Chainmail, who believed that the cause of unrest in the present, as in his beloved twelfth century, was the same: 'poverty in despair'.[14] Over the twelve intervening years the Gothic movement had gained stature, growing from a self-conscious indulgence into something nearer to the essential style of integrity and moral shape which Pugin and Ruskin were to eulogise.

Increasingly the message went out that the architecture of the Middle Ages was not something on which to improvise, but an object for serious study and imitation. This the Monmouth Gate expresses. It is not a version of the gatehouse of nearby St. Briavels Castle which it faintly resembles, but is copied from the Bourcette at Aachen.[15] This accounts for the strange tilt of its twin spires, the steep, highly un-English roof which links them and the grim dreariness of its facade. Time has not been kind to the Monmouth Gate. Its spirelet has gone, there are complex modern additions to the side and the present owner must bless Blore for the arrow-slits which now protect it from the glare and noise of night-time traffic. But at least it remains a monument to an aesthetic theory and a lost social purpose: the last tower of Mr. Chainmail and the Fortress of Beef and Ale.

CHAPTER NINE

'That Peculiar Mode of Building Which was Originally the Effect of Chance'[1]

This should not, strictly speaking, be a chapter. It will certainly be a short one.

The only justification for the study of the lodge as a separate building type has been its ability to take up current architectural modes and express them in a peculiarly intense and concentrated form. The effect, for example, of two Greek Doric columns, when they are part of a small three bay structure of genuinely humble reference, is quite different to their impact when spaced out across the facade of a major country house or court building. On a park gate lodge they appear both improper by the contrast with their usual pretentious contexts, and more satisfying because their essential simplicity has found a simple setting in which their form and fluting can be appreciated without the distraction of a massive severity of surrounding stone. It is the humble scale and function of the average lodge which sets up an attractive tension when it is made into a display case for formal motifs.

This is not the case when a *cottage orné* is used as a lodge. Because its essence is a *faux naïf* rustic simplicity, a thatched *cottage orné* can gain nothing in intensity when it is set up at a park gate. It has merely been placed in one strategic position rather than another. One function of a lodge was always to be a cottage. When a lodge is deliberately built to look like a cottage the valuable tension of design is lost because its other function, that of proclaiming the state of the park and house within, has been abandoned.

A reasonable number of such *cottage orné* lodges were built during the Regency and make an interesting contrast to the concurrent fashions for Gothic and neo-classical lodges. For that reason they must briefly be considered.

All three lodge styles of the early nineteenth century have their faltering origins in the first half of the previous century. In the 1790s poets, novelists and architects all rushed with headlong glee upon styles and themes which had been tentatively fingered for the past fifty years: Wordsworth after Thomson and Goldsmith, Mrs. Radcliffe after Walpole, the Reptons after Thomas Wright. The popularity of the thatched cottage may have been heightened because it provided a relief from the rigid angularity of neo-classical architecture. A classical lodge like Cothelstone that langorously exploited the curve was an exotic rarity, but when a small house was being built which was essentially nothing but a roof, and that roof a thick flexible blanket of thatch, rounded forms could be indulged in, like a sweet syrup.

· As far back as 1745 on that seminal site above Radway Grange, Warwickshire, Sanderson Miller had seen the picturesque potential of the inhabited roof two years before he completed his inhabited tower of Edgehill. The Miller cottage stands less than fifty yards away from the tower and as the drive now runs down through the tower complex the cottage rises just above the drive, presenting its most interesting roof scapes to travellers down that rocky road.[2] Whether Miller originally intended the cottage to be the lodge before another ambition thrust him on to build his tower cannot be known, but the cottage certainly has a relationship to both the village road and the Radway drive. It was on its rear elevation that Miller first tried out that device of slicing a roof down diagonally to cut through the stump of a round tower. The undulating slope which this produces must have pleased him for he repeated it in the rear elevations of his famous sham castle in Hagley Park, Worcestershire.[3] This suggests that early Gothick experiments and early cottage designs both had their roots in a desire to explore non-classical form.

124
One of the Slait Lodges at Badminton Park, Gloucestershire. Thomas Wright's design dates from 1748-56 when he was working for the 4th Duke of Beaufort.

Badminton Park, when Thomas Wright was working there between 1748 and 1756 for the widow of the fourth Duke of Beaufort, was another seed bed for contrived cottage simplicities.[4] Wright's buildings like the Slait Lodges on the Little Badminton road and his thatched cottage in Badminton village demonstrate that simplicity of form was the last aim of such cottage builders. Wright's cottage in the village owes much to his Root House or Hermit's Cell in the park proper. Its ogee Gothick dormers peep coyly from the great rug of thatch which spreads down almost to ground level, where rough tree trunks support it. The lower rooms are consequently intolerably dark. At the Slait Lodges, the further of which does stand at a gate into the

125
A *cottage orné* in Badminton village by Thomas Wright.

park, the exploration of form for form's sake is more apparent. Unmuffled by thatch the dormers jut up crisply and at each corner of the diminutive cottage is an octagonal turret with a slated cap.

These three cottages demonstrate how fine a line divides the *cottage orné* from the Gothick. Miller's Edgehill cottage is basically a very ruined tower keep with lancet windows; he simply draped the thatch over its high walls and low round turrets to achieve a free picturesque shape. Wright's Slait Lodges are a mistake. The symmetry of their corner turrets is too apparent. Thatch would have softened the over-exact outlines and in his Badminton village cottage, Wright hit upon Miller's device and dramatised the banal basic shape of the rectangular building into an amorphous creeping form simply by thatching it.

It is easy to talk, at this point, of vernacular forms being brought back into formal architecture to revitalise it. But the question needs to be asked, what vernacular? The cottage vernacular of the Cotswolds where Wright was building used limestone slates for its roofs and inclined to sharp gables and precise outlines, all quite unlike the thatched and hooded alien which Wright introduced into the midst of Badminton village. If, as seems likely, Wright had turned from the sharp slated symmetry of the Slait Lodges to his thatched creation between the years 1748 and 1756, this marks a very early appreciation for homely and softened cottage forms. It suggests that Wright was influenced by William Shenstone who was experimenting with cottages at the Leasowes in the 1740s.[5] In the Midlands thatch would have been the genuine vernacular and its effects may have begun to be appreciated from this source.

The potential freedom of form which such cottages could introduce to break up the prison of box and rectangle was not significantly exploited in thatched lodges. It was picturesque villages like Blaise Hamlet outside Bristol and Marford in Flintshire which showed what variety and charm of loggias, round-roofed privies and dormers was waiting to be exploited by an architect who would allow the internal machinery of a house to exhibit itself in its exterior shapes.[6]

Some cottage lodges remained trapped in the earlier garden building tradition of the octagon. The lodge to Wivenhoe Park, Essex, is an instance of this with the full Gothic treatment on its windows and doors but with the

126
A Regency ombrello lodge to Wivenhoe Park, Essex which has been stripped of its original thatch.

loggia device of the *cottage orné* carried out, not in rough tree trunks, but in sharp Tudor poles and under a battlemented eaves board. The twin octagon lodges, placed side by side at the Lion Gate of Scrivelsby Park, Lincolnshire, are particularly interesting as they may be by Humphry Repton who was working here in 1791. If they are they show how formal were his early notions of the Picturesque. They have lost their thatch which must originally have provided a heavy overhang though not a loggia. Repton, if it was he, devised no ingenious interpenetrating shapes for the neat little cottages but created a separate feature in the re-erection of the large Gothic arch which spans the drive entrance. The whole composition is incoherent and amateur.

It was only after Humphry Repton's son George Stanley had created, with John Nash, his demonstration pieces at Blaise that another Bristol landowner could have a gate lodge like that which once led into Broomwell House, Brislington. In this the Gothic tradition has been confidently linked with the *cottage orné*. The two tiers of thatching were not allowed to conceal the richly carved bargeboards and the various functional irregularities of the internal rooms were emphasised by the thatched slopes above them. The twisted brick chimney stacks of this Broomwell Lodge suggest a late date, perhaps 1830.

The average gate lodge of the earlier *cottage orné* enthusiasm was either a simple single storey rectangle with a loggia all around and a thatch draped over it or a two storey affair with two tiers of thatching. Examples of the

127
A pair of octagonal lodges, curiously sited by the Lion Gate to Scrivelsby Park, Lincolnshire. A possible Humphry Repton composition of 1791.

128
A contemporary print of the lodge to Broomwell House, Bristol.

simple type are found at Tawstock Court, Devon, Charborough Park, Dorset, Halswell House, Somerset, Combe Hay, also in Somerset, Ickenham House, Middlesex and Ugbrooke House, Devon. Their Wessex distribution is obvious though the neater finish of Norfolk reed resulted in some East Anglian examples with a much sharper outline. The Roudham lodge just outside East Harling with its lighter thatch uses logs for a rustic effect at the porch while a smaller outbuilding, once separate, produces a composition which can only be described in terms of mother and daughter — certainly an advance on the Scrivelsby pair. Most of these lodges have at least one distinctive feature. The Smoothway Lodge to Ugbrooke is a very rare survival of the wholesale primitive with walls of upright logs, but even this has Gothic windows so it would be quite wrong to press it as an illustration of Laugier's theories on the primitive origins of classical architecture. At Halswell the loggia has a floor composed of beach pebbles laid in decorative patterns and at Ickenham, where in Middlesex the rural feeling must have been wearing thin, the lodge has been given an architectural treatment of cruciform shape and windows with Tudor dripstones.

There is a natural intermediate stage between single and double storey thatched lodges where, as Wright discovered very early on, dormer windows can be set in the roof and the thatch peaked about them in pleasing variety. The Chain Bridge Lodge to Stuckeridge House, Devon is an instance of this. But at its height, when a full ombrello is attempted, the type can occasionally rise above merely pleasing qualities into something very close to real architectural forms. Gaunt's House at Hinton Martell, Dorset has such a lodge. It was probably built by William Evans of Wimborne to a Greek Ionic villa he designed for Sir Richard Carr Glyn and is, therefore, one

PLATE XXI

142

129
Rural primitivism. The Smoothway Lodge to Ugbrooke Park, Devon.

of the very rare thatched lodges which can be given a designer. The garden building tradition has survived, as at Wivenhoe, the lodge being a very rough approximation to an octagon. The fenestration is Gothic but Evans has wholly abandoned the incised shapes and outlines of the Wivenhoe architect and committed himself to a shape so organic as to be mushroom-like, yet so tense in its detail as to suggest a tethered balloon. Two porches with separate round thatched roofs prepare the eye for the thatched dome above the main house. This is anchored down to the house in a series of triangular peaks which are repeated on the porch roofs and caught up again in the arches of the Gothic fenestration.

130
Pebbled patterning in the loggia of the lodge to Halswell House, Somerset.

131
A tethered ombrello lodge to Gaunt's House, Hinton Martell, Dorset (c. 1809).

The limitation of this lodge is that all its effects come from deliberately applied design. The Repton cottages at Blaise were far more sophisticated because their decorative quality rose naturally out of the disposition of the rooms and the materials of the construction. In this way they anticipated the Arts and Crafts movement of the mid-nineteenth century.

PLATE XXI Thatcher at work on the Chain Bridge Lodge to Stuckeridge House, Devon.

PLATE XXII John Wood's free-form Palladian design in the Lower Lodge to Prior Park, Bath.

There are ombrello villas in south coastal towns like Lyme Regis, Sidmouth and Dawlish which play exactly the decorative tricks of the Gaunt's House Lodge. It was, moreover, a feature of the pattern books of the 1790–1820 period that their lodge designs are often expressly labelled as interchangeable. Papworth's steward's house would look well at a park gate or a gate lodge would, with a few additions, make a shooting box for a gentleman.[7] All this marks the first real faltering in the tradition of lodge building. To enliven villa design by 'vernacular' flexibility was an advance of a kind for house design in general, but for the separate tradition of lodge design it was harmful because the gap between a lodge and a small villa narrowed as a result of the inter-changeability. The essence of lodge design had always been a certain formality which distinguished it from ordinary small houses. In the next, mid-Victorian period, the lodge is often indistinguishable from the small suburban house with decorative features. The closing in of the types was inevitable. Once a lodge could serve as a gentleman's shooting box it could just as easily house a solicitor or a doctor in a town's new residential area. So, though the Arts and Crafts movement was to revitalise lodge design for a time, and though Victorian energy and wealth were to produce some gate lodges of intense decorative display and experimental flair, the building type had, after barely one hundred years of growth, passed its prime and begun to decline. This was inevitable as the demands of the new urban petty bourgeoisie created a field for experiment in the design of small detached houses so great that lodge design became quite overshadowed by it.

CHAPTER TEN

A New Florence in the West –
the Lodge as an Episode in the Italianate

THE LAST CHAPTER ended on a melancholy note, predicting the decline of lodge architecture as a result of the vogue for primping thatch. It was suggested that the destructive element in using the *cottage orné* as a lodge was the informality of the style, the lodge depending for its separate identity on a functional formalism which distinguished it from an ordinary small house. But the next wave of stylistic fashion, the Italianate, though like the cottage style, stemming from the fad for picturesque irregularity, had an invigorating effect upon lodge design. The lodge could respond to the Italianate for two reasons. It was an alien style, always artificial in an English landscape, and a lodge conceived in this style always stood apart and was therefore formal in its setting. Secondly the Italianate was a villa style where many parts: belvedere, loggia, balconied living quarters and arched entrances, composed the whole. This provided a rich source of detail for a lodge to concentrate into one small highly allusive building and so the lodge reassumed its function as a mood setter to, and essence of, the main house which it guarded.

One of the most interesting features about Italianate work in England has been the critical reaction to it in recent times. As Victorian architecture grew hugely in popular appreciation, the Italianate was bound to be carried along to some extent with the other favoured styles of the Victorian period. Was it not Victoria and Albert's own chosen style for Osborne House? But it has never achieved cult status as have Victorian Gothic, Romanesque or Queen Anne. No one has yet suggested pulling down Aston Webb's Edwardian classical front of Buckingham Palace to reconstruct Edward Blore's melancholy Italianate facade. Charles Barry's Trentham Hall in Staffordshire (1834–40) marked the apogee of the Italianate but it shows no sign, since its 1910 demolition, of becoming a legendary lost house like Gothick Fonthill.

In his *Thomas Hope and the Neo-Classical Idea,* where the origins of the Italianate are discussed in detail, David Watkin comments regretfully that the Italianate tended to be seen "merely as an example of 'the growing historicism' of the nineteenth century, but there is no reason why it should not be seen as the natural heir to English Palladianism, which is not normally described as an 'historicist style'."[1] This is a fair point. English Palladian was based, often very closely, on the sixteenth century architecture of the Veneto and yet its buildings have come to be accepted as natural parts of the English rural and urban scene. Meanwhile the very site of Thomas Hope's partly Italianate Deepdene in Surrey (1818–23) has been ploughed as if to expunge even the memory of his careful picturesque compositions.[2]

The fact is that British Italianate is not an easy architecture to define and write about, not easy therefore to appraise. It may be helpful to open with a consideration of two lodges, which are quite different in outline and in decoration, yet which can both be accepted as Italianate, to find what elements have made the style hard to assimilate and difficult to love.

132
The Pink Lodge to Alton Towers, Staffordshire. An early Italianate design of the mid 1820s.

The first is a lodge to Alton Towers, Staffordshire, always described, as the Pink Lodge. The history of Alton's multiple garden buildings is confused but this lodge, as its rough detail suggests, is probably a very early example of the Italian Style in this country. J.C. Loudon's *The Suburban Gardener and Villa Companion* of 1838 illustrates, without acknowledgement, something very like it[3] and Loudon's *Encyclopaedia* of 1846 is the authority for Robert Abraham having worked at Alton for the fifteenth Earl of Shrewsbury.[4] His knowledge of Abraham's time at Alton combined with his illustration of a design very close to the Pink Lodge allows an inference that the design he borrowed was by Abraham. Since the Earl died in 1827 the Pink Lodge, if it is by Abraham, must date from the mid 1820s at the latest. It is aggressively asymmetrical. Not only is the left hand tower much higher than the right with its coarsely detailed viewing platform or belvedere, but the fenestration of the two towers is wilfully discordant — the one gaping, the other pinched. What pulls the composition together is the spreading projection of the eaves of both towers and the pink paint on the rough brickwork. This, far more than Thomas Hope's carefully designed tower of 1823 at Deepdene[5] or Sir James Pennethorne's Italian villas of Park Village West, Regent's Park (1824 onwards)[6], seems to satisfy the original picturesque ideal of Uvedale Price by its play of outline and its unsophisticated directness. Aesthetically, it is not easy to digest. It demands attention but then fails to satisfy it by any detail or overall logic. Not only is its viewing platform set much lower than its roof would have permitted, but the building is down in a valley among woods commanding no views. The drive to Alton Towers is across the road and the Pink Lodge was used to receive coach visitors before they set off up the steep incline opposite, into the gardens under the earl's control. The zealous Roman Catholicism of the family may have influenced the choice of style, but one question which is rarely asked about English Italianate buildings is whether a cultivated Italian would accept them as Italianate. If so, of which period and of which Italian region?

To Sir Uvedale Price, the most influential theorist behind the Picturesque movement in architectural and landscape design, the word 'Italian' was imprecise. Wollaton was 'Italian' and picturesque, Nottingham Castle was 'Italian' and dull, only redeemed by its site.[7] The Italian style, as it began to evolve in early buildings like the Pink Lodge, was developed in an attempt to produce an acceptable modern version of Blenheim. Much of the Italianate's outlines and surface decoration are best appreciated if it is seen as a Vanbrughian Revival. Sir Joshua Reynolds had begun the reappraisal of Vanbrugh's *œuvre* in his Thirteenth Discourse. Uvedale Price completed it in his *Essay on the Picturesque*. What Price wanted to restore to architecture was a variety of roofline:

> I cannot but reflect with surprise, on the little attention that has been paid to the summits of houses in the country[8]

and he urged his reader to stand at evening across the lake at Blenheim:

> Whoever catches that view towards the close of the evening, when the sun strikes on the golden balls, and pours his beams through the open parts, gilding every rich and brilliant ornament, will think he sees some enchanted palace.[9]

But along with this richness above Price admired the way Vanbrugh's 'first point seems to have been massiveness as the foundation of grandeur,'[10] 'to produce richness and variety, and still to preserve the idea of massiveness'.[11] At the same time symmetry which 'particularly accords with the beautiful is in the same degree adverse to the picturesque.'[12]

If these requirements are added together they explain the oddity of the Pink Lodge. It has an open top structure, it is massive and it is asymmetrical, and since the earl had been working on his garden buildings since his succession in 1787 it could well be the earliest Italian picturesque structure in England.

Price's *Essay* explains a much later and initially surprising comment in J. Loudon's *Suburban Gardener*. Accompanying an illustration of a small lodge of cyclopean character he writes: 'it will be seen that massiveness is a leading feature in Italian lodges'.[13] As late as 1838 the Pink Lodge would be seen as typical of its style. T.F. Hunt's *Archittetura Campestre*, an 1827 pattern book already noted,[14] illustrates a lodge into which 'a campanile, a peculiar feature in Italian architecture, is introduced with a loggeta containing two rooms for a gate-porter or other domestic.'[15] A lodge design similar to this, simple to the point of bareness, was actually built at Tapeley House, Westleigh in Devon, overlooking the estuary of the Torridge. If Hunt was offering such designs in 1827 it suggests that campanile may have been becoming popular at least as early as Thomas Hope's Deepdene tower which was completed in 1823.

133
An urbane design for a rural lodge at Dowdeswell Court, Gloucestershire (1833-5).

The second lodge in this attempt to bracket the style is later than the Pink Lodge and quite unlike it. The Lower Lodge to Dowdeswell Court, Gloucestershire, was designed by the Cheltenham architect Rowland Paul in 1833–5. It is of a single storey, has no belvedere and has no picturesque outline. What marks the lodge as 'Italianate' is the proliferation of random detail thrust into the design at every point where a neo-classical lodge of the same general form would have been direct and bare.

The windows are round-headed and the rectangular shape into which they are illogically set has incised scroll patterns in the spandrels. Balusters and rusticated pilasters confuse the outline of each wing while the doorcase perversely blunts and decorates its essentially plain rectangle. Paterae cut off the top door angles, the brackets supporting the pediment are a floral tangle and the pediment itself, which begins straight and should continue straight to accord with the entablature, breaks into miniature volutes which support a shield with side swags of fruit. A feminine roundness and a dainty soften-

134 Charles Barry's vaunting Italianate viewing tower on Derry Hill near Bowood House, Wiltshire.

ing produces a not unpleasing contradiction of the basic classical form.

Whether either of these lodges is strictly of Italy is questionable, but the outline generalities of the Pink Lodge and the uninhibited fuss of Dowdeswell between them include the essential character of the British Italianate. The Pink Lodge is Italianate as the Picturesque theorists of the late 1790s had envisaged it; the Lower Lodge at Dowdeswell represents that element of fruity banker's classical decoration which became associated with the Italianate simply because the age enjoyed such detail.

When an architect like Charles Barry, with a real feeling for proportion and scale handled the style the result, his lodge for the third Marquess of Lansdowne, the Golden Gates at Derry Hill, Bowood in Wiltshire, was memorable. It relates to the little Tapeley lodge rather as a cathedral to a parish church and demonstrates how the style was changing its character. A tall belvedere tower on a main house produces a picturesque outline but also a theatrical air. On a lodge it can look exactly like what it really is: a place for a picnic with servants' rooms below. This is a revival of the gate lodge's old dual function as dining pavilion and gate guardian.

What was unpredictable in the Golden Gates was the nature of the surface decoration. Barry designed this lodge in the early 1840s[16] and as long ago as 1829 he had proved in his garden front to the Travellers' Club that he was competent in Venetian palazzo detail.[17] The top of his Golden Gates tower would be at home on Lake Como but most of the ornament on the lower sections is of that florid sub-classical, characteristic of the 1840s in England.

It was as the Italianate, a style originally devised to combine a complex outline with a massive simplicity, was developed into a style combining complex outline with complex surface decoration, that it became on occasions ineptly florid. As Uvedale Price had warned, anyone could throw up a conventional symmetrical house:

So tall, so stiff, some London house you'd swear
Had chang'd St. James's for a purer air.[18]

but a picturesque house, which would depend upon irregular elements tastefully disposed, would require a true architect working not on patterns but on his own judgements. The Italianate lodges are the proof of this; it is a style that tests its architects.

The lodge to Lucknam, Colerne in Wiltshire is early, of about 1830, and still relies on the cheerful irregularity of its tower, linked by an arch to a plain pedimented lodge house, for its effects. At Chatsworth, as late as 1840-2, John Robertson was still playing the game by the Picturesque book when he designed the Park Lodge on the grand formal approach from Baslow. The twin lodges each exploit three separate flat roof levels of first storey, second storey and tower emphasised by balustrading. But their actual surface decoration is chaste in the extreme, flat Doric pilasters for the porch and simple incised rectangular emphasis for the remainder. These are lodges which demonstrate how closely the Italianate was originally to the neo-classical, the

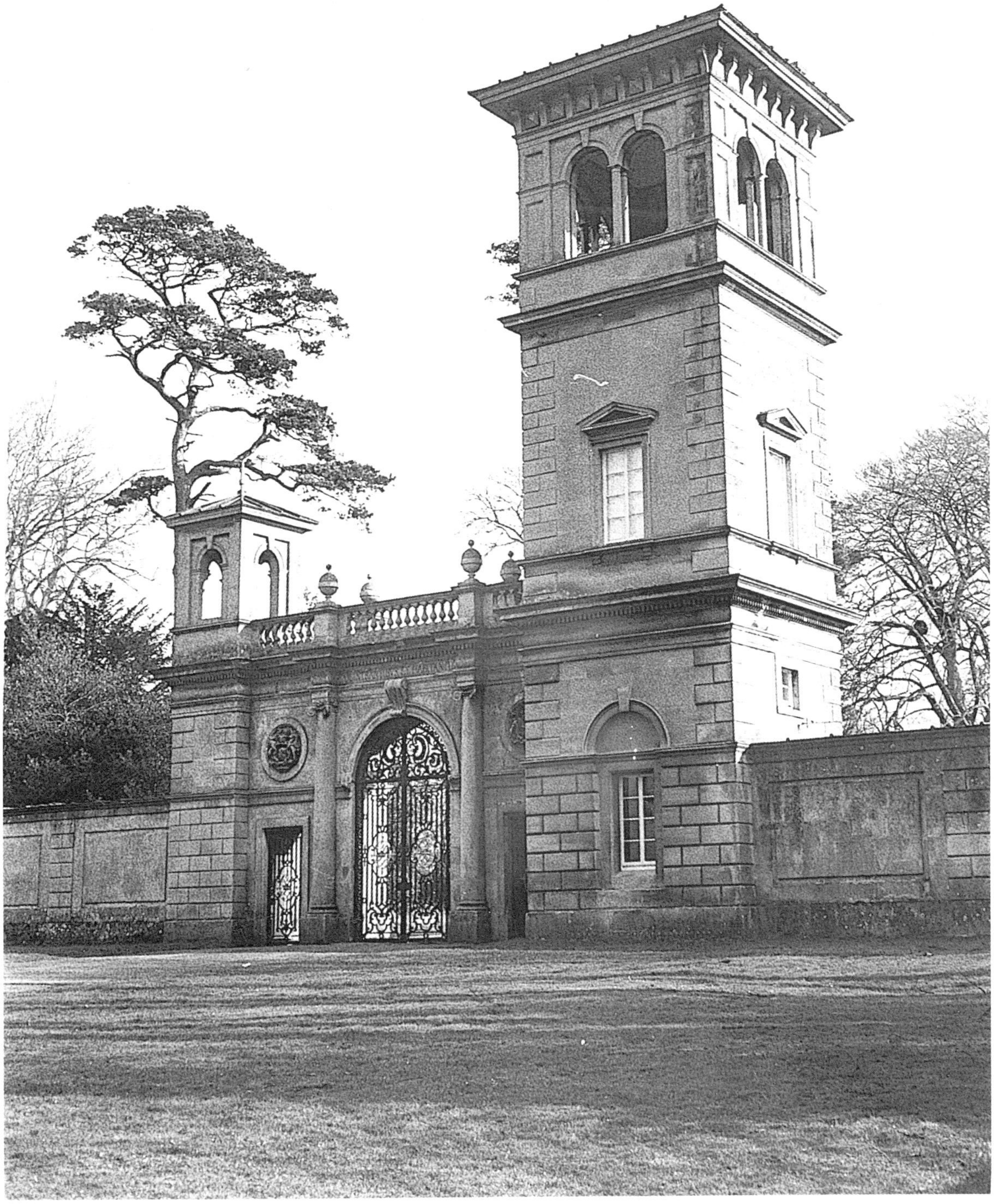

135
The Park Lodge to Chatsworth, Derbyshire, was built by John Robertson in 1840-2 for the Duke of Devonshire's physician.

Greek style which Uvedale Price saw as the epitome of beauty as opposed to the Picturesque.

At Great Witley in Worcestershire the lodges, south and north, to the vast Witley Court, handle their levels more busily than the Chatsworth lodges but they have to impress without the help of even a small belvedere, so there are two cake frills of balustrading, all over rustication, round-arched windows in square dormers and incised designs on the chimney stacks. They were designed in 1855 by Samuel Daukes when he had had considerable practice in the style and they succeed because their horizontal elements anchor a spacious lodge comfortably to the ground while the heavy patterning acts like a livery to suggest its official function.

P.C. Hardwick's lodge to Rendcomb House, Gloucestershire, will serve as an instance of how disastrously the Italianate could work when handled ineptly. It is a late design, of 1866, with all over rustication like the Daukes lodges, but its irregular and unimpressive single storey is capped with the sloping roof which Price had spoken so strongly against, and it comes as bathos after the fuss of the rustication. Placed next to this suburban elevation the stumpy tower with its melancholy round-headed two-light windows seems to dissociate itself from a neighbour to whom it is not logically connected.

The architect who took up the Italianate, handled its picturesque complexities and devised a decorative system which both enriched its surfaces and grew organically out of each building was Henry Edmund Goodridge

136
Inferior Italianate design at Rendcomb House, Gloucestershire (1866).

(1797–1864). Charles Barry designed larger Italianate houses (Trentham, 1834–40 and Cliveden, 1850–1) and taller belvederes than Goodridge, but it was on Goodridge's designing board that the style evolved 'muscular' characteristics that anticipate G.E. Street's later handling of the Gothic. Goodridge's work is generally confined to the south west, as he was of Bath by both birth and practice, and though he was an architect of the first rank he ought not to be numbered among the Victorian 'greats'. He was too consistent in his signature, too wedded to the one Italianate style to stand easily alongside eclectics like Edward Blore, Sir George Gilbert Scott and William Butterfield.

Monarchs do not always ascend thrones and die at the most appropriate time for the naming of architectural periods. If William IV had reigned neatly from 1820 to 1840 the urbane round-arched buildings typical of those years could then be styled 'Williamane' and not affronted with the alien title of 'Rundbogenstil'; and the arch architect of the Williamane would be Goodridge.

Uvedale Price's complaint, in his *Essay on the Picturesque,* about the flat monotony of Bath's rooflines must have been in Goodridge's mind when he designed his belvedere towers on Bathwick Hill. What is more impressive is the way in which he took up Price's enthusiasm for Vanbrugh's architecture.

There is an analysis in Price's essay of the various effects of rough and smooth surfaces in Nature. Goodridge seems to have carried this a stage further, considering similar effects in the rugged decorative surfaces of

137 Henry Goodridge's lodge to his own house, Montebello, Bath (1829).

Vanbrughian facades, and then applying his own highly individual versions of them on his buildings in Bath. Because the detailing of a Goodridge house is subtle and tightly organised, often applied to homely features like flues and chimney stacks, it is often demonstrated to better advantage in his several lodges on the suburban streets of Bath than on the larger houses behind them.

It was a town where, more than anywhere in England, the Italianate was likely to evolve into a native style, grafted onto the long standing and pervasive classical tradition of the place. In Queen's Parade Place there is a pair of Sedan Chair lodges of the 1720s, an early instance of the influence of garden buildings on commercial architecture, and these have an almost Vanbrughian over-emphasis to the keystones. At the foot of Church Street Hill there is a lodge to Prior Park which anticipates so many of Goodridge's tricks, such as letting a broad flat string course develop into a window architrave, that it would be tempting to attribute it to him were it not clearly shown on Thorpe's map of 1742, having been built by John Wood for Ralph Allen's mansion.[19]

PLATE XXII

Goodridge's own early style was naturally the neo-classical, though his four toll lodges of 1827 on the Cleveland Bridge betray a decorative restlessness with their stopped fluting of columns and the rustication which is lavished upon all the side walls and even on the rear wall of the portico. The whole discipline of the style was to separate the various elements of a design and Goodridge's later strength was his ability to unite them.

Montebello, the house on Bathwick Hill which he built for himself, is usually cited as his first Italianate work. In fact it is a picturesque dispersal of parts, like Hope's Deepdene, with an Italianate belvedere. This must be because it was begun in 1828, the year before Goodridge's converting visit to Italy. It is the lodge to Montebello which is truly Italianate. Angled precariously above the road to be viewed from below like a wayside chapel above Maggiore this little building is a *tour de force* of heavy compacted detail. Its round-arched belfry and chimney stack with bracketed top were to become signatures of Goodridge's work, most appealingly deployed perhaps in his lodge at Rode, out in rural Somerset. These were devices to give the air of consequence which he had lost by abandoning the classical column.

This Montebello lodge, soon to lose its proportions, as its parent house did long ago, through alterations,[20] is less subtle than his later lodges, more theatrical. A small blocked round window has a broad flat surround and four broad keystones. The door labours under a similar weight, and though it has Goodridge's favourite open pediment, the various emphatic features of the design are not pulled together as they are in his slightly later lodge to Bathwick Hill House just up the road.

At first sight this is plain to the point of dullness, but if studied it is full of subtle understatements: the batter of the lower wall to counter the slope, the deep thin cutting of the rustication and the trick which he had been taught by the Prior Park Lodge of linking the elements by letting string courses serve two purposes. This device, incidentally, had been the strength of John Carr's fine North Lodge at Wentworth Woodhouse. It was in buildings like these, where the rhythms had to grow from functional design and not from applied decoration, that a new style was almost born. Architects were, as Professor Mordaunt Crook has said of James Wyatt, 'poised between historicism and experimentation.'[21] Goodridge's practice is an unusually clear and moving instance of this.

Students on the Goodridge lodge-trail in Bath: Ashley Lodge in Widcombe, Henley Lodge on the Weston Road, Brookfield Coach House a little further on down the same road, Kelston Knoll Lodge and Kelston Park

139
An essay in Romanesque eclecticism. The entrance to Lansdown Cemetry, Bath (1848) by Henry Goodridge.

Lodge, will soon learn what features and handling to anticipate. In addition to those already mentioned, there are the balconies with chunky stone fretwork, the chimney flues boldly bracketted out (encircling a window at Rode!) the incised rectangles between the eaves brackets and rusticated pilasters framing the elevations; everywhere there is texture and depth but not of the conventional fruit, swags and garlands type on which his contemporaries depended.

138
The lodge to Merfield House, Rode, Somerset, before recent alteration.

PLATE XXIII

Vanbrugh was not Uvedale Price's only architect hero. He had also a strong feeling for Piranesi, and it was when Goodridge moved out into the green hilly countryside to the west with the Kelston Knoll Lodge and the Kelston Park Lodge that he felt free to evoke both architects in one building. The Kelston Knoll Lodge only adds a rockface finish to his usual devices; it is the Kelston Park Lodge which most strongly shows his genius.

To begin with it is superbly sited looking south, down over its very inferior parent house and the wide Avon valley. Its second asset is that it is almost invisible. Like so many other fine lodges, though more unreasonably than most since its size and outlook would command a small fortune were it auctioned, it is a ruin. Thick, glossy ivy and sprouting trees cloak its massive walls and the brilliant detail of Goodridge's design only reveals itself section by section to those ready to pull back the branches and swat the swarming insects. Even its gates lie flat in thick grass, still preserving palmettes of acanthus leaves in solid metal bolted to their square rustic bars. There is no

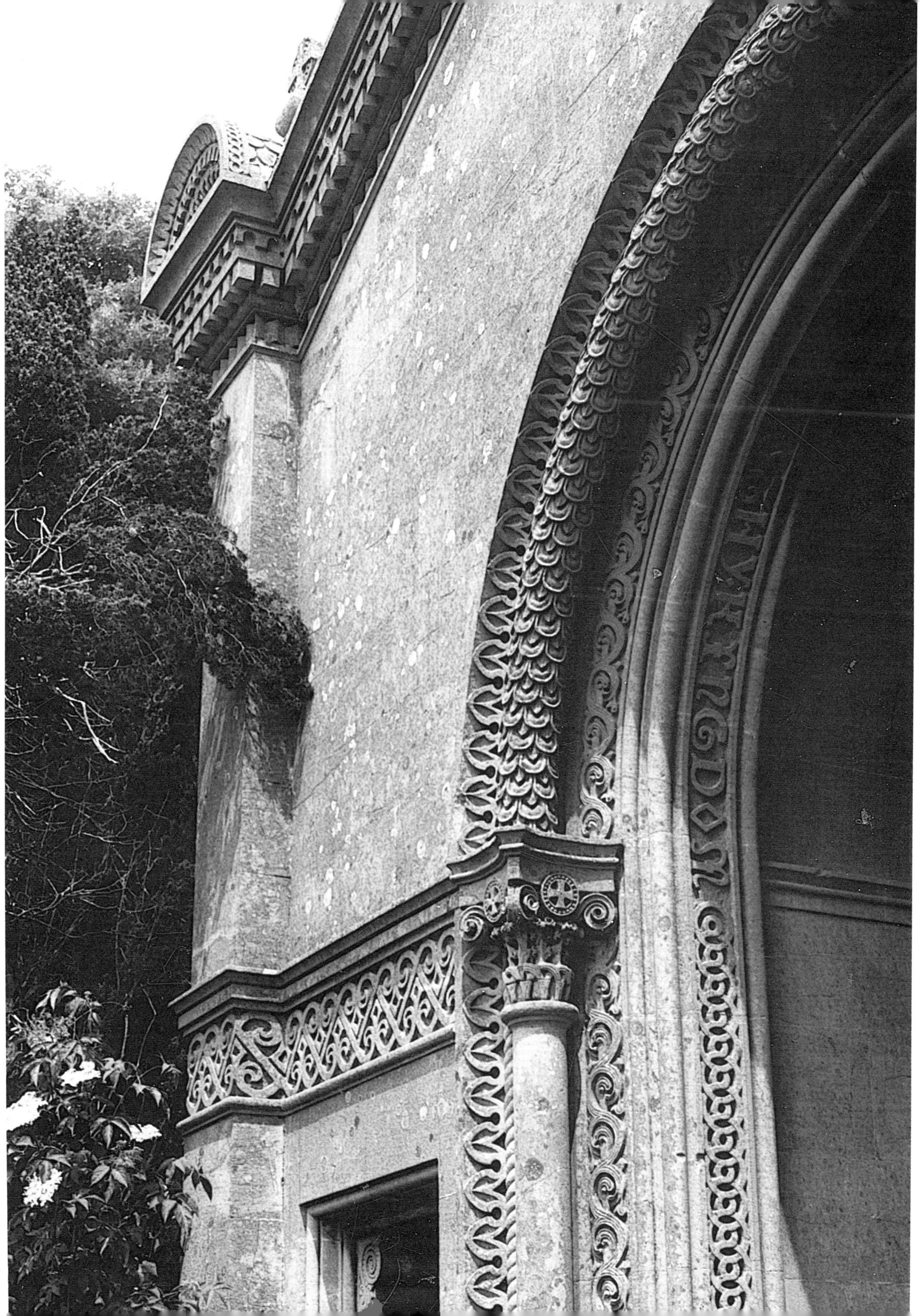

better instance of the danger of being an architect not quite early enough for the Georgian accolade, not quite late enough to be a famous Victorian. Only the Lulworth Castle lodges have an equal claim on national generosity for work of preservation; and Goodridge built so massively, just as Uvedale Price directed, that the restoration would be easy. Even standing as it does now in a young thicket, the Kelston Park Lodge is still intact.

Its walls are of grey green rockface finish, the quoins standing out even further, all in sharp contrast to the smooth flat section window surrounds and string coursing. The Piranesian air is given by the basement windows which scowl at grass level under a heavily bracketted open pediment. Most of the keystones are doubled for emphasis, an echo across the years of the Sedan Chair lodges. At ground floor level the windows, such as can be seen, are segmental-headed with three lights, each light with its massive keystone. Above the door, and a shape only in the cloaking glossy leaves, is a belfry without a bell. Inside there is a living room, a lower kitchen lit by the Piranesi windows and two bedrooms. Even the carpets survive in this unvandalised rural place.

What can be confidently stated about this extraordinarily hidden lodge is that its elevations are of great strength and irregular invention. Only the lodge at Rode in Somerset comes near to it in quality.

Goodridge's last lodge in this heartland of the Italianate was never completed and has only a gate with hollow side walls. It is an appropriate place at which to end because it is a cemetery lodge and sadly symbolic, as though a contrived finale to his life's work. Goodridge himself lies within under the evening shadow of the composite tower he built for William Beckford. The gateway, built in 1848, has none of the functional muscularity of his domestic lodges. The tides of eclecticism have swept over him and he has designed a columned cavern of sinuous Italian Romanesque with only a hint of his perverse individuality. Over the doorways tormented lettering declares like a prophecy of the new historicism to which he has abandoned himself: 'The Gates of Death Resurgent' and across the vaults is carved, with gloomy relish, an epitaph for the tutelary spirits of native English architecture: 'Till the heavens be no more they shall not awake'.

CHAPTER ELEVEN

The Lodges of High Victorian Historicism

*'It is an architect's business to understand all styles,
and to be prejudiced in favour of none.'* Thomas Hopper

The epigraph to this chapter stands as one of the most cynical and destructive comments ever made by a practising architect on his profession.

From the Renaissance to the Bauhaus all architectural styles have been historicist, but it was after the Regency that British architects acquired a cold-blooded facility in the imitation of every style and period on which an illustrated manual had been published or careful sketches made. Historicism is effective if, like eighteenth century Palladianism or Goodridge's Italianate, it has been fused through into a new and individual style, or if, like Anthony Salvin's Gothic, it accepts the original disciplines of the style from which it borrows wholesale.

In between these alternatives lies a wasteland. Thomas Hopper could claim better than most to understand all styles and to be prejudiced in favour of none. Gothic conservatories, Norman castles and classical houses flowed easily from his office. So he came to stand as a model for the next, the Victorian, generation of architects of how to gain a whole world of rich commissions by eclectic dexterity and still to lose his own soul.

His lodge at the Llandegai approach to Penrhyn Castle, Caernarvonshire, repays examination. To begin with it avoids the stimulating pressure of combining a visible living unit with a castle tower. Then it cheats twice historically. The round corbelled out turrets are two centuries later than the Norman arch between them and an arch this wide would never be placed in a military structure, it belongs to a church. The composition is symmetrical and quite misses the picturesque. Finally it suggests a contemporary prison entrance.

Perhaps this is a purist and unreasonable assault but it exposes some of the perils of half-way historicism. The lodge does not satisfy by proportion and it does not delight by authenticity or by incorrect audacity.

It is no longer fashionable to abuse Victorian architecture, and only Victorian lodges, of which there are an enormous number, are within the scope of this book. Within that field however, the authors must be frank and state that while, in their opinion, there are some fine Victorian lodges, many are very bad indeed and are inferior versions of historical styles, partly comprehended and then misapplied. After 1865–70 the sky began to lighten

140 Misapplied historicism. Thomas Hopper's Llandegai lodge to Penrhyn Castle, Caernarvonshire.

and the influences of the English vernacular enlivened the lodge again. It will be no part of this book to denigrate Norman Shaw or the Arts and Crafts, they are essentially Edwardian in style, Queen Victoria having for the convenience of architectural nomenclature, mistimed her death by almost forty years.

Not that Edward, Prince of Wales was any kind of architectural hero. Indeed, if the views just expressed seem unreasonable and arbitrary, it will be worth pausing for a moment before plunging into the main historicist sea to look at a lodge in Sandringham village street. Prince Edward must be held responsible for this as it was built around 1875 during the reconstruction of the house and estate by A.J. Humbert which began in 1870.

This lodge surely illustrates an absolute collapse of taste. Even forty years before it would have been unthinkable, yet in 1875 it was built to house the servants of an affluent Prince of the blood. Symmetry has been lost without picturesque gain, Scots baronial detail has been carried out in Norfolk flint with brick patterning, a gable from Bruges has lodged between the pepper

PLATE XXIII Kelston Park Lodge, Somerset. A Goodridge design now choked by rampant ivy.

PLATE XXIV Ruthlessly direct Pugin Gothic at Peper Harow, Surrey (1843).

PLATE XXV Anthony Salvin's handling of surface textures and geometrical form in the Gatehouse to Peckforton Castle, Cheshire (1844-50).

PLATE XXVI In his East Lodge (1894) to Shere Manor House, Surrey, Sir Edwin Lutyens allowed the building to grow organically from its site on the village street.

pots and a porch from a *cottage orné* has settled over the door. The banal fenestration, without rhythm or form, is the most dispiriting of all the depressing detail. It is an aesthetic disgrace and it is a Victorian lodge. Anger at its creation seems reasonable and there is real interest in tracing the collapse of aristocratic taste which must have preceded it.

There are two main stylistic streams of Victorian lodges: the 'Bethan — Tudorbethan, Elizabethan, Jacobethan — and the Muscular Gothic, the latter developing from a sense of impatience at the flaccidity of design in the former. Between the two flowed a third indeterminate stream of different styles; neo-Norman, Picturesque survival, French chateau and German schloss, a gutter flow to which the Sandringham lodge belongs and a muddy testimony to a period of fragmented taste.

141
An instance of royal taste. A lodge to Sandringham House, Norfolk.

Now that their mullions and gabled outlines have become commonplace, not only in houses but in schools, mental institution's and hospitals over the whole country, it is not easy to appreciate the early 'Bethan lodges as the delightful and socially advanced novelties which they were in the beginning. They have their origins long before Victoria was even born. Humphry Repton's gauntly proportioned but completely novel Tudor Lodge at Woburn was devised in 1811 to sit beside a supposedly Tudor rose garden at a park entrance.[1] The great show of black and white timbering in its upper storeys is the first in a particular 'Bethan line which was to flower, in the hands of architects more versed in the vernacular, into the Arts and Crafts half timbering of the latter nineteenth century. But the Atcham Lodge to Longner Hall, Shropshire is much more typical of the first essays. It was built by John Nash in 1805 very early in his career when he showed every sign of becoming a provincial architect with a practice in Wales and the border. There are no less than three Nash lodges within a quarter of a mile of each other at this point and the whole cluster is less than a mile from his sadly

142 John Nash's east lodge to Longner Hall, Shropshire (*c*.1805). An early example of 'Bethan design.

lodgeless Cronkhill. The Burtons of Longner, for whom Nash had just built a dashingly picturesque Tudor style house, were moved, either by neighbourly or competitive feeling, to have a lodge in the same brisk style to make a show opposite the shoddy Gothick lodges to Lord Berwick's Attingham.

As this Longner lodge is the first halt on a line with many hundred stations it is worth some consideration. It is a single storey brick lodge with stone dressings, four pinnacled gables and two central chimney stacks — an interesting rather than an impressive outline. It has large three light windows in wooden frames and is deliberately designed to look like a modern house in Tudor dress rather than an ancient relic. Two features may explain the consequent popularity of the type. It looked well in brick when brick had become the economic building material, and it was copying a relatively recent style in which lodge keepers' families could be housed in decent comfort without scrambling up towers to bed or flitting in night gowns across the drive to their beds in a classical cube. This point needs to be stressed in the nineteenth century's favour. Lodges of that time indicate a far more responsible attitude to working class accommodation.

One result of this move towards larger lodge houses was that fewer pairs of lodges were designed and that when they were built, as at Westonbirt, Gloucestershire, by Lewis Vulliamy (1863–70), both were sizeable two storey houses with an assortment of projecting bay windows on all sides, designed to catch the sun and provide civilised comfort. Taste may have declined but social enlightenment increased; the rich began to express their wealth by concern for their employees rather than by a show of columns at the gate.

Another lodge of this type, the south west lodge to Aqualate Hall, Staffordshire, has been attributed to Nash who enlarged the Hall in 1808. Its pinnacling resembles that of Longner's lodge, but if it was by Nash, then there has been a bewildering leap in mood from the insouciance of Longner

143 A stylistic echo of its main house. The lodges to Westonbirt House, Gloucestershire by Lewis Vulliamy.

144 Westonbirt House, Gloucestershire, built 1863-70 (Country Life).

to the grave propriety and hard-edged mouldings of Aqualate. Its careful Perpendicular detail and the elaborate wit of its gatepiers suggests as late a date as 1850. Even Pugin would not have been displeased by its crisp outlines and it is hard to imagine Nash designing a building that Pugin would have liked.

145
Two houses in one gatehouse. A rich Tudor design of 1829 at Port Eliot, Cornwall, by Henry Harrison.

Far more typical of the easy going 'Bethan line is the eastern Port Eliot lodge at St. Germans in Cornwall. It was designed by Henry Harrison for the second Earl of St. Germans when he was building an entrance hall and porch for the main house. Its general scheme is ingenious in that it is two separate houses, both well lit and of respectable proportions, which contrive, by means of a linking arch, to look like a Tudor gatehouse. They stand four square, conventionally quatrefoiled, battlemented and bayed, a rich yet superlatively uninventive composition; and it is possible, looking at their structural pretence, to understand the fury such creations roused in Augustus Welby Pugin and why he wrote and built so desperately against this tide of pleasant mediocrity.

Stirrings of original design troubled the 'Bethan calm from time to time. The Morrisons' dull little South Lodge to Combermere Abbey, Cheshire, thrusts out a side arm with cautious Perpendicular fenestration to view the drive and ends with a porch mildly hinting at a chantry chapel. Lewis Vulliamy's Nansawn Lodge to Tregothnan House, Cornwall, stages a dramatic introduction to the long panoramic estuary drive to the Earl of Falmouth's seat. Its conventional, shaped central gable is filled with a blast of heraldry in a Gothic frame and, instead of the cliché of twin Tudor chimneys, four aggressively angular stacks rocket up behind it, while the great gate beneath has an enormous bronze boar for a knocker. But this was a mid-1840s lodge when Pugin's influence will at least have made a conventional architect feel the need for movement.

At Charlton Park, Wiltshire, in the mid-1830s the influence of the old eighteenth century convention of a classical twin set of lodges is strong in a 'Bethan pair. The lodges are trim Tudor designs but a Jacobean motif of a pointed urn has been used to supply the rhythm and emphasis that a classical lodge would not have needed. Six of these exotic vases create a profile link between the gatepiers and the rooflines while another eight ball finials create a counterpoint around them.

More representative of the type, for a last glance, is the North Lodge to Dorfold Hall just outside Nantwich in Cheshire. It is large but lies low; its brick is patterned in diamond shapes and four demurely shaped gables sport an undisturbing tracery of round arches in stone dressings. From this unexceptional and civilised design of 1862 it is easy to see that the next stylistic move in the same decade will be to explore the native English vernacular, keeping the cosy appeal of brick but livening up the facades by functional irregularities and the roofline by the play of sloping roofs rather than these toy-like gables. Landowners who commissioned lodges like that at Dorfold would take naturally to Norman Shaw, but the authentic 'Bethan line of stone and brick and shaped gable historicism was to go lumbering on in parallel development right into the next century, with buildings like the Lion

146
Dramatic heraldry on the Nansawn Lodge to Tregothnan House, Cornwall. Lewis Vulliamy's work of 1842-8.

147
Neat neo-Jacobean lodges to serve an authentic Jacobean house, Charlton Park, Wiltshire.

148
The consistent popularity of 'Bethan design demonstrated at Dorfold Hall, Cheshire (1862).

Gates Lodge (1894) to Welbeck Abbey and the Kingston Lodge to Ham House, Surrey, of *c.* 1900.

After this insipid charm it is invigorating to turn to a pair of gatehouse lodges like Pugin's at Peper Harow in Surrey (1843) and Salvin's to Peckforton Castle in Cheshire of 1850. Here form comes to life again, convenience is thrown out through the narrow pointed windows and the wrestle of the designer's mind can still be sensed.

166

149
The lodge as a minor country house at the Lion Gate to Welbeck Abbey, Nottinghamshire (1894).

It is a fine point which is the superior of two very closely matched designs. The Peper Harow lodge is the more disturbing while Salvin's lodge is more satisfying. The structural integrity of the great castle, Peckforton, which he built high on a sandstone ridge has been widely praised[2] but his lodge has all the thought and care of the castle in a smaller compass. As the eye runs down the side turret, first the conical cap is broken by a narrow dormer to sharpen the profile, then the curved face is left absolutely plain until the last possible moment, allowing it to impact as a bold shape and texture of fine masonry. When it is finally corbelled back, instead of retreating into a square, it recedes into a triangle which cuts like a ship's prow into its retreating circles. The great gable over the gate arch is reserved and undisturbed to let the recession of arches and the fine vaults within hold the attention. Salvin has been as ruthless as any twenty century modernist in his determination to let form speak for itself and to avoid decoration.

PLATE XXV

Pugin's gate tower at Peper Harow is part of a group with barns, millpond and bridge that evoke northern France in rural Surrey. His lodge is slightly earlier than Salvin's and has just the same single-minded insistence on form. Pugin's side turret is not articulated to its gable with anything like Salvin's clean drama and his actual gate arch first straddles then hits the side walls to change direction with a visual shock. Instead of a vista of vaults, the passageway narrows to the right and ends with a much smaller arch. Everywhere there are these unpredictabilities — buttresses that offer symmetry then withdraw the promise, a belfry crammed awkwardly behind the cap of the turret. The composition is curiously homely in spite of its first arrogant assault on the eye, the heraldry is slight and more religious than aristocratic. Very few of Pugin's buildings live up to the claims of his writing but this is one where expense was not spared and vulgar ostentation was not demanded; it must stand among his very finest achievements.

PLATE XXIV

The Gothic gatehouse lodges which followed these were less interested in

150
Pietistic detail from the Peper Harow Gatehouse by A.W.N. Pugin (1843).

an authentic medieval image and more intent upon experiment, for that reason perhaps more aptly termed 'muscular'. They try harder and tend to achieve less. Most of them are content with a token archway at the side and concentrate upon the form of an unpierced Gothic house at the side, thereby forfeiting the drama of the cavernous vault. E.F. Law's gateway to Moreton Pinkney Manor, Northamptonshire (1860), fails to work much consequence from its side house. Using exactly the same elements that Salvin used at Peckforton, Law merely demonstrates the difference between a mediocre architect and a great one. Yet another return to Cheshire must be made to find real muscularity.

The East Lodge to Cholmondeley Castle is dated 1854. Its arch is a

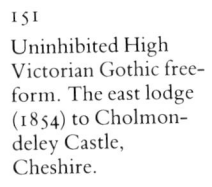

151
Uninhibited High Victorian Gothic free-form. The east lodge (1854) to Cholmondeley Castle, Cheshire.

conventional side piece but the lodge is among the most restless house designs in the country. As with Pugin's work (and this has no architect) nothing can be taken for granted: octagonal tower, stepped gables, pyramidal caps and sculptural chimney stacks, all crowd into its profile. One lean symmetrical element is permitted in a narrow bay window which corbels out meagrely above twin lancets. The remainder of the road elevation is almost windowless leaving, like Peckforton, the textures of the masonry and the angularities of the design to carry the building. It is a very large lodge, whether it is a very well-lit lodge or an easy machine in which to live is less certain, and this is a general criticism of the whole muscular series. They hold the eye but do they satisfy their inhabitants?

Lodges like this at Cholmondeley or Henry Clutton's slightly earlier pierced gate tower, the Aisholt Lodge at Over Stowey in Somerset of 1857, sum up between them the whole puzzle of Victorian architecture. Just what did their architects think they were achieving? The Cholmondeley Lodge suggests no Gothic period or even country of origin, so it has no discipline of authentic historicism. Clutton's gigantic lodge of grey-green stone has the immediate appearance of an embattled gateway, of perhaps the fifteenth century, but then the eye takes in the vast archway and realises that it is round and not pointed and that it rises without demarcation straight out of the double buttresses. The canopy over the heraldic achievement writhes like plasticine, not like Perpendicular work. Both lodges are successes in their

152
A French design in rural Buckinghamshire by Hippolyte Destailleur for the Waddesdon Rothschilds (c.1880).

visual impact but quite irresponsible and incoherent if anyone is looking to them for a movement in architecture which is going anywhere and will have successors.

It is at this point that the bland 'Bethan bungalow at Dorfold needs to be recalled. That was of 1862, the last two lodges were 1854 and 1857 respectively. They represent, with their wild free form and desperately overweighted statements, the end of a line, and Dorfold for all its banality represented gentle charm and habitable potential. The stylistic pattern of the last half of the century is already determined; the road will lead from Norman Shaw to Lutyens.

There remains only to mention a few of the inconsequential but often delightful lodges of the third, the 'gutter', stream of oddment styles. Their lodges lead nowhere but to omit them would be wholly to misrepresent the period whose essence was self-confident experiment and excess.

Neo-Norman has already been given its measure. For the Picturesque survival a lodge enthusiast cannot do better than to visit Edensor, that village of lodges at the gate to Chatsworth. The last house before the gate is a slightly ludicrous castlette: Norman, Tudor, Scottish, essentially a pleasing skyline. It was designed by John Robertson in 1842; he worked with Joseph Paxton here and was responsible for several designs in Loudon's *Encyclopaedia* of 1846, a sign of the enduring popularity of the mild, old Regency Gothic.

After some of the lodges in this chapter it is not surprising that, when the infinitely wealthy Baron Ferdinand de Rothschild wanted a home in England with a lodge to guard it, he employed a Frenchman, Hippolyte Destailleur, to design one. The proof of his good sense still stands at the crossroads just east

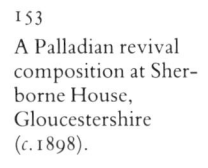

153
A Palladian revival composition at Sherborne House, Gloucestershire (*c.*1898).

of Waddesdon in Buckinghamshire. It is wholly French, mannered but relaxed, a lodge for a gentleman who might also be a valued servant.

Lastly, not only as a reminder of the continuous appeal of the Palladian through all the years of trial and error, but because the lodge pair for all its pastichery is as harmonious and outrightly beautiful as anything the eighteenth century ever achieved, there is the pair of lodges to Sherborne House, Gloucestershire, on the A40. They were probably designed by a London architect called King in 1898, an improvisation, though the suggestion of the word is too casual, on the gatepiers to the hunting lodge at Sherborne on the other side of the road.[3] Between two belts of beech trees and across a vast green curve of grass these diminutive buildings make such a poetry out of modest symmetry that they control the whole generous landscape with just three bays and a single storey.

No doubt it is unjust to the High Victorian episode to conclude it with its antithesis but if there is a lesson to be read from these lodges, then their photographic images will be allowed to make it.

CHAPTER TWELVE

The Last Lodges

Modern architectural journalists have learnt their trade in a hard school. Since the 1930s, but particularly since the war, they have been paid to persuade the public that wholly charmless structures often built on the cheap, with untried materials, represent significant form and offer a new aesthetic. They have been aided in this by the adjacent critical confusion in the world of art and sculpture, but can claim real credit themselves for perfecting a type of article for architectural journals which wreathes impeccably dense jargon around brilliantly lit and angled photographs. This technical breakthrough in communicating uncritical praise is called 'hype' and can be applied retrospectively to the architecture of the past as well as to the street structures of the present. One imaginatively handled exhibition at the Hayward Gallery in 1981 was almost sufficient to establish Edwin Lutyens as 'the greatest English architect' and topple Sir Christopher Wren from a pillar where he had become a rather tiresome fixture. It is necessary, particularly when estimating the architecture of the recent past, to be wary of these hypes. The last half of the nineteenth century was a period when great wealth was available to be put into sticks, bricks and stones and many able architects emerged to tempt this money into their own projects. Though certain architects have come to be associated with certain styles, almost every architect followed Thomas Hopper's dictum and would turn his hand to anything. As the last chapter noted, the line of 'Bethan historicist continued strongly into the next century, long after it had lost mere novelty, and there was Queen Anne, old English, neo-Baroque, neo-Georgian and a variety of pastiche foreign styles from which to choose.

The architects of that time have served their penitentiary period in despised oblivion and are now eagerly studied and generously praised. The odd point that William Morris quit Philip Webb's Red House with indecent haste and spent the rest of his life in a rented fifteenth century manor and an eighteenth century riverside house is overlooked. George Devey's 'seminal influence' is traced and his lacklustre historicism praised as 'an adaptation of Elizabethan brick vernacular to the requirements of the nineteenth century',[1] which is one way of saying that his houses had plumbing, corridors and bedrooms for the maids. William Butterfield, Ernest George and Aston Webb have their admirers and there is a torrent of well-informed praise for Norman Shaw, Eden Nesfield, Lethaby, Godwin, Mackmurdo, Mackintosh and Voysey. In one sense all buildings are interesting, if only as examples of outrageous cheek or human folly, and the architecture of pre–1900 is more humanly scaled and approachable than that which immediately preceded it, so it earns its new modishness. But its modern exegesis should be read with two cautions. One is against the over-praise of one architect at the expense of equally worthy and often superior contemporaries whose life spans may not be so accessible to journalistic dramatisation because they were not addicted to alcohol or fretted by sexual impotence. The second is a caution against regionalism. Two lodges will serve to underline the first caution.

There is a Lutyens lodge to Shere Manor House in Surrey, praised in the relevant Pevsner volume as 'very free, high-spirited massing of 1894, with a big bold chimney'. It is indeed an admirable house commanding its corner site with just the correct additional distinction of form to separate it from the village cottages. A batter anchors it and allows it to zigzag irregularly up-hill on two elevations with a variety of angles yet still look as if it had grown organically. The front is jettied out dramatically with the cliché of the undercut porch, rather weakly supported by a single beam and brace. In all it is vintage early Lutyens, inventive, sculptural, seductively habitable.

PLATE XXVI

But it needs to be assessed alongside another lodge on the busy A519 in Staffordshire, the West Lodge to Trentham Hall. Slightly larger than the Lutyens lodge, it has exactly the same qualities: the anchoring chimney, the appealing changes of direction to give depth to the roadside elevation, the jettied front, the rich variety of textures — tile hanging, stone, brick, plaster and half timbering. The handling of the jettying in the Trentham lodge is actually stronger and more spatially convincing than Lutyen's flat upper storey. Yet this lodge, a sophisticated and mature example of free-style old English, is dated 1859: it is thirty five years earlier than Lutyens's work, easily antedates the usually accepted first Arts and Crafts work and is distinctly closer to William Morris's ideal than the Red House which Philip Webb was building for him in the same year.

W.E. Nesfield, who set up practice in 1858 and worked in the north-west and designed later at Trentham, could have been the architect; his early

154
An extremely early example (1859) by an unknown architect of the free-style Old English usually associated with George Devey. The West lodge to Trentham Park, Staffordshire.

173

sketches show similar feeling. Whoever designed it had achieved, before a much trumpeted movement began, most of the objectives of that movement.

If the question is asked why the Trentham lodge has been ignored and every detail of much later ingenuities by Lutyens examined, it will raise the second of the two cautions — that of regional bias.

Most of the able writers and certainly most of the successful publishers are London based. A very large proportion of the work of Norman Shaw, Voysey and Lutyens is found in the south east, a brief car ride from the capital. This could be the reason why all Shaw's fine detail from Kent and Sussex farmhouse vernacular has been so extensively noted and admired.[2] It is the style of the writers' rural bolt holes. Staffordshire is too rude and crusted a county to inspire either Georgian poets or Queen Anne fanciers. The Dukes of Sutherland deserted Trentham and their fine lodge seventy years ago to live in politer places.

The dramatic magpie timbering of the Welsh border counties was as rich a source of 'Old English' detail as any Surrey title hanging. The Trentham lodge proves this; but western architects like John Douglas, who were mining this source in the late 1870s, have received little attention, certainly no exploration in a book. London, like Paris, distorts the cultural vision. Douglas's work will be examined in the next chapter, but a lodge like that to Brockhampton Court in Herefordshire can represent this strand of design equally well.

155
A rich example of Welsh Border black and white design at Brockhampton Court, Ross, Herefordshire. The work of Faulkner Armitage (1893).

174

It was designed in 1893 by Faulkner Armitage, a Manchester architect, and is as sincere an expression of Arts and Crafts ideals in its wholly authentic woodwork as is Lethaby's stone church of 1901–2 which stands across the road. Deeply coved in its upper floors, then heavily hooded in its eaves, the lodge resounds with heavy patterning of quatrefoils and diamonds. Where a stone lodge of the period would have been undercut and opened out by a loggia, this takes the roofline down in a great sweep over the porch, a favourite Douglas trick. For all its structural integrity the building never pretends for a moment to be of the sixteenth century. It is an exuberant contemporary extension of an earlier mode.

The west is strewn with similar Arts and Crafts half timbering. There is a nimble footed hexagonal lodge in the style to the Grove just north of Craven Arms, Shropshire, and a cheerful black and white cricket pavilion of a lodge with a shaped gable by the Davies gates to Chirk Castle, Denbighshire. The style even reaches down into Dorset where the south east lodge to More Crichel House risks one timbered overhang on its otherwise solid surfaces. At Marbury Hall near Malpas, Cheshire, the lodge is an acid comment on the victorians' feeling for outline and linear patterning. Half a mile away on the same lane stands a genuine sixteenth century yeoman's house in the style, low, rounded and patterned strictly into structural squares and rectangles. The lodge, of 1861, takes up the style, cuts the studs and braces into decorative trefoils and diagonals and rises sharp, angular and jettied out. It is an uneasy alien in a countryside where it could have been as natural as the trees if the architect had not been so confident of his ability to improve on the past.

In a sense these half timbered lodges are the baroque phase of the Arts and Crafts, as opposed to the classic or standard Norman Shaw type of brick and tile. Two such pieces of truly riotous timbering have intruded into the heartland of Norman Shaw suburbia in Buckinghamshire. The North Lodge to Dropmore House and the Beaconsfield Lodge to Hall Barn can hardly be called half timbering since every square inch of the latter, and the greater part of the former, have been turned into display cabinets for a collection of English and foreign carved work. This must have taken some assiduous collector years of travel to acquire. The Hall Barn lodge stages its own particular version of the jettied out stage and loggia supported on a Solomonic wooden pillar carved intricately with vines and birds. The whole extraordinary structure should be removed bodily to the Victoria and Albert Museum and set up as a worthy exhibit in its great gallery of fakes.

There is never any danger that lodges of this type will look like anything but lodges. A *cottage orné* did not change when moved to a drive entrance but lodges like that at Brockhampton are modelled on the timbering of inns such as the Feathers at Ludlow or the Royal Oak at Tenbury. The style of their originals was intended for display and attention and is thus perfectly functional in a lodge. It is hard at this point to resist a much wider question on the whole fitness of the Arts and Crafts aesthetic for large houses. The concepts of the movement should logically result in park gate lodges in the style being aesthetically more satisfying than their main houses and this is not very far

156
At Hall Barn, Beaconsfield, Buckinghamshire the lodge has been given an eccentric overlay of authentic antique woodwork.

from the truth. The whole idea of taking form and detail from small farmhouses and then extending them across a major elevation is illogical. Philip Webb's Clouds, Wiltshire, and Standen in Sussex are often praised for their casual composition when a dispassionate judge might say that they were a confusion of interesting oddment facades and roofs pulled together by plain contiguity.[3] It may be heresy to write it but several of Lutyens's large early houses fail in coherence. Berrydown at Ashe in Hampshire looks like three separate houses side by side with a row of shops underneath[4] and his Pleasaunce at Overstrand in Norfolk has some of the visual suggestion of Edward Prior's seaside terrace at West Bay, Dorset.[5] Nesfield's lodge to Kinmel Park, Denbighshire is unquestionably a finer artistic whole than the long, incoherent garden front of the main house where he has contrived to

PLATE XXVII C.F.A. Voysey's intensely original south lodge to Norney Grange, Shackleford, Surrey (1897).

PLATE XXVIII An early Lutyens lodge in the mood of Ernest George at Park Hatch, Hascombe, Surrey (1890).

PLATE XXIX The vertical thrust of this lodge to Chinthurst Hill, Wonersh, Surrey is a typical Lutyens response to the topography of the site.

PLATE XXX At Plumpton Place, Sussex in 1928 Lutyens fused rustic simplicity with classical formalism in his entrance gateway and lodges. (By kind permission of Roger White).

unite the fissiparous qualities of the Arts and Crafts to the frail symmetries of Queen Anne.[6]

So much of the early work was for houses in shaded London streets where an array of individual facades was natural. As a result the architects seem to have grown accustomed to this visual disunity, which can indeed be pleasing, and they cheerfully dragged whole streets of Chelsea into rural parkland.

Lodges in the Arts and Crafts style have the advantage that they work within just the general dimensions of the farm cottages from which Shaw and Nesfield collected details on their sketching expeditions. They tend as a result to excel their main houses.

Even Charles Annesley Voysey's celebrated Perrycroft (1893–4) at Colwall on the Malverns, which is lauded for its reserved horizontals, its simplicity and the unifying roof line, looks, if one is honest, more like two houses on a street corner than a single residence.[7] The shorter its main elevation the more efficiently a Voysey house works, and one of his very finest designs is a lodge of 1897, the earlier of two lodges to Norney Grange Shackleford in Surrey. PLATE XXVII

If the half timbered work can be accepted as a baroque phase of the Arts and Crafts then Voysey's designs are its neo-classical. In the Norney Grange lodge the horizontal simplicity drawn originally from cottages has been applied to a cottage-sized structure. The result is a humble perfection, one of the great lodges, except that 'great' is a wholly inappropriate term to express its elusive and disturbing asymmetries. It stands under tall trees against dark rhododendrons, with a smug goblin smile on the five light rounded bay of its upper storey. Almost everything else is roof, a whole ski-slope of it to the drive, with a long row of rough mullions sweeping round to upset the initial symmetrical impression of the elevation to the road and provide a functional lookout to the gate. This road front is jettied out twice and the rounded bay which centres it has to balance, or unbalance, the crude low bay to one side and an abrupt cut in the roof-line to the other, though the cut is partly compensated by a pronounced batter in the ground floor.

This lodge is the archetype of literally thousands of houses in middle class suburbs of the 1900–40 period: individual but reserved, the peasant ideal raised to gentility. What needs to be stressed is that the lodge does not copy from the suburbs; the suburbs copy from it.

The difference between a late lodge like that at Norney Grange and an early one of the Norman Shaw vernacular type is one of degree rather than kind. Both weave primitive simplicities into sophisticated simplicities, with a Japanese feeling for the rightness of a window here and a tiled surface there, all in superficially random placing. The Star Lodge on the Aylesbury drive to Hartwell House, Buckinghamshire, makes an interesting contrast to the handling of Norney Grange.

Where the Norney Grange roof overlapped the lodge in one fold, throwing all attention onto the elements of the elevation which remained, the roofs of the Star Lodge are themselves the dominant elements, creating a pattern of sloping triangles and wedges of dark tile above chalky pale stone. The

177

157 In the Star Lodge to Hartwell House, Buckinghamshire. The decorative patterning springs entirely from the subtle handling of functional detail.

front elevation is symmetrical and thrusting; the side to the road is wilfully random in fenestration. As the geometry is insistent and bold the textures are delicate: tiles, diamond paned windows in square bays and random clunch masonry. A flint infilling under a strainer arch emphasises the only curve in the whole composition, and a coved eaves, finely outlined, stresses the limits of the roofs. There is no hint of historicism; the lodge depends upon the vernacular, dynamised into both rhythmic and arbitrary pure form. If Edward Godwin was ever allowed to design a lodge it was this.

Since the same architect is quite capable of a lodge in free form vernacular picturesque and one in the new symmetrical neo-Georgian, it is perhaps artificial to keep a distinction between the two main styles. No great gap in years separates Norman Shaw's wholly asymmetrical stone lodge to Flete House in south Devon (1879–83) from his matching brick pair in neo-Georgian, the Tittenley lodge of 1885 to Shavington Hall in Shropshire. The first hurls the whole book of picturesque devices at the visitor. An elegant stone bow curves over a loggia with a wooden settle and an *œil de boeuf* spy window, a double bayed projection juts out through a broad secondary roof skirt and a wooden porch hurries away round the corner to provide a veranda to the south. Even the central chimney stack mounts on a crow-stepped gable. At Shavington the chimneys are rigidly central, stone quoined with ball finials on pyramidal roofs, and every feature below them is repeated in the same order — Diocletian windows above, Venetian below, all on the other side of the drive.

The contrast between the two lodges is so extreme as to urge that the two styles deserve separate treatment even if their architect dextrously overlaps. Picturesque asymmetry can impose itself on virtually any style if the architect is sufficiently determined, and the usual way to attack a box shape was through the porch.

While Thomas Harris was taking a huge bite of loggia out of the corner entrance to his chunkily Jacobean lodge to Stokesay Court, Shropshire in 1890, Lutyens was doing much the same thing far more deftly in his first

158
Very early neo-Georgian design in the pair of lodges by Norman Shaw at Shavington Hall, Shropshire (1885).

lodges, the pair, unused and dilapidated at the time of writing (even a great name is no safe insurance) to Park Hatch at Hascombe in Surrey. Harris was so determined to destabilise his heavy lodge that he shifted its shaped gables off centre and canted a triangular bay out into the drive. Lutyens seemed satisfied to work with the controlling symmetry of a pair, darkened all the main rooms with a deep loggia on wooden Doric pillars, and brightened up the end gables with otherwise irrelevant half timbered patterning which he had picked up from Ernest George. Only the eclecticism hints at his later strength, but the lodges were erected 'by Joseph Goodman with money taken as prizes for Sussex Cattle', so possibly funds were limited.[8]

Lutyens did better in his Chinthurst Hill lodge (1893–5) at Wonersh in the same stockbroker land, stepping it up hill and compensating for the sharp recession of the elevation by a monumental chimney out of Repton's period. As at Shere the recessed porch is weakly supported, and at Lascombe in the same year he consciously remedied this fault by doubling the pillars, heightening the base and adding a decorative brick buttress.

PLATE XXIX

In justice it has to be said that the relatively unknown architect H. Paxton Watson's Milford Lodge to Witley Park, Surrey, of 1896 puts Lutyens' mild mannered houselets in the shade. It is a grand house of the period in miniature: gabled gatehouse, domed octagonal tower and bayed 'Bethan block, all jostled rudely but amusingly into one fair sized lodge. Its main house, built for a suicidal financier, the gentry type of Surrey, has gone, so the lodge recalls its lost quality.

The North of England has its asymmetries — Norman Shaw's Cragside for instance, but its native vein was more conventional. N.R. Mills of Banbury provided a large East Lodge for Wykeham Abbey in the North Riding in 1904, and the impression it gives is one of asymmetry because the

159
The Milford Lodge to Witley Park, Surrey, is an ingeniously compressed design of 1890 by H. Paxton Watson for stockbroker land

side to the road is in severely stripped-down classical while the drive elevation is Jacobean and even more dour. Both are, however, within themselves, rigidly symmetrical and determined not to acknowledge what is going on around each others shoulders. In the same area at Welburn Hall in 1890

160
A northern version of Norman Shaw. The East Lodge to Wykenham Abbey, North Riding by N.R. Mills (1904).

Walter Brierley had managed to clamp a Cotswold style picturesque lodge with battlements into symmetrical order, so Yorkshire seemed not to share the tastes of Surrey. In the same spirit, when working for a northern landowner, Romaine Walker was allowed to build an asymmetrical lodge by a roaring stream at the valley drive to Grantley Hall, West Riding, but he had to phrase his 'looseness' in wholly classical form with matching gable

161
The lodge to Grantley Hall, West Riding has had formal classical detail applied to an informal ground plan.

ends and a loggia porch balanced on one prim pillar of fluted Doric: a true marriage of the rival styles.

Norman Shaw was quite capable of neo-Georgian formality, as was noted earlier in his 1885 lodges to Shavington, but the final effect of all their repetitive detail was oddly unlike anything which the eighteenth century produced. It is notorious that for all its ecclesiology the nineteenth century rarely produced, or perhaps wished to produce, a church which could be mistaken for a genuine produce of the Middle Ages, so perhaps its neo-Georgian was infected with the same perversity. Nevertheless, Shavington was an incongruous opening to a style which has tended to be the target for more mockery than most.

This is probably because it has usually been deployed, in its gate lodges at least, in a few stagey details and has rarely been thought through in a scholarly way. It is, however, virtually the only lodge style still acceptable in the second half of the twentieth century. With a cabinet minister, Mr. Heseltine, recently commissioning the eminent historicist architect Quinlan Terry to build a changing room for his garden at Thenford, Northamptonshire in high English baroque, with a whole row of half engaged Corinthian columns, there is hope that the tradition of aristocratic ostentation and good taste may be having a new lease of life. Perhaps a neo-classical triumphal arch with side lodges is to follow.[9]

The best neo-Georgian lodges of this century are those which take themselves most seriously. Ernest George and Yates built a brick octagonal lodge to Moor Place, Esher in 1905 which seems to come straight out of John Miller's *County Gentlemen's Architect* of 1787. John Belcher's pair of lodges to Cornbury Park, Oxfordshire, are a satisfying suggestion of the kind of lodge which Hugh May would have built for the Earl of Clarendon if Clarendon had lived in a lodge-building period, which of course, he did not. At least the gate piers are correct.

Easily the most scholarly of all such modern pastiche lodges is that to Raynham Hall, Norfolk. This is a 1930s building which uses the flint, brick and voluted gables of William Edge's Caroline main house with such restraint and workmanship as to deceive until a very close inspection has been made. Lord Faringdon commissioned another unpredictably sober lodge, this time in astylar Augustan from Geddes Hyslop, for Buscot Park, Oxfordshire in 1934–5.[10]

As serious architectural scholarship made its Germanic advances of the post War period, an actual James Wyatt drawing of 1778, discovered in Northampton Public Library was translated in 1956, under the supervision of Sir Albert Richardson, into lodges and gate piers for Kelmarsh Hall in Northamptonshire. In this case the design, a pedimented gable with a window framed in an arch, was so conventional that the similarly scaled

162
The increasingly sophisticated historicism of the period is exemplified in this lodge of 1901-5 by John Belcher to Cornbury Park, Oxfordshire.

Bromfield lodge to Oakley Park, Shropshire, whose facade C.R. Cockerell treated in wholly self-conscious classicism, is to be preferred. In this Oakley lodge all the detail of pediment, arch and pilasters has been fined down, but the door in the middle has been set into such a deep recess that a monumentality results from its shadows and an 1826 lodge fulfils its old function of impressing without any apparent effort of detail or stoney mass.

That early foreshadowing of the neo-Georgian gave Lutyens a precedent. At Nashdon, Buckinghamshire, where he was working to a tight budget for the richly named Princess Dolgorouki, he devised a paper thin pair of servants' lodges, one on each side of an entablature on Doric columns. The design relies for life on the butterfly ground plan, the punctuating chimney stacks and a slight perversity in the fenestration. Basil Ionides the interior decorator fell back on the traditional facade furniture of the early lodges when he designed a lodge for his home Buxted Place, Sussex. Thus

163
Highly convincing pastiche design of the 1930s in the lodge to Raynham Hall, Norfolk.

his drive elevation of giant, or baby giant, Ionic pilasters, toy Doric portico and shrunken Diocletian pediment light is in just the same tradition of design and feeling as the Gothick lodge to Downton Hall examined in the third chapter of this book. Both are perfectly ordinary houses with a carefree show of applied detail fixed with a little cement to their outward faces.

The psychological motivation which created the building type from garden pavilions to fill the void of the lost gatehouse has proved enduring. When Edward Hudson, Editor of *Country Life* and therefore a shrewd guardian of landed interests, was having a Sussex farmhouse transformed into a 'gracious home' for him, Plumpton Place by Edwin Lutyens in 1927–8, he not only retained and deepened the moat, but had a lodge composed by that great purveyor of architectural fantasies. The range of retainers' flats is in the Sussex vernacular like a long barn of weatherboarding with a low tiled roof. But in the centre, where a way leads through into an open courtyard the bridge across the moat and the main house in its idyllic isolation, a trumpet had to be sounded because this was the lodge, the entry point to a sanctum. The trumpet which Lutyens sounded with emphatic wit shall end the chapter on the true note of nonsense and charm: a white arch boldly outlined against the creosoted weatherboarding and supported on four white Ionic columns. It is wholly and deliberately out of place in its setting, a gesture of tradition and elegance in a range of vernacular charm — two opposed aesthetic pleasures boldly linked for the delight of those informed enough to comprehend them, a sure gate marker to an area where life is to be lived in elegant detachment, a stage removed from the prosaic realities of the world shut out.

PLATE XXX

CHAPTER THIRTEEN

One River and Two Parks of Lodges

As THE RIVER Dee leaves the Welsh mountains in the Vale of Llangollen it flows into a series of deeply incised loops below the hanging woods on the southern limits of Wynnstay. A century ago the park had wild turkeys, a herd of buffalo, Chinese cattle and pigs with curly coats. Now the Wynns of Wynnstay have left for one of their lesser seats and there is only a boys' public school in the Hall and its immediate gardens. The rest of the park is farmed though still, in places, nobly wooded. Roads and long walls of mustard coloured stone bound it on the west and north. On the south it drops down three hundred feet to the river, to the east it crosses a lane and mixed farmland to end indeterminately at the kennels of the Wynnstay Hunt. The steep-sided Nantybelan valley running north south into the Dee divides the old park area roughly in two.

It is a romantic but ingeniously desecrated place. Immediately to the west lie the wreck of old coal mines and brickworks, an active chemical works with reeking vats and council housing. A railway viaduct in the same crusted buff stone and Telford's Pontcysyllte aqueduct stride across the valley before a closing in of mountains behind the castle-crowned cone of Dinas Bran. It is a curiously complex setting: industry, history and class divisions tangled evocatively together in a setting of much original beauty.

Twelve miles to the north by road, but many more by the insistently winding river, the Dee, now prone to flooding and well into its lowland stage, flows along the eastern edges of another park, that of Eaton Hall in Cheshire. The park is almost flat, a part of the Cheshire plain, and its central area is appreciably smaller than the original Wynnstay, but spreading out like a radiant star or a great spider, are four prodigious drives between belts of fine trees. They reach out arms of forest across the rich but meagrely timbered dairyland. The shortest drive is three miles long, the longest is five — an eight mile span from Hawarden to Bruera. One vaults the Dee in a single iron span, several leap arrogantly over roads on stone bridges. In the last century there were deer and the rides are still alive with rabbits, squirrels and pheasant. There is a private golf course, much grass meticulously manicured and, instead of a school and forlorn dilapidation there is, as in some Nancy Mitford novel, a very rich duke in residence, for Eaton is the seat of the Grosvenor dukes of Westminster.

The lodge systems of the two parks are so strikingly contrasted in their styles and in their pattern of development that they merit a comparative chapter to themselves. The Wynns were Welsh and Tory; the lodges at their

164 Pompeo Batoni's group of the 4th Sir Watkin Williams Wynn (the left hand figure) with two of his companions on the Grand Tour 1768-9. (By kind permission of the National Museum of Wales).

park gates were built piecemeal over two centuries, an organic growth, and their masterpiece is a late classical pavilion. The Grosvenors were English and Whig. With one exception, the dazzling collection of lodges in and around their park was put up by one man, Hugh Lupus Grosvenor, the first Duke, between 1877 and 1898, and the finest is a late Gothic gatehouse.

Because Wynnstay has lost its baronets and Eaton has kept its dukes, it should not be presumed that the comparison between the two estates is in any way an unequal one. Until 1761 the Grosvenors, like the Wynns, were only baronets and, if the 1745 Rebellion had gone against the Hanoverians and a Stuart had reigned again, the third or 'Great' Sir Watkin Williams Wynn would certainly have become a duke for his loyalty to the Jacobite cause and would thus have anticipated the Westminster's ducal creation of 1874 by more than a century. As it was, the fourth Sir Watkin was so rich and splendid in life style that George III offered him an earldom which he refused because it was more evocative to be 'Sir Watkin' in North Wales. This was while the Grosvenors were still mere barons eagerly scrambling their way up the peerage.

In the perverse economic style of the period both families were vastly wealthy. Sir Watkin owed £100,000 after Robert Adam had finished his superb town house in St. James's Square in 1775. Lord Grosvenor slightly excelled him, owing £151,000 in 1779. Both continued to prosper on spreading acres and teeming veins of ore; the Grosvenors being perhaps more fortunate in that their mines were decently distant from Eaton at Halkyn in Flintshire while the Wynns had to delve on and even under their doorstep. 'Have you thought anything abt. the coals in the neighbourhood of Wynnstay ... they will certainly be of great value to me' the fourth Sir Watkin wrote to his agent in February 1777.[1] And so they proved to be.

The interesting feature about the Wynnstay lodges is just where they stood in the table of priorities of a Welsh aristocrat whose pockets brimmed with money. The fourth Sir Watkin succeeded the third in 1749 when he was only five months old. He inherited a modest Smith of Warwick house and a park which, according to *A Pocket Book of Mapps of Demesne Land Etc. belonging to Sir Watkyn Williams Wynn Baronet*[2], had two lodges, one to Ruabon where there is now no true gate lodge, and one to Oswestry near Newbridge on the site of a later lodge and a drive entrance which has been incorrectly described as created in response to the craze for the Picturesque. This drive has in fact always been the London approach to the house even before Telford created the Holyhead road.

A current rent roll of £30,000 a year and a long minority left the fourth Sir Watkin very rich indeed as he came of age. His Grand Tour, part of which he spent with the fifth Duke of Devonshire (1768–9), cost £8,643.12s.9d. and he had fifteen thousand guests to dinner to celebrate his twenty first birthday in 1770 at a further cost of £1,621.17s.11½d. The Wynns, however, then and throughout the next century, were essentially Welsh as well as European in their culture. They spoke Welsh at home and took as much pride in their descent from the Welsh princes as the Grosvenors did in theirs — from a nephew of William the Conqueror. The fourth Sir Watkin's first enthusiasm was for music. He paid John Parry, the blind harpist, a retainer of 100 guineas a year; he was the treasurer and force behind the Ancient Concerts and the ambitious Handel commemorations of 1784; orchestras and bands accompanied all his lavish and frequent entertainments. His second enthusiasm was for acting, he was a friend of David Garrick and built a private theatre at Wynnstay before he constructed a single garden building. Architectural improvements came only third to these relatively non-visual arts. It is significant that, though Welsh, he spent his first fortune on his London townhouse; though in 1770 he had commissioned first Robert Adam and then James Byres to design palaces to supplant the Francis Smith house at Wynnstay. Eventually, late in his short life span (he died aged forty) he turned to park improvements. There was room for these. In 1756 Lord Lyttelton had commented on Wynnstay 'it stands in the middle of a very pretty park; but if the park was extended a little farther, it would take in a hill, with a view of valley, most beautifully wooded; and the river Dee winding in so romantic and charming a manner, that I think it exceeds that of Festiniog or any confined prospect I ever beheld.'[3]

Capability Brown is recorded as having been at Wynnstay in 1778 and 1779,[4] but if the grand avenue from Ruabon was being laid in 1777 it is likely that he was there in that year also, when 'there are nineteen men employed in the Park who are making a gravel walk of 1,738 yards.'[5] This suggests that Sir Watkin saw his priority as being to impress the locals of Ruabon and not to encompass the views to the south. Brown died in 1783, and in the same year John Jones, a local mason, was paid £32.10s. 'of the ballance of his account for building the gate at the bottom of Wynnstay Park',[6] so by 1783 an existing lodge to Ruabon had been pulled down and replaced by the present clumsy arch in a sub-Adam manner. There is a small gate lodge next to this with a Gothick door, but essentially the Jones gate uses the whole replanned village square of Ruabon as a park gate marker leading from Wynnstay to Ruabon church.

Work continued on the park but still away from the great vistas to the south west. Instead a drive was pushed to the east and marked by the

165
James Wyatt's sober Roman Doric Kennels Lodge to Wynnstay Park, Denbighshire.

Kennels or Park Eyton Lodge three quarters of a mile from the house. This is an impressively chaste neo-classical building with a tetrastyle Roman Doric portico. Sir Watkin had been elected in 1776 as a member of the Society of Dilettanti whose drinking toast was 'Grecian Taste and Roman Spirit', so he predictably favoured such a style rather than Gothick ventures; but the authorship of the lodge is uncertain. Brown had built a Doric Dairy in the park which was complete by 1783, but his last work as recorded by John Byng, the Wynn Agent, was near the house; works 'in the lower part of the park' were 'under the direction of a late servant of Lancelot Brown'.[7] This was the cartographer John Evans (1723–95) of Llwyn y groes, so he may have designed the lodge. However, in 1785 James Wyatt began to work at Wynnstay and his Bath House is also in severe Roman Doric lacking, like the Kennels Lodge, the relief of paterae which Brown had applied to the entablature of his Dairy. Wyatt is, therefore, the likeliest author of the Kennels Lodge and of the equally severe apsidal fronted lodge which, with a set of rusticated gatepiers, marks the point where the drive to the Kennels 'leaps'

166
Rhos y Madoc Lodge Wynnstay. An 18th century solution to the problem of carrying a drive across a minor road.

the public lane to Rhos y Madoc. The sad wreck of what was once a columned gateway in this same Roman Doric survives further down this lane. Only one of the four columns remains standing. The lodge and chapel on each side of it are later and it is another pointer to the fourth Sir Watkin's Dilettanti predilections.

The fourth Sir Watkin died late in 1789 and there followed another long minority during which the Wynn economics restabilised, aided by the fifth Sir Watkin's marriage in 1817 to Lady Henrietta Clive, daughter of the first Earl of Powys, by which time he commanded an income of £62,000 a year and could indulge in further park improvements. The most interesting of the Wynnstay lodges date from this time.

The young Sir Watkin had already made a gesture in a classical direction by building, on his return from action in Ireland in 1800, a memorial tower at Nantybelan to his dead comrades of 'the bloody Britons', the fencible cavalry regiment of the Ancient British Light Dragoons which he had led. The tower was modelled on the Tomb of Caecilia Metella on the Via Appia. But at some point near 1820, the dates are not exact, he built two lodges, one

167
Benjamin Gummow's coarsely detailed Waterloo Tower, Wynnstay, set above a lost park entrance.

notable and Gothic, one an accepted masterpiece and largely classical.

The Gothic lodge was also a viewing point, the Waterloo Tower, and therefore, like the Edgehill Tower, rarely accepted in its second function as a park gate lodge. It stands on a high point in the south west of the park, commanding the prospects over the Vale of Llangollen which the earlier park works of the fourth Sir Watkin had curiously avoided. Because Jeffry Wyatville had designed the classical Nantybelan memorial tower his name is attached to the Waterloo Tower of twenty years later. But Benjamin Gummow was working at Wynnstay at this time and his name is usually attached, quite rightly, to any coarse Gothic garden building in East Wales of this period. The Waterloo Tower is coarse in detail but satisfying in outline. The tall, octagonal turret, from which a house flag always flew when Sir Watkin was in residence, rises far above the three storey square tower itself. As a lodge it is of great interest because it has outworks of walls and turrets designed to frown down at the drive which is cut deep into the rock below the tower. The whole complex thus marks a continuity in the idea of the lodge as a mood creator, linking up with Miller's Edgehill Tower and Brown's Convent Lodge at Tong. The gateway which once led carriages into this 'horrid' experience has been blocked but the site of it can be traced in the lane leading up to Newbridge.

Even more impressive is the C.R. Cockerell lodge which stands by the drive from the new bridge over the Dee. This building, admirably appraised by David Watkin,[8] must stand among the best gate lodges in Britain as perhaps the finest of all, with only Kent's Worcester Lodge at Badminton as its rival. Unlike Kent's prodigy it is not a palace in miniature but quintessentially a gate lodge, grim and guarding yet suggesting power and opulence beyond it up the hill. Both Dr. Watkin and Peter Howell see the Newbridge Lodge designed as a prelude to a picturesque drive up out of the wooded gorge of the Dee.[9] This is not easy to follow. There was already a lodge at this point before the Francis Smith house was altered and a lodge of Gothic or at least of *cottage orné* design would surely have been the likeliest introduction to a drive that had been conceived as a Picturesque experience. The

168
The Newbridge Lodge, Wynnstay. A superbly atmospheric composition of 1827-8 by C.R. Cockerell.

Newbridge lodge has an overwhelming impact but the three deeply recessed arches of its substructure and the tomb-like finials of its rusticated side piers suggest far more the nightmare authority of Piranesi's *Carceri* than the Payne Knight subtleties of landscape appreciation. The lodge is wholly unregional, of no local reference, though admirably designed to dominate the wild prospect which it commands.

Though Wyatt's Wynnstay was lost in the fire of 1858, this lodge must always have been too fine for its main house. Its most likely *raison d'etre* is that it was conceived in 1820 by Cockerell for the fifth and temporarily affluent Sir Watkin when he was expecting a royal visit, which never took place, from George IV in 1821. The lodge and the stout ironwork of its gates are more appropriate to a palace forecourt than a romantic rapture and it would have been from that point that the King would have approached.

A 'Great Room' for the Hall was designed by Cockerell for the same non-event and he actually supervised the building of the lodge and the room in 1827–8, the urgency of the occasion having passed away. What is additionally pleasing about this lodge is its enduring functional ability to house and give pleasure to its occupants. The scowling arches of its lower storey may well be a crypto porticus reminiscent of Guilio Romano or Ledoux's *Barrières*[10], but their gloom is lightened by their southern aspect, and the old couple who enjoy the lodge at present take their summer tea in its shade, while appreciating the swell of hills and the stilted viaduct across the river.

After this achievement the other lodges of Wynnstay are inevitably anticlimactic, though Gummow did design a pair with square-headed Gothic windows to Acrefair which are unique in that their modestly pleasing facades turn wholly inward to the park. To the main road and the scarred industrial landscape beyond they present only rounded and windowless backsides of soot-blackened stone.

The fortunes of the Wynns declined in the later nineteenth century just when the Grosvenor wealth by wise investment was ascendant. The old exits from the park were gently abandoned and a pair of generous but characterless stone lodges was set up on the northern park wall to give motors a convenient exit to the outside world. Finally three imposts of death duties within the space of five years enforced the abandonment of the house and a retreat to the mild rural seat of Llangedwyn in Montgomeryshire.

The present contrast between Wynnstay and Eaton is absolute and exhilarating. To observe the real impact of lodges and their function in a park it is necessary to find at least one ducal family with the kind of wealth and accompanying power which the Whig dukes of the eighteenth century once wielded. If only as an illumination of past English history, such a family and such a park should survive, glitteringly untroubled by the need to lure tourists in to traipse the rooms of the house or to make the park into a menagerie.

The most remarkable feature of Eaton is that the lodges rather than the house itself are the attraction of the park. The structure of the estate with its lengthy rides projected north to Chester, west to Hawarden, south west to Pulford and east to Aldford and Bruera demands a heavy punctuation of

PLATE XXXII 27 The most ambitious and romantic of John Douglas's lodges to Eaton Hall. The Eccleston Hill Lodge of 1881–2.

outlying lodges. But at Eaton, until the very end of the nineteenth century, the eighteenth century tradition of building lodges, within the park bounds yet marking certain functional changes of usage, was kept up. As a result it has the richest collection of lodges, though not the widest stylistic variety of them, in Britain. Welbeck may have had thirty five lodges in its heyday but only one of them was of much architectural consequence. At least twelve of Eaton's lodges are of real quality. They were put up within a limited space of years, the reign, for in Cheshire such a term is not excessive, of the first duke, 1869–99, so some analysis of his education and nature is directly relevant.

The eighteenth century record of the Grosvenors has already been noted. The baronet of 1622 became baron in 1761, earl in 1784 and marquess in 1831. With estates in Cheshire, Flintshire, Wiltshire, Dorset and West London, a dukedom was impending. The second Marquess of Westminster, father of the man who was to become the first Duke of Westminster in 1874, was a man with a romantic sense of family tradition, an educational martinet and a sincere aesthete. This romanticism is manifest in his christening his son Hugh Lupus after that Earl of Chester, nephew of the Conqueror, who was uncle to the first Gros Veneur. Almost the first instance of art patronage by this Hugh Lupus Grosvenor when he succeeded his father as third Marquess in 1869, was to commission a mounted bronze statue of his namesake from G.F. Watts to stand in the forecourt of the Eaton Hall which Waterhouse was to build for him. His essentially Pre-Raphaelite aestheticism, later to be demonstrated in his lodges, is shown by his offer to cross a Percheron mare with an English thoroughbred in order to produce, in the course of time, an exactly correct model for Watts to use for Hugh Lupus's warhorse. In just such a spirit of visual integrity Holman Hunt stood in a trench, his feet warmed by straw, in order to paint for 'The Light of the World' orchards in the cold dews of early morning with total authenticity.

Eaton park is a late flowering of the Pre-Raphaelite spirit and one reason for this must be the intensely Ruskinian education which the second Marquess gave his son. To read an account of the long holiday, fourteen months in all from June 1835 to August 1836, which the Marquess, his wife, young son and two elder daughters took through Germany, Italy and France, is to be reminded irresistibly of Ruskin's travels a little earlier in a similarly close and earnest family group. The Grosvenors were rigorous in their enjoyment of art: churches, palaces and above all the great collections of paintings in Dresden, Munich, Rome, Florence and Paris. They absorbed them all and their son was not merely tagged at their heels through the galleries, he was taught, like another Ruskin, to use his eyes actively and to draw. Later, as a young man, he made his own Grand Tour, like the fourth Sir Watkin, and over much the same territory, but with a romantic and Gothic bias where the Wynn had been a classicist.

There followed Oxford and a dutiful acceptance of the family seat of Chester, where he was returned unopposed as a Liberal M.P. in 1847. Marriage to Constance Leveson-Gower, his first cousin and a daughter of the Duke of Sutherland, came in 1852. The next seventeen years were

PLATE XXXI The neo-Georgian lodge of 1969 to Tythrop House, Buckinghamshire.

PLATE XXXII The most ambitious and romantic of John Douglas's lodges to Eaton Hall. The Eccleston Hill Lodge of 1881–2.

eminently conventional. He produced a large family, became for a time M.F.H. to the Cheshire hunt, set an example in the Yeomanry and Volunteers, shot regularly in Scotland, supported Gladstone in the Commons and attempted to restrain his wife's lavish expenditure. His father 'lived for the

169 A portrait of Hugh Lupus Grosvenor, 1st Duke of Westminster. (By kind permission of the National Portrait Gallery, London).

pleasure of getting money which he had not the heart to enjoy',[11] and in consequence kept his son on a tight financial rein.

When his father died suddenly of a malignant carbuncle in 1869 Hugh Grosvenor, now third Marquess of Westminster, came into possession of an enormous fortune after seventeen years of debts and difficulties. He was far from profligate by nature but he had a keen sense of ducal style as well as for ducal duties. In his will the old marquess had left Fonthill Gifford in Wiltshire and Motcombe in Dorset, the seats where he had passed most of his time, to his widow, so the new marquess had to make do with Cliveden, Halkyn Castle near the Flintshire mines and Eaton Hall. His strong feeling for propriety and tradition impelled him to make Eaton once more the main seat of the family but Eaton Hall was an architectural problem of some urgency.

William Porden had rebuilt it in 1804–12 for the second Earl, a spiny fantasy, unarchaeological yet allusive, airy and inventive, the culminating achievement of Gothick design.[12] It was finished moreover with a complete set of ambitious Gothick lodges, gate towers for the most part. That on the Chester approach was pinnacled and bepointed, those on the Belgrave and Eccleston drives were symmetrical and castellated. The first Marquess, writing anonymously in *The Eaton Tourists,* a light-hearted guide book of 1824, claimed that these lodges 'impressed a proper feeling of grandeur upon the mind'.[13]

Certainly every detail of Porden's Eaton did this; unfortunately it was so cold and comfortless that female Grosvenors were obliged to wear thick

170
The Pulford Lodges to Eaton Hall. Vigorous neo-Jacobean work by William Burn of 1846-51 for the 2nd Marquess.

trousers under their skirts when they were in residence. It was for this reason that Fonthill and Motcombe were so popular with the first and second Marquesses. The return to Eaton and thick underwear was made only for ceremonial occasions. William Burn had tinkered with the house in 1846–51, damaging its appearance and building a pair of lodges for the Pulford approach. These are the only early lodges to have survived to the present day: single storey rectangles with spirited Jacobean applied detail, they have shaped gables and emphatic ball finials to hold down a moulded cornice of almost baroque projection. All their ornament is slightly larger than life and as a result draws the eye most effectively.

It seems likely that it was the inconvenience of Porden's Eaton combined with the sense of financial limitation from which he had long been suffering which led the new third Marquess to make the one real but disastrous error of architectural judgement in his life. This was to commission Alfred Waterhouse, a nationally established architect, and not John Douglas, a local Cheshire architect, to design and build a new Eaton Hall. He took this decision in 1870, very soon after he had succeeded. This suggests a degree of urgency and architectural frustration in which the personality of the marquess's first and spendthrift wife may have been involved.

1870 was a bad year for making a major decision on architectural styles. Fashions were just about to turn away from the muscular Gothic in which Waterhouse had made his name towards the reviving traditionalism of Philip Webb, Eden Nesfield and Richard Norman Shaw. It was in 1870 that Shaw began to build Cragside in Northumberland for the armaments millionaire Lord Armstrong, and in Denbighshire, the next county to Cheshire, Nesfield had begun to build a vast Queen Anne house at Kinmel Park in 1868. Examples of the new style on the scale which Eaton would require were therefore to hand and everything in Hugh Grosvenor's later architectural patronage suggests that his instincts were Aesthetic and favoured romantic, traditional, Arts and Crafts solutions to building needs. But in 1870 he made in haste the decision which he repented at leisure; he chose Waterhouse's retardaire scheme and spent £600,000 on it.

It is becoming fashionable now to regret the fact that the third Duke had most of this fourth Eaton Hall pulled down in 1961. Less would be heard of this nostalgia if the Grosvenors had not gone on to put up a fifth Eaton Hall which is equally indigestible. There is a consistency in the architectural conservatism of the Grosvenors. The last three Eaton Halls were all designed in a style recently fashionable but which was just becoming discredited.

Waterhouse's Eaton was not merely retardaire in design, it was an open confession that he had been unable to design a single integrated house appropriate to a rich aristocrat.[14] The main block contained the state rooms, the clock tower provided a feature to distract attention from the mediocrity of the elevations and a private wing to the north east, structurally quite separate, housed the Grosvenor family. The result was an ugly public building next to an ugly private house. The only redeeming note was the Golden Gate, ironwork of about 1710 by the Davies Brothers which had survived from the second Eaton. Waterhouse doubled this in length and

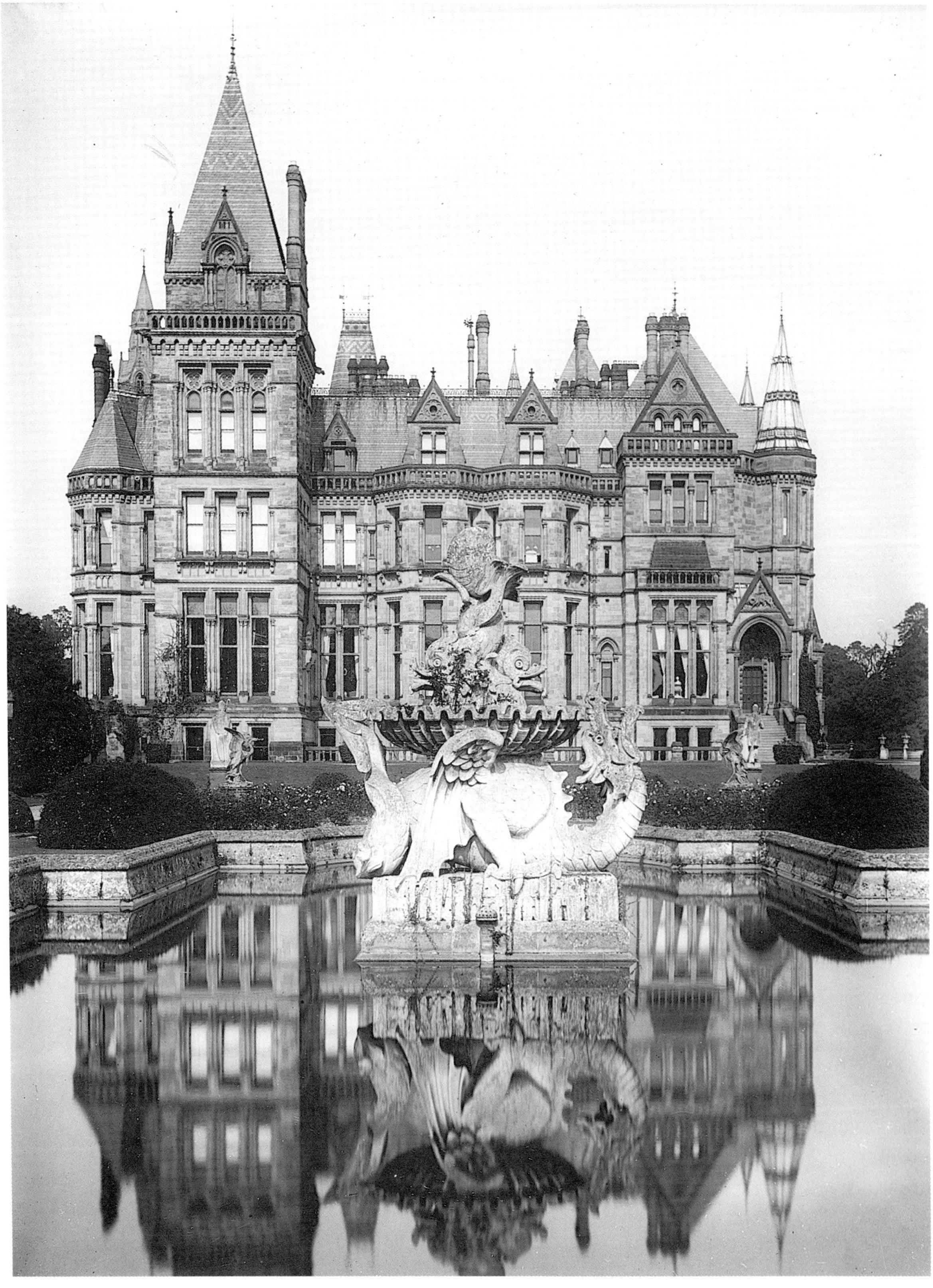

built single room stone lodges of inappropriate sub-Gothic design at each side of them. These still stand in front of the new fifth Eaton.

There was no outstanding beauty of detail in Waterhouse's facades to redeem the overall clumsiness of outline, and stylistically it was illogical to confine French Gothic arches within the symmetry of a French Renaissance facade and roof line. Yet all this was what the third Marquess, who was first Duke by the time it was finished in 1882, should have expected when he employed someone whose real claim to fame was that he had designed Manchester Town Hall. The duke never liked his new home and was heard to say that if his grandson and heir had any sense he would pull it down and start again. This of course happened after his grandson's death with results which can be seen.

Not quite everything in the design of the fourth Eaton has to be counted as loss. The reason for this lies in the compromising talents of John Douglas, the local architect who had hoped to design the new hall and was ready to work alongside Waterhouse when his ambition was disappointed.

As late as 1866 Douglas had designed the church at Aldford, one of the estate villages, in just the hard edged muscular Gothic style that was Waterhouse's forte, but in 1870 Douglas showed himself to be thoroughly at home in the up-and-coming Arts and Crafts vernacular tradition by designing a cottage for the estate at the south west corner of Eccleston churchyard. The

171
The fourth Eaton Hall, Cheshire built by Alfred Waterhouse between 1870 and 1883 (Royal Commission on Historical Monuments (England)).

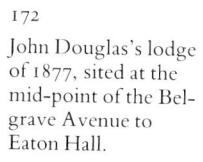

172
John Douglas's lodge of 1877, sited at the mid-point of the Belgrave Avenue to Eaton Hall.

cottage has half-timbered gables, tile hung walls and mingled brick and stonework. This, rather than the alien French Gothic angularities of the Hall, must have been the style for which the first Duke was looking. It became only the first of a long chain of brilliant lodges and park buildings which Douglas and later the firm of Douglas and Fordham went on to build around the Hall. They were clearly an aesthetic compensation for the central disaster of the place. These Douglas lodges were an imaginative union of the knightly and traditional forms appropriate to a gentleman's residence of the period. By demonstrating them within the modestly generous limits which the duke thought correct for his servants, they provided perfect prototypes for suburban middle class houses over Cheshire and the surrounding counties. This does not mean that the duke was suburban in his aestheticism, but that the middle class subordinates were ducal in theirs. The Douglas lodges at Eaton are a perfect instance of an aristocrat expressing the architectural spirit of his times in buildings of concentrated fantasy and modest size which then served as models for the homes of another class.

In 1873 Douglas put up two houses on the Eaton estate. The first was a Park Keeper's house set beside what was then the surviving Porden lodge on the Eccleston drive. It is a setpiece of conventional Cheshire vernacular: a black and white house so skilfully done that only the flair of a gable roof continued down over the porch and the dramatically coved eaves line reveal it as a piece of self-conscious vernacular revival. The second Douglas house of this year was the important one. In this, the Eaton Lodge on the Chester approach, Douglas first used the pinnacle and turret forms which bristle over Waterhouse's Hall, but linked and softened them into a comfortably sprawling picturesque composition by hipped gables, half timbering and a sensitive feeling for materials.

Four years later in 1877 Douglas built a second lodge, another uncannily accurate foreshadowing of standard suburban middle class houses. This went up at that point on the straight two miles of the Belgrave Avenue where the park limits and a lodge had been in the eighteenth century. It is the earlier Eccleston cottage writ large with a tile hung gable and the upper stage jettied out on a breastsummer carved richly with roses. On this occasion Douglas has dropped the Waterhouse motif of the conical capped turret and even his own favourite device of blue diapering in the brickwork, relying for diversity of form on a subtle patterning of gables — a dormer window gable leading to the roof line of the side wing and that leading, by the slanting line built into the chimney stack, to the main roof gable.

The dormer gable has painted pargetting and in the same year Douglas covered the upper walls of his semi-detached lodge pair on the Aldford drive with large floral panels of painted pargetting. This was a decorative device which he repeated in 1882 on another semi-detached lodge pair on the Eccleston sub-drive to the Chester approach, but here he abandoned the mawkish floral design for bold mannerist arabesques covering whole gable ends and the surrounds of the jettied out windows. The fact that two of the Douglas lodges are semi-detached, though given the full Arts and Crafts treatment of vernacular detail, is another instance of their applicability to, and potential influence upon, suburban forms.

It was in 1881 that the most brilliant burst of lodge building began at Eaton with the North Lodge (1881), the Garden Lodge (1881–3), the overwhelming Eccleston Hill Lodge (1881–2), the Stud Lodge (1883) and The Paddocks (this last not a lodge but linked stylistically and in mood) of the same year. All were by Douglas.

This is an episode of garden building comparable with that at Alton Towers under the sixteenth and seventeenth Earls of Shrewsbury or of Lord Cobham's building in the great days of Stowe, and it is natural to look for explanations. One must be that the work on the Hall itself, complete by 1882, was beginning to run down and there were craftsmen at hand and money to spare. Though the Hall cost £600,000, the Westminster's rent roll from the London estates alone was £250,000 a year at this time and rising. More personally, the duke's first wife had died in 1880. The duke favoured the Pre-Raphaelites, buying their paintings and tapestries for the Hall and Burne-Jones was a guest on occasions, and there was a note of melancholy Pre-Raphaelitism in his own life. His official biography based upon 'full access to the unpublished Grosvenor archives at Eaton and in London' dismisses the first Duchess thus:

> Pleasure-loving Constance had not been his ideal mate and in temperament he and she were very different. Nor, in the later years of their marriage, can he have been unaware of her infidelities.[15]

He had then played a handsome dutiful Arthur to this wife's Guinevere. In 1882 he married a second time, his son-in-law's sister Katherine, the youngest daughter of Lord Chesham. This marriage was notably happy though his wife was thirty two years younger than he was. They promptly began a second family from which the present duke is descended. So between 1880 and 1882 the duke was without a wife and this was the period of the lodge building burst.

There was moreover, another significant woman in the Eaton social scene. This was Sibell, Lady Grosvenor. A daughter of the Earl of Scarborough, she was a beautiful, vivacious woman who had married Victor, the duke's eldest son. He was an epileptic and, after fathering three children, he died in 1884. Sibell, as well as being a beauty, was deeply religious and mystically inclined. The duke was devoted to his daughter-in-law, who lived nearby in Saighton Grange, and heartily approved her second marriage three years after in 1887 to the brilliant and amorous George Wyndham. Wyndham became private secretary to Arthur Balfour in the same year and Balfour was the leader of that remarkable social group; élitist, confident, mystically chivalrous, delicately adulterous, known as 'The Souls'.

Wyndham, who later became Secretary for Ireland in the Balfour government, was, of course, one of the Souls, as were his sister Lady Elcho and his wife Lady Grosvenor. Lord Curzon, the Duchess of Rutland, Lady Plymouth, Lady Windsor, Lord and Lady Pembroke, Alfred Lyttelton and St.

John Brodrick were all of the group as, in a sense, was their guru, the poet Wilfrid Scawen Blunt. Burne-Jones was their chosen painter and the *Morte d'Arthur* their lay-bible, their enthusiasms ran to Wagner, Rodin, intellectual games after dinner and bicycling. Love affairs typically conducted in gardens and 'gracious' homes were another favourite pursuit and they had a keen feeling for a storied and traditionally English visual background for their amours. Curzon leased Montacute as a proper setting for his 'sin on a tiger skin' with Elinor Glyn. Lady Windsor fell in love with George Wyndham at St. Fagans Castle, Glamorgan and he wrote appreciatively from her house: 'an enchanted land of Arthurian romance, Eizabethan with gables, built within the enceinte of a Norman fortress. There is a plesaunce and terraces and fishponds and mazes of cut yews.'[16]

George Wyndham did not become a settled feature of the Eaton scene until his marriage in 1887, but it had already a Pre-Raphaelite artistic bias and Sibell Grosvenor had been there since she married into the family in 1874. The gardens at Eaton certainly had their plesaunces, terraces, fishponds and mazes in plenty. After the lodge building of 1881–3 they also had their Arthurian towers and turrets, in forms more traditional and acceptable than the stark array on the Hall. It was then that Eaton must have become a correct setting for 'Souls' with Arthurian predilections and, since the duke personally approved all building plans he must, either personally or under the influence of those close to him, have decided on the form and spirit of these romantic buildings.

The first of the great Eaton lodges of this period, the North Lodge, is the only substantial lodge in the whole park which suggests some of the spirit of Waterhouse's lost Hall. In a way this is unfortunate, as it is a more satisfying composition than anything that has been pulled down and so may suggest lost excellences which never existed. Supposedly designed by Waterhouse himself, it is a four storey round tower all of stone under a sharp conical roof crowned with a spirelet. It stands aggressively at the entrance to the vast stable area where Waterhouse relaxed and allowed half timbering to mingle pleasantly with the stonier Gothic. The outline of the lodge is reaffirmed by a round stair turret and modified by a low side block, but its most effective additions are a dormer window pedimented with the sunflower blazon of the Aesthetic Movement and a very tall chimney stack. This is reminiscent of the one Nesfield added to his famous lodge at Kew and contradicts the general fifteenth century French air of the building, tempering its otherwise firm historicism. How much of a hand Douglas actually had in this exhilarating design can only be guessed. To be fair to Waterhouse its details are hard and the linking of the stair turret to the main tower is muscular enough to be of his design.

PLATE XXXII

The next and most ambitious of all Eaton's many lodges, the Eccleston Hill Lodge, is wholly of Douglas's design — a melancholy masterwork which straddles the wide main approach from Chester but stands isolated in the middle of the park, appearing to link forest with green forest like a sudden enchantment from the *Morte d'Arthur* or the *Faerie Queene*. In this lodge Douglas has enlivened the faintly bromide charm of his vernacular

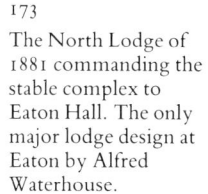

173 The North Lodge of 1881 commanding the stable complex to Eaton Hall. The only major lodge design at Eaton by Alfred Waterhouse.

magpie work by adding the main living unit in that style to a three storey gatehouse tower. The gate arch is pure Waterhouse with ribbed stone vaulting and crisp moulding but the actual gate of writhing black iron twists up to finials of the triumphant Aesthetic Movement sunflowers. Above are two storeys loaded with armorial devices and topped by a pin cushion of tourelles and a hipped roof so vertiginous as to swoop up into a blunted spire. There was never a lodge which created a mood more effectively than this. It must have come like a harsh trumpet blast to the visitor approaching from Chester: French romance rendered into English forms, its only flaw a rather uneasy point in the design where the Douglas cottage leans upon the stair turret of the gatehouse.

174 Mannerist pargetting on Douglas's semi-detached lodges of 1882 at Eccleston side drive.

The Garden Lodge which lies within a stone's throw of the North Lodge is a return to Douglas's soft compositions in timbered picturesque. Acceptable but unmemorable, it underlines the need for the hard outlines and historicist fantasy of Waterhouse. The logical advance from the Eccleston Hill Lodge is not technically a gate lodge at all but a house of distinctive character. This is demurely and quite inappropriately styled 'The Paddocks' and was built by the side of the public road to the Eccleston Lodge to house the duke's agent in a style more suited to King Ludwig of Bavaria. More properly it should have been styled the Castle of Fayremonde and shipped bodily to London in 1898 to serve as a backdrop to the Art Workers' Guild Masque of 'Beauty Awakening', staged in October of that year by Walter Crane to heighten the aesthetic sensibilities of the City Aldermen.[17] It would be a generous gesture if the hedge concealing the Paddocks were lowered so that one of the most remarkable houses of the century could be enjoyed more readily.

Last of the lodges of the great years and the least remarkable is the Stud Lodge, a lively half timbered octagon on a round base with an eight-sided conical roof. As usual Douglas uses a chimney stack to cloak the join between this bold turret and the delicately patterned house beside it.

The Eaton lodges of the 1890s represent a slight falling off. Douglas

175
The Stud Lodge at Eaton Hall. A John Douglas design of 1883.

himself was rarely employed. The highly complex lodge at the Belgrave approach is by the firm of Douglas and Fordham (1899). It has all Douglas's tricks of twisted brick chimneys and blue brick diapering but it is no substitute for the Porden gate tower which it replaced. This lodge and the similar busy Overleigh Lodge (1898) at the gates of Chester are signs that the duke in his seventies was losing that stimulating medievalism which had

176
The Eccleston Lodge to Eaton Hall. A late work of 1894 by the Douglas Fordham partnership.

impelled him in the early 1880s. Both these later lodges stand so far to the side of their wide rides as to be almost invisible from the road. The gate towers which they replaced would have dominated these key drives with far more authority.

The Eccleston Lodge of 1894 is another Douglas and Fordham design and, while it has the characteristic restlessness of the period, projecting, jettying and opening unpredictably on all three public facades, the bold timbered patterning of its great gable does much to tie the quivering stone and red and blue brick together.

Though there are many more lodges at Eaton it is right to leave the park by the Dee, for there on the banks of the deep brown river is that rarest of

177
The River Lodge by the Iron Bridge in Eaton Hall Park. This building of 1894 was built as a reception point for boats from Chester.

lodges, a river lodge. In the last century it was the goal of Chester's pleasure trippers, both lodge and tea-house in the days when even the rowdiest Lancashire trippers could not persuade the first Duke to close his gates, and when servants of the Hall were strongly adjured to treat all visitors with absolute courtesy. Now the River Lodge stands quietly at the top of the boat steps, a simple exercise in the Douglas manner, two timbered black and white gables over a ground floor of red and blue brick. As a final tremendous flourish of ducal style, by the side of the lodge and perfectly framing it, John Hazeldine's Iron Bridge launches the Aldford drive across the Dee in one daring leap on spandrels of elegant Gothick trefoils, the last true relic of Porden's lost Eaton and testament of a period when drives and lodges were an art form in their own right.

NOTES TO THE TEXT

INTRODUCTION

1 Page 78.
2 Humphry Repton, *Observations on the Theory and Practice of Landscape Gardening*, 1803, 142.
3 Both of these lodges are illustrated in Barbara Jones, *Follies and Grottoes*, 2nd. ed., 1974, 393 and 224.

CHAPTER ONE

1 These views, though scattered throughout the country in private collections, have been brought together in John Harris, *The Artist and the Country House*, 1979.
2 A panorama of the gardens at Hampton Court by van Wyngaerde is given in Roy Strong, *The Renaissance Garden in England*, 1979, plate 8.
3 Smythson's plan for Wollaton is illustrated in Strong, *Renaissance Garden*, plate 26.
4 Canto 12 verse 83.
5 For a discussion of Eizabethan banquets and the taking of dessert in summerhouses see Mark Girouard, *Life in the English Country House*, 1978, 104–7.
6 A view of Crewe Hall by Wenceslaus Hollar is given in Harris, *Artist and the Country House*, plate 24.
7 A drawing of Campden House in its original form showing the garden buildings is in the British Museum and illustrated in C. Whitfield, *A History of Chipping Campden*, 1958, plate 18.
8 Tallard's garden is discussed in Miles Hadfield *A History of British Gardening*, 1960, 155–6 and is illustrated on the end papers of the same book.
9 Quoted in Hadfield, *British Gardening*, 165.
10 Kip's view of Hamstead Marshall is given in *Country Life*, 29 March 1913.
11 See *Country Life*, 20 May 1965.

CHAPTER TWO

1 From the Temple of Flora at Stourhead.
2 Princesse Radziwill (ed.) *Memoirs of the Duchesse de Dino 1831–50*, 1909, volume i (1831–5), 56–7.
3 *Characteristicks*, ii, 98.
4 *Paradise Lost*, Book 4, 135–42 and 579–81.
5 Visitors entered the park at Rousham through a Palladian gateway on the public road to the west designed by Kent. Next to it is a Gothic seat and a castellated structure also by Kent which acts as a park boundary marker and which could be mistaken for a lodge. Jennifer Sherwood in the revised Oxfordshire volume of the *Buildings of England* calls it a lodge and her lead is followed by David Jarrett in *The English Landscape Garden*, 1978 who gives an illustration of the building on page 40. On inspection, however, the structure is a castellated barn with, at its base, a sheltered seat that might just conceivably have been used by a welcoming servant in fine weather.
6 John Summerson, *Architecture in Britain 1530–1830*, 1977 edition, chapter 20.
7 For information on the Gothick proposals for Sutton Place see *Country Life*, 14 February 1914.
8 Quoted by Hadfield, *British Gardening*, 165.
9 Ibid. 165.
10 See C.H. Collins Baker and Muriel Baker *The Life and Circumstances of James Brydges, First Duke of Chandos*, 1949, 183.
11 For Kip's view of Dyrham see Atkyns, *Gloucestershire*.
12 For the dating of the Boughton arch and lodges see *Country Life*, 11 March 1971.
13 The Setterington views are illustrated in Harris, *Artist and the Country House*, plates 196a–c. Richard Hewlings attributes the addition of these pavilions to William Thornton who made drawings for living accommodation to be added to the stables at Ledston.
14 Bound together as 'The Kingsweston Volume of Drawings', Bristol Record Office 33746.
15 Elton Hall, Peterborough, Nos. 193 and 198. Design No. 193 is illustrated in an article on the Kingsweston drawings by Kerry Downes in *Architectural History*, volume 10 (1967), figure 28. No. 198 is illustrated in H M Colvin and M J Craig, *Architectural Drawings in the Library of Elton Hall*, 1964, plate XXa.
16 Christopher Gotch, 'Mylne and Kingsweston', in *Country Life*, 23 January 1953. The gate appears in a Rococo vignette on Isaac Taylor's survey map of the estate of 1771 held in the Bristol Record Office.
17 Penpole Gate was demolished in

September 1950. Two photographs taken before and after World War II are given in *Country Life*, 24 November 1950, Correspondence.
18 Both estate map and watercolour are in the possession of Mr. Charles Wynne Eaton. The watercolour is reproduced in *Country Life*, 30 July 1943.
19 Suggestions of Christopher Hussey in his *Country Life* article.
20 Geoffrey Beard has found payments to Kent (1745–7) in the Badminton Papers.
21 Kent's design for the Holkham Triumphal Arch is preserved at Holkham and is illustrated in Margaret Jourdain, *The Work of William Kent*, 1948, 95, figure 23.
22 For Kent's designs for Esher, see John Harris in *Country Life*, 14 May 1959.
23 These lodges to Claremont are shown to be on an oil painting dated 1742–5 by John Harris which is illustrated in his *Artist and the Country House*, plate 193. The plate is wrongly captioned as Esher Place and we are grateful to Mr. Harris for pointing this out to us. One of Kent's garden buildings for Claremont appears on Rocque's 1738 engraving of the grounds so the lodges are presumably of the same date. They have been incorrectly attributed to Henry Holland in the second, revised edition of the *Buildings of England: Surrey*. Holland was working at Claremont much later (1771–4).
24 A drawing for these is preserved at Holkham and is illustrated in Laurence Fleming and Alan Gore, *The English Garden*, 1979, 97.

CHAPTER THREE

1 1966 edition, 227.
2 Oxford University Press edition, 1980, volume 2, 127.
3 Edmund Burke, *A Philosophical Enquiry into the origin of our ideas of the Sublime and the Beautiful*, 1757.
4 A drawing of the gatehouse by Paul Sandby is given in Kerry Downes, *Vanbrugh*, 1977, plate 104.
5 Quoted in *Country Life*, 25 October 1924.
6 W.S. Lewis (ed.) *Horace Walpole's Correspondence*, 1973, volume 35, 279.
7 Both cottage and arch are illustrated in *Country Life*, 13 September 1946.
8 Quoted in *Country Life*, 13 September 1946.
9 For Keene's Gothick work at Enville see Timothy Mowl, 'The Case of the Enville Museum' in *Journal of Garden History*, volume 3, no. 2, 134–43.
10 The two-light windows with dripstones are nineteenth century alterations. Miller's original 'y' tracery fenestration survives in one window in each lodge facing the Court.
11 Repton, *Observations*, 142.
12 We are grateful to Roger White for the information on Carr's Raby Castle lodge design.
13 As the lodges are dated on the stonework 1785, those built by Joseph Towsey of Blandford for Thomas Weld in 1792–3 must have been erected on another entrance to the park.
14 Repton, *Observations*, 145.
15 Ibid., 145.
16 Ibid., 145.
17 Ibid., 142.
18 Ibid., 144.

CHAPTER FOUR

1 Caption to Plate 40 in Joseph Gandy's *'The Rural Architect'*, 1806.
2 The temple is illustrated in *Country Life*, 19 June 1958.
3 Howard Colvin in his *Biographical Dictionary of British Architects 1600–1840*, 1978 edition, has pointed out that if the date were amended to MDCCXLII, 1742 would be an early date for Lightoler and John Halfpenny to have been in collaboration. We suggest that the numerals be amended to MDCCLVII as 1757 is a much likelier date for the contents of the pattern book.
4 Richardson's date of birth is not known, but he was described as an 'apprentice' in 1759 when witnessing John Adam's will.
5 Richardson, *New Designs*, 14.
6 Parkyns, *Six Designs*, Advertisement.
7 Ibid., 14.
8 Ibid., 12.
9 Ibid., 15.
10 Ibid., 15
11 Ibid., 15
12 Elsam, *Rural Architecture*, 52.
13 Soane's Langley Park lodges and gateway are illustrated in Dorothy Stroud, *John Soane*, 1961, plates 20, 21 and 22.
14 Brown's unexecuted design for these lodges is given in Dorothy Stroud, *Capability Brown*, 1975, plate 30c.

15 For Brown's layout for Packington and his triumphal arched lodge see Stroud, *Capability Brown*, plates 5a and 6b.

16 Repton's Red Book for Prestwood House, Staffs.,(Hereford Record Office) captures this attention to detail exactly. Produced for Edward Foley in 1791, Repton proposed a lodge 'partaking of the stile in which the house itself is built; this Lodge will be so placed as to meet the Eye and become a very picturesque object from both roads'. His accompanying plate shows a charming building in the West Midlands Gothick style which would have echoed perfectly the parent house. It is not known if this was executed and the house itself was demolished in 1922.

17 See John Summerson, 'The Vision of J.M. Gandy, in *Heavenly Mansions*, 1949.

18 Harrison designed Gothic vaulting for Chirk Castle about 1820 and the lodges may well be his work being stylistically in his more usual neo-classical manner.

19 Papworth, *Rural Residences*, 1818, plate 4 and pages 18–19

20 Dearn, *Designs for Lodges*, 1823 edition, plate 20.

21 Ibid., 6.

22 Hunt, *Archittetura Campestre, 16.*

CHAPTER FIVE

1 See Chapter 2, note 21.

2 Hawksmoor's Woodstock gate is illustrated in Kerry Downes, *Hawksmoor*, 1969, plate 166.

3 Everard (1723–92) appears to have designed a Tuscan garden temple at Ince Blundell Hall and as the gateway is in the Tuscan Doric style he may well have designed both buildings. The temple is illustrated in *Country Life*, 17 April 1958.

4 For the political influences in the garden layout at Stowe see George Clarke, 'Grecian Taste and Gothic Virtue: Lord Cobham's gardening programme and its iconography' in *Apollo*, June 1973.

5 Repton's design is given in Dorothy Stroud, *Humphry Repton*, 1962, 100.

6 There is a design by Wyatt for the 'Sodbury entrance at Dodington Park' dated 1798 in the RIBA Drawings Collection and the archway is illustrated in Christopher Hussey, *English Country Houses: Late Georgian*, 1958, plate 65.

7 See RIBA Drawings Collection, Catalogue C-F, 95 and figure 71.

8 John Rutter in his *Delineations of Fonthill and its Abbey* of 1823 attributes the gateway to Inigo Jones on the strength of local tradition. This does not seem so wild an attribution when the gateway is compared to a drawing by Jones for an archway structure, possibly for Newmarket Place, Suffolk, illustrated in John Harris, *The Palladians,* 1981, plate 120. The tripartite compositions with lower lean-to additions are identical and both have heavy rustication and balustrades on the pavilions. However, in his 24 November 1966 *Country Life* article on Fonthill, Mr. Harris suggests that the gateway is of Alderman Beckford's time, a view shared by James Lees-Milne in his *William Beckford,* 1976, 14.

9 Soane's Tyringham lodge is illustrated in Stroud, *Soane* plate 99.

10 Page 276. Hardwick's drawing for the Propylaeum is given in *Seven Victorian Architects,* ed. Jane Fawcett, 1976, plate 37, and the arch as built forms the frontispiece to the same book.

CHAPTER SIX

1 Jolivet's map is illustrated in *Country Life*, 20 June 1974.

2 John Donowell is given as the architect of West Wycombe House in the fifth volume of *Vitruvius Britannicus*. Gervase Jackson-Stops in his *Country Life* article on West Wycombe attributes a drawing for Daphne's Temple preserved at the house to Donowell.

3 We are grateful to Roger White for informing us of Vardy's drawing for these lodges which is preserved at Hackwood House.

4 Paine designed a banqueting house for Forcett in 1762 and may also have designed the lodges. They are unlikely to date from Daniel Garret's work at the house (c.1730–40).

5 The Phyllis Court pair probably date from c.1765 when the house was partially demolished and rebuilt.

6 Mitchell is the likeliest architect for the Ramsbury lodges as they are identical to those he designed for Cottesbrooke, Northants, and the families of the two houses were related.

7 Christopher Hussey attributes the lodges to Adam in *Country Life*, 12 June 1937. But the pattern of rustication and quoining on the gatepiers and lodges corresponds closely with that of the stables, and a drawing for these as they were built exists at Newby, signed William Belwood.
8 James Paine, *Plans, Elevations and Sections of Noblemen and Gentlemen's Houses*, volume 2 1783, plates 68–71.
9 Brettingham was working at Holkham from 1734 and claimed to have designed the East Lodge in his *The Plans and Elevations of the late Earl of Leicester's House at Holkham*, 2nd ed. 1773.
10 For illustrations of these architects' work see Helen Rosenau, *Boullée and Visionary Architecture*, 1976.
11 The lodge is at the end of the former east drive. A drawing for it attributed to Repton and corresponding to the building as erected is in the RIBA Drawings Collection, catalogue volume O-R, 120.

CHAPTER SEVEN

1 See J.S. Curl, *A Celebration of Death*, 1980, chapter 7.
2 Quoted in *Life of Benjamin Robert Haydon*, ed. Tom Taylor, 1853, volume 1, 93.
3 The temple is illustrated in J.M. Crook, *The Greek Revival*, 1972, plate 48.
4 Nicholas Revett added a fluted Doric portico to Standlynch House, Wilts. in 1766 and an Ionic portico to West Wycombe's west front in 1771. The first house to be newly built using the Greek Doric order was Osberton House, Notts, of 1805.
5 Byfield (c.1756–1813) was building a Gothic chapel at Brockhampton in 1799 but could just as easily turn his designing skill to Greek Revival forms as at the Session House in Canterbury.
6 See Chapter 13.
7 For Hope's views on the designs for Downing see David Watkin, *Thomas Hope and the Neo-Classical Idea*, 1968, 61–4.
8 Ibid., 63
9 Curl, *Celebration of Death*, 208, with an illustration of the entrance.
10 See Chapter 4, note 18.
11 Wilkins did prepare a severe Greek Doric design for a park building in 1815 which is illustrated in *Great Drawings from the Collection of the Royal Institute of British Architects*, eds. J. Harris, J. Lever and M. Richardson, no date, plate 33. This is captioned as a lodge or mausoleum. The latter is the more probable.
12 Translations were published in 1762, 1763, 1768, 1776 and 1798 and were frequently reprinted in periodicals.
13 *London Chronicle*, 16, 1764, 564–88.
14 *Universal Museum*, 4 February 1768, 56. Translation by Fuseli of Winckelmann's *Beschreibung des Apollo in Belvedere*.
15 William Blake, *An Island in the Moon*.
16 There are drawings by Wilkins for the lodges at the Hereford and Ledbury entrances to the park in the Hereford County Record Office, B 30/1 nos 11–12 etc.
17 The publication was a major source book for neo-classical decoration.
18 For example at Chesthunt Nunnery, Herts. (c. 1802) and at Balgowan, Perthshire (pre 1807).
19 Revett's temple is illustrated in Crook, *Greek Revival*, plate 77.
20 There is an identical pair at the south east corner of the park.
21 The lodges were built for Thomas, first Viscount Anson.
22 Revett's engraving is illustrated in Crook, *Greek Revival*, plate 10.
23 A photograph of Silverton Park is given in *The Destruction of the Country House*, eds. R. Strong, M. Binney and J. Harris, 1974, plate 138.
24 M.A. Laugier, *Essai sur l'Architecture*, 1753. For further information on Laugier see W. Herrmann, *Laugier and Eighteenth Century French Theory*, 1962. Sir William Chambers's *Treatise* of 1759 drew on Laugier in connection with the origins of primitive architecture.

CHAPTER EIGHT

1 Thomas Rickman (1776–1841), who has already been referred to as the father of archaeological Gothic categories, published his definitive *An Attempt to discriminate the Styles of English Architecture from the Conquest to the Reformation* in 1817. He was patronised by the Church Building Commissioners and designed many churches in a rigidly mechanical Regency Perpendicular.
2 An oil painting of the lodge is in the

possession of Mrs. Jennings of Babington House, Somerset.
3 First published in 1819.
4 Thomas Hopper (1776–1856), ranged from neo-Norman and Gothic through Greek Revival to Elizabethan and Tudor Gothic. Edward Blore (1787–1879), achieved structures in neo-Romanesque, Gothic, neo-Jacobean, Greek Revival and Elizabethan.
5 Midford Castle was built *c.* 1775 for Henry Disney Roebuck. The architect is not recorded but John Carter's design for a castle which appeared in the *Builder's Magazine* of 1774 corresponds with slight modifications to the building as erected. There were substantial Gothick additions made to the castle by Charles Conolly in 1810 which included a porch, conservatory, chapel and priory. The porch particularly relates in style to the lodge so it is reasonable to assume that the latter dates from 1810. For further information on Midford see *Country Life,* 3 March 1944.
6 Henry Wood was a Bristol statuary mason whose recorded architectural works are few. A drawing for the Lower Lodge at Ashton Court signed by him and with an 1802 watermark is in the Bristol Record Office, AC PL/74.
7 John Nash is recorded as having built a cottage for Lord Macclesfield and it may well be this lodge. See *The Buildings of England: Oxfordshire,* 1974, 763.
8 The Mythe Bridge dates from 1823–6.
9 The canal was opened in 1827. Telford had almost completed the working drawings in 1823, but these do not survive and Robert Mylne took over the work soon after. It is not known, therefore, whether Telford or Mylne designed the Doric canal keepers' houses. The best surviving example is at Splatt Bridge, Frampton on Severn which is illustrated in *The Buildings of England, Gloucestershire (The Vale and the Forest of Dean),* 1980 edition, plate 81.
10 The mansion of Sir Thomas Champneys was pulled down in 1856 and replaced by an Elizabethan style house designed by T.H. Wyatt in 1855–8. A boat house and rotunda survive from Sir Thomas's time.
11 *Gentleman's Magazine,* 1828, ii, 357.
12 Of the village buildings two particularly recall the style of the Court. They are the village pub, Ye Olde Hostelrie, and a cottage formerly called the Antient Cruys.
13 Drawings for the house by Blore are in the RIBA Drawings Collection, photographs of which are in the Hereford Record Office, F61/1–5. Wordsworth's remark is recorded in *The Buildings of England: Herefordshire,* 1963, 169. For photographs of the Court see *The Destruction of the Country House,* plate 171, and Peter Reid, *Burke's and Savill's Guide to Country Houses,* volume 2, 1980, 31.
14 Quoted in Marilyn Butler, *Peacock Displayed, A Satirist in his Context,* 1979, 221.
15 This stylistic comparison is given in an 1884 sale catalogue in the possession of the Hereford Record Office.

CHAPTER NINE
1 Subtitle to James Malton's *An Essay on British Cottage Architecture* of 1798.
2 The cottage is illustrated in *Country Life,* 13 September 1946.
3 Miller's sham castle at Hagley is illustrated in Terence Davis, *The Gothick Taste,* 1974, plate 28.
4 For Wright's work at Badminton see *Country Life,* 9 September 1971.
5 Shenstone designed the Leasowes so that vistas should open up past his Priory ruin to the cottages and slender spire of Halesowen church.
6 For a discussion of Marford see *Country Life,* 22 February 1979.
7 See Chapter 4.

CHAPTER TEN
1 Watkin, *Thomas Hope,* 183.
2 The house was enlarged by Hope's son Henry Beresford Hope, the contents were dispersed in 1917 and the building was demolished in 1967.
3 Figure 324 on page 729.
4 J.C. Loudon, *Encyclopaedia of Cottage, Farm and Villa Architecture,* 1846, 784–9.
5 The tower is illustrated in Watkin, *Hope,* plate 68.
6 For Pennethorne's authorship of the Park Villages see Summerson, *Architecture in Britain,* 520.
7 Uvedale Price, *An Essay on the Picturesque as compared with the Sublime and the Beautiful,* 1796 edition, volume 2, 259.
8 Ibid., 2, 258.

9 Ibid., 2, 254.
10 Ibid., 2, 252.
11 Ibid., 2, 265.
12 Ibid., 1, 64.
13 Page 728.
14 See Chapter 4.
15 Plate 3, page 6.
16 There are three designs for the lodge preserved at Bowood: two by Barry and one by T.H. Wyatt. The Wyatt design, dated 1841, is in Moorish-Gothic but both Barry's designs are Italianate: one for the lodge as erected and an earlier version with symmertically placed two storey pavilions either side of the entrance.
17 For an illustration of this front see Summerson, *Architecture in Britain*, plate 412.
18 Price, *Essay on the Picturesque*, 2, 211.
19 Mr. Francis Kelly has informed us that the structural ribs in the top floor room are identical to those used by Wood in two houses at Combe Down. Wood was not the classical purist that he is often labelled and the mixed style of the lodge may be entirely due to him. But it should be remembered that Goodridge was working at Prior Park in 1829–34 and may have applied the quirky details to the original lodge when it was extended at that time.
20 The lodge has already been marred by a nineteenth century addition and it is proposed to destroy Goodridge's original conception further by adding another section to this extension, completely ruining the vertical thrust of the building. Listed building status has not prevented this desecration, work is now (June 1984) in progress.
21 Crook, *Greek Revival*, 76.

CHAPTER ELEVEN

1 An engraving of the lodge and a recent photograph of it are given in Dorothy Stroud, *Humphry Repton*, 1962, 143.
2 See Mark Girouard, *The Victorian Country House*, 1979 edition, 154–63.
3 The hunting lodge, Lodge Park, was built about 1640 and King added lodges to it in 1898 when it was converted into a dwelling. There is a design for these lodges in the Gloucester Record office, D678, and King may well have been asked to design an even grander entrance for the main house.

CHAPTER TWELVE

1 Alistair Service on St. Alban's Court, Nonington, Kent, (*c*. 1860–4) in *Edwardian Architecture*, 1977, 16.
2 Andrew Saint, *Richard Norman Shaw*, 1976.
3 Clouds and Standen are illustrated in Roger Dixon and Stefan Muthesius, *Victorian Architecture*, 1978, plates 37–9.
4 Berrydowne is illustrated in Roderick Gradidge, *Dream Houses: The Edwardian Ideal*, 1980, plate 8.
5 For the Pleasaunce see Gradidge, *Dream Houses*, plate 11, and for Prior's Pier Terrace see Service, *Edwardian Architecture*, plate 51.
6 The lodge is illustrated in Mark Girouard, *Sweetness and Light: The Queen Anne Movement 1860–1900*, 1977, plate 21.
7 For Perrycroft see Duncan Simpson, *C.F.A. Voysey: an architect of individuality*, 1979, plates 14a-b.
8 Inscription on the right hand lodge on entering.
9 Quinlan Terry's design for the Heseltines is discussed with lavish illustrations in the *Architect's Journal*, 14 December 1983.
10 Hyslop found an austere neo-classical lodge on one side of the drive and built another to face it in identical style.

CHAPTER THIRTEEN

1 Quoted in T.W. Pritchard, *The Wynns of Wynnstay*, 1982, 38.
2 Preserved at the Wynnstay Estate Office, Ruabon.
3 Quoted in *Country Life*, 6 April 1972.
4 Stroud, *Capability Brown*, 183.
5 Pritchard, *Wynns of Wynnstay*, 104.
6 Ibid., 104.
7 *The Torrington Diaries*, ed. by C. Bruyn Andrews, volume 1, 175.
8 David Watkin, *The Life and Work of C.R. Cockerell, R.A.*, 1974, 164–5.
9 Peter Howell in *Country Life*, 6 April 1972.
10 Watkin, *Cockerell*, 164.
11 A newspaper comment quoted in Gervas Huxley, *Victorian Duke: The Life of Hugh Lupus Grosvenor, First Duke of Westminster*, 1967, 72.
12 For an illustration of Porden's Eaton see Huxley, *Victorian Duke*, plate 4.
13 Page 102. One of Porden's lodges, the Grosvenor Lodge, existed as late as 1901 when it was mentioned in an

14   article on the grounds in *Country Life*, 20 April 1901.
14   Waterhouse's Eaton Hall is illustrated in Dixon and Muthesius, *Victorian Architecture*, plate 25.
15   Huxley, *Victorian Duke*, 120.
16   Quoted in Mark Girouard, *The Return to Camelot: Chivalry and the English Gentleman*, 1981, 211. We are indebted to this work for much of our information on the Souls.
17   See Gradidge, *Dream Houses*, 41–3.

LIST OF ILLUSTRATIONS

COLOUR PLATES

I The Triangular Lodge, Rushton Hall, Northamptonshire.
II The Bottle Lodge at Tixall, Staffordshire.
III The Pyramid Gate, Castle Howard, North Riding.
IVa The White Gates, Leeswood Hall, Flintshire.
IVb The Black Gates, Leeswood Hall, Flintshire.
V Triumphal Arch to Holkham Hall, Norfolk.
VI The Carrmire Gate, Castle Howard, North Riding.
VII The Convent Lodge, Tong Castle, Shropshire.
VIII The Lodge to Redbourne Hall, Lincolnshire.
IX The main lodge to Hartwell House, Buckinghamshire.
X Lodge to the vanished houses of Fonthill, Wiltshire.
XI Lodge to Phyllis Court, Henley-on-Thames, Oxfordshire.
XII Old Lodge, Trelissick, Cornwall.
XIII Lodges to Arnos Vale Cemetery, Bristol.
XIV Hanover Gate to Regent's Park, London.
XV Milford Lodges, Shugborough Park, Staffordshire.
XVI Lodge to Ammerdown Park, Somerset.
XVII West Lodge, Sheffield Place, Sussex.
XVIII Lower Lodge, Caerhays Castle, Cornwall.
XIX Lullington Gatehouse to Orchardleigh Park, Somerset.
XX Lodges to Rushton Hall, Northamptonshire.
XXI Chain Bridge Lodge, Stuckeridge House, Devon.
XXII Lower Lodge, Prior Park, Bath.
XXIII Lodge to Kelston Park, Somerset.
XXIV Gatehouse to Peper Harow, Surrey.
XXV Gatehouse to Peckforton Castle, Cheshire.
XXVI East Lodge, Shere Manor House, Surrey.
XXVII South Lodge, Norney Grange, Surrey.
XXVIII Lodge to Park Hatch, Surrey.
XXIX Lodge to Chinthurst Hill, Surrey.
XXX Gateway and lodges to Plumpton Place, Sussex.
XXXI Lodge to Tythrop House, Buckinghamshire.
XXXII Eccleston Hill Lodge, Eaton Hall, Cheshire.

BLACK AND WHITE ILLUSTRATIONS

INTRODUCTION

1 Woodbridge Lodge, Rendlesham Hall, Suffolk.
2 The main lodge, Onslow Hall, near Shrewsbury, Shropshire.
3 Lodge to Blithfield Hall, Staffordshire.

CHAPTER ONE

4 Porter's Lodge Tower at Denbigh Castle, Denbighshire.
5 The Porter's Lodge, New College, Oxford.
6 The entrance gate and side lodges at Hardwick Hall, Derbyshire.
7 Gatehouse, Stanway House, Gloucestershire.
8 Banquet house to Campden House, Gloucestershire.
9 The Gate Lodges to Campden House, Gloucestershire.
10 Gatepiers at Hamstead Marshall, Berkshire.
11 Forecourt piers of Coleshill House, Berkshire.
12 Westwood Park, Worcestershire.
13 Shipton Moyne, Gloucestershire.
14 Lulworth Castle, Dorset.

CHAPTER TWO

15 Lodge to Woburn Abbey, Bedfordshire.
16 Entrance Lodge to Sutton Place, Surrey.
17 Gate lodge at Ham House, Surrey.
18 Bath Lodges to Dyrham House, Gloucestershire.
19 Forecourt gateway to Boughton House, Northamptonshire.
20 Pavilions and gateway at Ledston Hall, West Riding.
21 Kingsweston House, Gloucestershire.
22 Penpole Gate, Kingsweston House, Gloucestershire.
23 Brington Lodges, Althorp, Northamptonshire.
24 Black Gates Lodges, Leeswood Hall, Flintshire.
25 Oxford Gate, Stowe House, Buckinghamshire.
26 Lodges to Esher Place, Surrey.
27 Lodges to Claremont, Surrey.
28 Worcester Lodge to Badminton House, Gloucestershire.

CHAPTER THREE

29 Clearwell Castle, Gloucestershire.

30 Steeple Lodge to Wentworth Castle, West Riding.
31 Outwork tower to Stainborough Castle, West Riding.
32 The Hawking Tower, Boughton Park, Northamptonshire.
33 Sanderson Miller.
34 The Edgehill Tower, Warwickshire.
35 The Round Towers, Arbury Hall, Warwickshire.
36 Griff Lodges, Arbury Hall, Warwickshire.
37 Lodge to Siston Court, Gloucestershire.
38 Cottage, Downton Hall estate, Stanton Lacy, Shropshire.
39 East Lodges, Bowden Park, Wiltshire.
40 Lodges to Gisburn Park, West Riding.
41 Lodge at Fillingham Castle, Lincolnshire.
42 North entrance lodge to Lulworth Castle, Dorset.
43 Lodge to Blaise Castle, near Bristol.

CHAPTER FOUR
44 Batty Langley's 'Dorick gate' design.
45 A 'Gothick Temple' design, Batty Langley.
46 Batty Langley's 'Temple design, adapted to a gate lodge at Castletown House, County Kildare.
47 'Gothic Portico' design by Batty Langley.
48 The 'Portico' design used at Tottenham Park, near Marlborough, Wiltshire.
49 A 'Gothic Lodge' design by the Halfpenny brothers.
50 Lodge or keeper's house by Timothy Lightoler.
51 Dairy Lodge by Timothy Lightoler.
52 Spiers Lodge, Warwick Castle, Warwickshire.
53 Triumphal arch with side lodges by John Carter.
54 Screen from George Richardson's *New Designs in Architecture*.
55 Lodges and Gateway from George Richardson's *New Designs in Architecture*.
56 Designs for the park at Belmont, Herefordshire, by George Parkyns.
57 Plate from Joseph Gandy's *Designs*.
58 Steward's lodge or cottage designed by J.B. Papworth.
59 Gate lodge as a tenement block designed by Thomas Dearn.
60 Single-bedroom lodge designed by Thomas Dearn.
61 Plate from *Half a Dozen Hints* by T.F. Hunt.
62 Early Italianate lodge design by T.F. Hunt.

CHAPTER FIVE
63 The Lion Gate, Ince Blundell Hall, Lancashire.
64 Corinthian Arch at Stowe, Buckinghamshire.
65 Triumphal arch, Harewood House, West Riding.
66 Triumphal arch at Carden Hall, Cheshire.
67 Gatehouse to Berrington Hall, Herefordshire.
68 Triumphal arch, Greenbank, Chester.
69 South Lodge, Tabley House, Cheshire.
70 Arched Screen with twin lodges, Studley Royal, West Riding.
71 Entrance screen, Syon House, Middlesex.
72 Apleyhead Lodge, Clumber Park, Nottinghamshire.
73 Triumphal arch, Attingham Hall, Shropshire.
74 Knutsford Lodge, Tatton Park, Cheshire.
75 Gateway to Fonthill, Wiltshire.
76 North Lodge, Kedleston Hall, Derbyshire.
77 Gateway to Bryanston House, Dorset.
78 Grand Lodge, Heaton Park, near Manchester.
79 Propylaeum, Euston Station, London.

CHAPTER SIX
80 Lodge and Temple, West Wycombe Park, Buckinghamshire.
81 Lodges at Hackwood Park, Hampshire.
82 South Lodge, Kedleston Hall, Derbyshire.
83 Higher Lodges, Milton Abbey, Dorset.
84 East Lodge, Thornton-le Street Hall, North Riding.
85 Stag Lodge, Saltram house, Devon.
86 Lodge pair, Painshill, Surrey.
87 Skelton Lodges, Newby Hall, West Riding.
88 Lodges to Weston Park, Staffordshire.
89 North Lodge to Wentworth Woodhouse, West Riding.
90 East Lodge, Holkam Hall, Norfolk.
91 Lodges to Hooton Hall, Cheshire.
92 The Tern Lodge, Attingham Hall, Shropshire.

CHAPTER SEVEN
93 Oxford Lodges, Basildon Park, Berkshire.
94 Lodges to Brockhampton Park, Bromyard, Herefordshire.
95 Cambridge Lodge, Audley End House, Essex.
96 The Rostherne Lodge, Tatton Park, Cheshire.

97 Doric Lodge, Wentworth Woodhouse, West Riding.
98 Lodges to Chirk Castle, Denbighshire.
99 West Lodge, Stoke Edith, Herefordshire.
100 The Honey Pots, Carden Hall, Cheshire.
101 Mausoleum entrance, Trentham Park, Staffordshire.
102 Bath Lodge, Dodington Park, Gloucestershire.
103 The Mere Lodge, Tatton Park, Cheshire.
104 The Smithy Lodge, Heaton Park, near Manchester.
105 Lodges at Ottershaw Park, Surrey.
106 Gate opener's Lodge, Regent's Park, London.
107 Queen's Gate Lodge, Hyde Park, London.
108 Lodge to Wrelton, North Riding.
109 Lodge to Pellwall House, Shropshire.
110 Lodge to Cothelstone House, Somerset.
111 North-west lodge to Heath House, Tean, Staffordshire.
112 The Hope Dale Lodge to Millichope Park, Shropshire.

CHAPTER EIGHT
113 Lodge at Bryn Kynallt, Denbighshire.
114 North Lodge, Newark Park, Gloucestershire.
115 Lodges to Alscot Park, Warwickshire.
116 Tower lodge, Cholmondeley Castle, Cheshire.
117 Upper Lodge, Caerhays Castle, Cornwall.
118 Lodge to Midford Castle, Somerset.
119 The Combe Lodge to Ashton Court, Bristol.
120 Lodge, Mostyn Hall, Flintshire.
121 Toll-house, Mythe Bridge, Tewkesbury, Gloucestershire.
122 Forecourt of Lullington Gatehouse, Orchardleigh Park, Somerset.
123 Gatehouse to Goodrich Court, Herefordshire.

CHAPTER NINE
124 One of the Slait Lodges, Badminton Park, Gloucestershire.
125 A *cottage orné* lodge, Badminton village.
126 Lodge to Wivenhoe Park, Essex.
127 Lodges at Scrivelsby Park, Lincolnshire.
128 Lodge to Broomwell House, Bristol.
129 Smoothway Lodge, Ugbrooke Park, Devon.
130 Lodge to Halswell House, Somerset.
131 Lodge to Gaunt's House, Hinton Martell, Dorset.

CHAPTER TEN
132 Pink Lodge, Alton Towers, Staffordshire.
133 Lodge at Dowdeswell Court, Gloucestershire.
134 Viewing tower, Derry Hill, Bowood House, Wiltshire.
135 Park Lodge, Chatsworth, Derbyshire.
136 Lodge at Rendcomb House, Gloucestershire.
137 Lodge to Montebello, Bath.
138 Lodge to Merfield House, Rode, Somerset.
139 Entrance to Lansdown Cemetry, Bath.

CHAPTER ELEVEN
140 Llandegai Lodge, Penrhyn Castle, Caernarvonshire.
141 Lodge to Sandringham House, Norfolk.
142 East Lodge to Longner Hall, Shropshire.
143 Lodges to Westonbirt House, Gloucestershire.
144 Westonbirt House, Gloucestershire.
145 Gatehouse, Port Eliot, Cornwall.
146 Nansawn Lodge, Tregothnan House, Cornwall.
147 Lodges, Charlton Park, Wiltshire.
148 North Lodge, Dorfold Hall, Cheshire.
149 Lion Gate, Welbeck Abbey, Nottinghamshire.
150 Gatehouse to Peper Harow, Surrey.
151 East Lodge, Cholmondeley Castle, Cheshire.
152 Lodge to Waddesdon Manor, Buckinghamshire.
153 Lodge to Sherborne House, Gloucestershire.

CHAPTER TWELVE
154 The West Lodge, Trentham Park, Staffordshire.
155 Brockhampton Court, Ross-on-Wye, Herefordshire.
156 Lodge to Hall Barn, Beaconsfield, Buckinghamshire.
157 Star Lodge, Hartwell House, Buckinghamshire.
158 Lodges, Shavington Hall, Shropshire.
159 Milford Lodge, Witley Park, Surrey.
160 East Lodge, Wykeham Abbey, North Riding.
161 Lodge, Grantley Hall, West Riding.
162 Lodge, Cornbury Park, Oxfordshire.
163 Lodge, Raynham Hall, Norfolk.

CHAPTER THIRTEEN
164 Portrait of the 4th Sir Watkin Williams Wynn with two of his companions by

Pompeo Batoni.
165 Kennels Lodge, Wynnstay Park, Denbighshire.
166 Rhos y Madoc Lodge, Wynnstay Park, Denbighshire.
167 Waterloo Tower, Wynnstay Park, Denbighshire.
168 The Newbridge Lodge, Wynnstay Park, Denbighshire.
169 Portrait of Hugh Lupus Grosvenor, 1st Duke of Westminster.
170 Pulford Lodges, Eaton Hall, Cheshire.
171 Waterhouse's Eaton Hall, Cheshire.
172 Lodge on Belgrave Avenue to Eaton Hall, Cheshire.
173 North Lodge, Eaton Hall, Cheshire.
174 Douglas lodge 1882, Eaton Hall, Cheshire.
175 The Stud Lodge, Eaton Hall, Cheshire.
176 Eccleston Lodge, Eaton Hall, Cheshire.
177 The River Lodge, Eaton Hall, Cheshire.

GLOSSARY

ABACUS: See ORDERS.

ACANTHUS: A fleshy leaved plant conventionalized in the decoration of classical capitals.

AEDICULE: A small PEDIMENTED structure originally a shrine; hence frame for a niche.

ANTAE: Flat PILASTERS at either end of a row of columns.

ANTHEMION: Ornament in Greek architecture resembling honeysuckle often incorporated with ACANTHUS.

APSE: Semi-circular or polygonal recess often at end of presbytery, choir or aisle of a church.

ARCHITRAVE: 1. Lowest member of the ENTABLATURE (see diagram) resting directly upon capitals of supporting columns. 2. Moulding surrounding door or window.

ARTISAN MANNERISM: A non-courtly style of architecture of the seventeenth century in which elements of Elizabethan, Jacobean, Mannerist and Classical styles are used indiscriminately.

ARTS AND CRAFTS: Movement in the late nineteenth century inspired by the teaching of William Morris and Ruskin, to revive handicrafts and improve standards of design.

ASHLAR: Masonry walling made of large smooth even blocks.

ASTYLAR: Term describing a facade without PILASTERS or columns.

ATTIC STOREY: 1. A stage above the principal ENTABLATURE of a classical building. 2. The 'attic' in modern speech, space used loosely to mean garrett.

BALL FINIAL: See FINIAL.

BALUSTER: Individual element of a balustrade; short post or pillar supporting a handrail or COPING.

BAROQUE: Movement of the seventeenth and early eighteenth centuries. Architecture characterised by exuberant decoration and massing and complex composition.

BARONIAL: Scottish Revivalist style of the nineteenth century inspired by Scottish fortified architecture.

BARREL VAULT: See VAULTS.

BATTER: A slight tilt of a wall from its base upwards

BAY: Compartment or section in a building marked on the outside by windows, inside by columns.

BEAUX ARTS: Rich classical style favoured by the Ecole de Beaux Arts in late nineteenth century France.

BELVEDERE: Small structure of Italian derivation erected on the roof to give a good view.

BREASTSUMMER: A massive horizontal beam spanning a wide opening such as a fire place or a projecting gable.

BUCRANE/BUCRANIUM: A carved ox head or skull, usually garlanded, used decoratively in classical architecture.

CARYATID: Sculptured female figure used in Greek architecture instead of a column to support an ENTABLATURE, loosely, columns and pilasters, carved wholly or partly in human form.

CHAMFERED: An angle or edge of stone or wood block cut off diagonally.

CLERESTORY: Storey of aisled basilica or church above the range of arches or columns, pierced by windows. Applicable to domestic buildings.

CLUNCH: A type of chalk, strong enough to be used as building stone.

COADE STONE: Artificial stone resembling terracotta manufactured in London from 1769 onwards.

COMPOSITE: See ORDERS.

COPING: The uppermost course of masonry or brickwork in a wall, usually sloping, to throw off rain.

CORINTHIAN: See ORDERS.

CORNICE: Projecting horizontal section at top of ENTABLATURE, also any projecting ornamental moulding crowning an external facade or internally at junction of wall and ceiling.

COVE: Large concave moulding especially that produced by the arched junction of wall and ceiling.

CROCKET: A Gothic decorative feature, based on foliage projecting at regular intervals from spires, pinnacles, canopies, GABLES, etc.

CROW-STEPPED GABLE: See GABLE.

CUPOLA: A small dome on a circular or polygonal base crowning a roof or turret, frequently used to light a staircase.

CURVILINEAR: See TRACERY.

CUSP: Projecting barb-like motif formed by the junction of foils. Used to ornament Gothic tracery.

CYCLOPEAN MASONRY: Irregular blocks of stone; has come to mean any polygonal masonry of a very large size.

DADO: Usually the finishing of the lower part of an interior wall from floor to waist height, often decorated with a frieze or similar device.

DECORATED: English Gothic architectural style c.1290–1350 characterised by foliage carving and complex window tracery. Much use of the OGEE ARCH.

DENTIL: A small square block used in series in IONIC, CORINTHIAN, COMPOSITE, and more rarely, DORIC cornices.

DIAPERWORK: Surface decoration or a small repeated geometric pattern prevalent in the later middle ages.

DOGTOOTH: A four-armed star-shaped motif prevalent in Early Gothic architecture.

DORIC: See ORDERS.

DORMER WINDOWS: A window placed vertically in a sloping roof and with a roof of its own.

DOSSERET: French term for an additional high block or slabs on top of an ABACUS (see diagram).

DOUBLE PILE: A type of house plan popularised by Sir Roger Pratt in the seventeenth century in which the house is two rooms deep, the series of rooms separated by a longitudinal corridor.

DRIP MOULD: A projecting moulding to throw off the rain, on the face of the wall above a window.

EARLY ENGLISH: The earliest form of GOTHIC architecture in England c.1180–1260.

ELEVATION: The external faces of a building; also used to mean a drawing made in projection on a vertical plane to show any one face of a building.

ENTABLATURE: Upper part of an ORDER · consisting of ARCHITRAVE, FRIEZE and CORNICE.

EXEDRA: Small apse-like termination to a room or hall.

FAN VAULT: See VAULTING.

FINIAL: Ornamental feature, generally stone, places on top of pinnacle or apex and base of gable. BALL FINIAL — a finial terminated by a small stone sphere.

FOLLY: A deliberately functionless building or ruined structure, popular in the eighteenth century to add an element of the picturesque to the landscape.

FRETTING: Geometrical ornament of horizontal and vertical straight lines repeated to form a band.

FRIEZE: Middle division of an ENTABLATURE, between the ARCHITRAVE and the CORNICE, usually decorated but may be plain.

GABLE: The vertical, triangular portion of a wall at the end of a ridged roof, from the eaves level to the apex. A CROW-STEPPED GABLE has stepped sides.

GIANT ORDER: See ORDER.

GIBBS SURROUND: The surround of a doorway or window made up of alternately large and small blocks of stone, named after the architect James Gibbs.

GOTHIC: Style of architecture prevalent in Europe c. 1130–1550. Salient features are the use of RIB-VAULT, the flying buttress and the pointed arch; in its most refined forms, a structural unity and a dissolution of walling to gain large windows.

GOTHICK: Eighteenth century use of Gothic forms to create a Romantic mood in a building without recourse to Gothic precepts of design.

GOTHIC REVIVAL: Movement to revive the Gothic style belonging chiefly to the eighteenth and nineteenth centuries. Distinguished from Gothick by a more correct archaeological use of motifs.

GROIN VAULTS: See VAULTING.

GROTTO: Man made and highly stylized cave, popular in the eighteenth century as a feature in the gardens of country houses.

HEXASTYLE: See PORTICO.

HIPPED/HIP: The external angle formed by the meeting of two floating roof surfaces.

IN ANTIS: See PORTICO.

INTERSTICES: Intervening spaces between members of e.g. a vault.

ITALIANATE: Nineteenth century revivalist style of architecture evoking Renaissance Italy.

JETTIED CONSTRUCTION: The projection of an upper storey beyond the storey below found in timber framed buildings. On their outer ends is placed the sill of the walling for the storey above.

KEYSTONE: The central stone of an arch or rib vault.

LIGHTS: Openings between the MULLIONS of a window.

LINTEL: A piece of stone or timber laid horizontally across a doorway or window opening.

LOGGIA: A gallery open on one or more sides, sometimes pillared; it may also be a separate structure, usually in a garden.

MACHICOLATION: A projecting parapet built on the outside of fortified buildings with openings in the floor through which to drop lead etc onto assailants.

MANNERISM: The style current in Italy from Michelangelo to the end of the sixteenth century when strict canons of classical design were being relaxed or reversed.

MANSARD ROOF: Roof made up of two planes, the lower being longer and steeper than the upper.

MULLION: Vertical strip, usually of masonry dividing a window into two or more LIGHTS.

NEO-CLASSICAL: A term describing the architecture of a movement which began in the 1750s as a return to the principles of Greek or Roman Art and Architecture.

NEO-GEORGIAN: A late nineteenth and twentieth century revival of the principles of Georgian house design, i.e. a domestic architecture of restraint and symmetry decorated with classical details especially round doorways.

OCULUS: A round opening in a wall, often used as window.

OEIL-DE-BOEUF WINDOW: A round or oval window.

OGEE ARCH: A pointed arch made up of two curves, each of which is made up of a convex and concave part.

Andrea Palladio, introduced by Inigo Jones in the early seventeenth century, and later made popular by Lord Burlington and his followers.

PALMETTE: A fan-like ornamental motif composed of a number of thin strips coming together at the base, in the manner of a palm frond. Mainly used as a FRIEZE decoration.

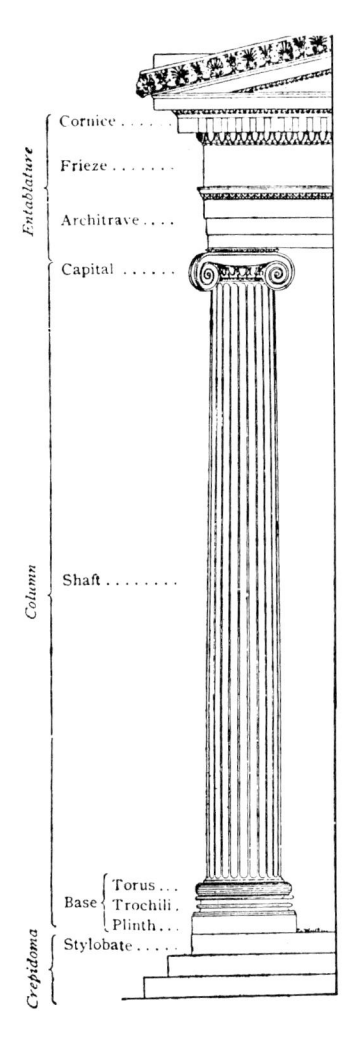

The Orders. Jacomo Barrozzio da Vignola: 1507–73. Reproduced by kind permission of the Architectural Association.

Corner of an Ionic facade

ORDERS: In classical architecture a system of architectural design comprising a column with base, shaft, and capital supporting an entablature. The whole ornamental according to five ordained styles: DORIC, TUSCAN, IONIC, CORINTHIAN or COMPOSITE (see illustration). GIANT ORDER — an order where the columns rise from the ground through two or more storeys.

PALLADIAN: In English architecture, the classical style of the Italian architect

PARGETTING: The covering of buildings, usually timber-framed, with a durable plaster of lime, the surface of which is often decorated with ornate patterns.

PATERA: A circular ornament sunk into a wall, decorated with stylized foliage or petals.

PEDIMENT: Originally a low pitched triangular GABLE over a PORTICO used in classical architecture and frequently used later to decorate doorways and windows.

BROKEN PEDIMENT — one in which the apex of the triangle is removed, leaving a roughly arc-like shape though other shapes are possible. SEGMENTAL PEDIMENT — one made of an arc of a circle, almost always used over doors or windows.

PERRON: A platform in front of a doorway of a house, church or civic building, reached by a flight of steps.

PERPENDICULAR: A late GOTHIC architectural style, unique to England. It evolved around 1330 and was general until *c.* 1540. Characterised by windows dominated by vertical lines hitting the arch, giving a grid iron appearance.

PIANO NOBILE: An Italian renaissance term, signifying the principal floor of a house containing the reception rooms, the whole raised on a basement storey.

PILASTER: A flat column set against the surface of a building, built into it and projecting not more than one third of its surface breadth.

POLYCHROMY: The use of several colours of brick or stone to decorate the surface of a building.

PORTICO: A roofed structure supported by columns, attached to a building normally as an entrance feature. PORTICO IN ANTIS — One in which the columns are in a plane with the walls of the building i.e. the PORTICO does not project beyond the building. A HEXASTYLE portico is one with six columns. A TETRASTYLE portico is one with four columns.

PYLON: Originally the pyramidal, truncated, rectangular towers used to flank an entrance in Egyptian architecture; often used now to mean any large isolated structure.

QUATREFOIL: A four-lobed ornament used mainly in Gothic architecture, as a surface decoration, also found in window tracery.

QUEEN ANNE: English domestic architecture of the early eighteenth century, admired for its simple grace by Norman Shaw and revived by his office in the late nineteenth century.

QUOINS: Dressed stones at the corner of a building, sometimes imitated by groups of brick in wholly brick buildings.

REGENCY: The style of architecture prevalent under George IV as King 1820–1830 or as Prince Regent 1811–1820, epitomised by the works of John Nash.

REPOUSSÉ: Metalwork beaten into relief by hammering from the reverse side, used, for example, in ornamental lead troughs.

ROCOCO: A very ornate, light, mid-eighteenth century style of art and architecture, following the more weighty BAROQUE. In England it was mainly confined to interior design, plasterwork and furniture, while a PALLADIAN style was almost exclusively used for the exterior of major buildings.

RUSTICATION: The use of massive elements of masonry mainly in the basement storey of a building, to give an impression of strength. Originally the blocks were rough hewn; in later styles the surface would be smooth with artifically large courses cut between the blocks. VERMICULATED RUSTICATION — the surface of the rusticated blocks is heavily channelled with curved, irregular grooves, giving an impression of the surface being riddled with worms

SASH WINDOW: One made of sashes i.e. sliding wooden panels of glass set in grooves.

STRAINER ARCH: An arch inserted across the width of the building to support a weight above, often used in medieval churches e.g. Salisbury, to support the central tower.

STRAPWORK: Elizabethan and Jacobean surface ornament composed of interlacing strips giving the impression of punched and studded leatherwork, sometimes used to create an ornate skyline.

STRING COURSE: A projecting course of stone or brick running horizontally across a building.

SWAG: A carved representation of drapery and/or foliage hanging from two level points.

TETRASTYLE: See PORTICO.

THERMAL WINDOW: A semi-circular window divided by two MULLIONS, derived from classical baths.

TRACERY: The ornamental pattern filling the head of a Gothic window of two or more lights; also applied to the surface of buildings as decoration.

TRANSOM: A horizontal strip of masonry dividing up a window.

TREFOIL: A three-lobed figure in TRACERY or a three-lobed carved leaf.

TRIGLYPH: See diagram. Elements in a DORIC frieze, which separate the METOPES.

TUDORBETHAN: An imprecise nineteenth century revival of sixteenth and seventeenth century styles, mixing Tudor, Elizabethan, and Jacobean motifs.

TUSCAN ORDER: See ORDERS.

TYMPANUM: The triangular rounded area within a pediment and the area above a doorway, enclosed by the LINTEL and the surrounding arch.

VAULT 1. BARREL or TUNNEL VAULT: vault in continuous semi-circular or more rarely, pointed sections. 2. GROIN VAULT: composed of the intersection of two tunnel vaults at right angles, giving four compartments. 3. RIB VAULT: vault with stone ribs projecting from the groins i.e. the intersecting planes of the vault. 4. FAN VAULT: complex late medieval vault in which all ribs are of same length and the same distance apart, and of the same curvature. Sometimes the interstices or panels between the fans are decorated with pendants i.e. projecting ornamental features.

VENETIAN WINDOW: A classical window made up of three parts, the central part wider and taller than the other two and arched. Also used for doorways.

VERMICULATED RUSTICATION: See RUSTICATION.

VITRUVIAN SCROLL: A repeated classical motif made up of features reminiscent of waves terminated by scrolls.

VOLUTE: A spiral scroll used in the IONIC capital. Also used as a linking motif in classical architecture.

WEATHERBOARDING: Overlapping strips of wood cladding a building.

SELECT BIBLIOGRAPHY

Primary Sources

Robert Atkyns, *Gloucestershire*, 1712
Rev. A. Barry, *Life and Works of Sir Charles Barry*, 1867
Matthew Brettingham, *The Plans and Elevations of the late Earl of Leicester's House at Holkham*, 2nd ed., 1773
John Carter, *The Builder's Magazine*, 1774
T.D.W. Dearn, *Designs for Lodges and Entrances*, 1811, 2nd ed., 1823
Charles L. Eastlake, *A History of the Gothic Revival*, 1872
Richard Elsam, *An Essay on Rural Architecture*, 1803
Benjamin Ferrey, *Recollections of A.W.N. Pugin and his father Augustus Pugin*, 1861
Joseph Gandy, *Designs for Cottages, Cottage Farms, and other Rural Buildings including Entrance Gates and Lodges*, 1805
Joseph Gandy, *The Rural Architect*, 1806
Edward Gyfford, *Designs for Small Picturesque Cottages*, 1807
William & John Halfpenny, *The Country Gentleman's Pocket Companion and Builder's Assistant for Rural Decorative Architecture*, 1753
William & John Halfpenny, *A New and Complete System of Architecture*, 1759
W. & J. Halfpenny, T. Lightoler & R. Morris, *The Modern Builder's Assistant*, date uncertain
Thomas Hopper, *Hopper versus Cust on the New Houses of Parliament*, 1837
T.F. Hunt, *Half a dozen Hints on Picturesque Domestic Architecture*, 1825
T.F. Hunt, *Archittetura Campestre*, 1827
Batty Langley, *City and Country Builder's and Workman's Treasury of Designs*, 1740
Batty Langley, *Ancient Architecture Restored and Improved*, 1741–2
Timothy Lightoler, *The Gentleman and Farmer's Architect*, 1762
J.C. Loudon, *The Suburban Gardener and Villa Companion*, 1838
J.C. Loudon, *Encyclopaedia of Cottage, Farm and Villa Architecture*, 1846
Robert Lugar, *Architectural Sketches for Cottages, Rural Dwellings and Villas*, 1805
John Miller, *The Country Gentleman's Architect*, 1787
Charles Nash, *The Goodrich Court Guide*, 1845
J.P. Neale, *Views of Seats of Noblemen and Gentlemen in England, Wales, Scotland and Ireland*, 1818–29
James Paine, *Plans, Elevations and Sections of Noblemen and Gentlemen's Houses*, volume 2, 1783
John B. Papworth, *Rural Residences*, 1818
George J. Parkyns, *Six Designs for improving and embellishing grounds*, 1793
R. Payne Knight, *An Analytical Inquiry into the Principles of Taste*, 1805
Uvedale Price, *An Essay on the Picturesque as compared with the Sublime and Beautiful*, 1796 edition
A.W.N. Pugin, *Contrasts*, 1836
Humphry Repton, *Observations on the Theory and Practice of Landscape Gardening*, 2nd ed., 1805
George Richardson, *New Designs in Architecture*, 1792
Thomas Rickman, *An attempt to discriminate the Styles of English Architecture from the Conquest to the Reformation*, 1817
Thomas Miller Rickman, *Notes on the Life of Thomas Rickman*, 1901
P.F. Robinson, *Rural Architecture or A Series of Designs for Ornamental Cottages*, 1823
John Soane, *Plans, Elevations and Sections of Buildings*, 1788
John Vardy, *Some Designs of Mr. Inigo Jones and Mr. William Kent*, 1744

Secondary Sources

B. Sprague Allen, *Tides in English Taste 1619–1800*, 1937
Ian Anstruther, *The Knight and the Umbrella*, 1963
Clive Aslet, *The Last Country Houses*, 1982
Elizabeth Aslin, *The Aesthetic Movement*, 1981
C.H.C. Baker & M.I. Baker, *The Life and Circumstances of James Brydges First Duke of Chandos*, 1949
John Betjeman, *London's Historic Railway Stations*, 1972
A.T. Bolton, *Architecture of Robert and James Adam*, 1922
John Brandon-Jones and others, *C.F.A. Voysey: architect and designer 1857–1941*, Exhibition Catalogue, Royal Pavilion, Brighton, 1978
Marilyn Butler, *Peacock Displayed, A Satirist in his Context*, 1979
G.F. Chadwick, *The Works of Sir Joseph Paxton 1803–1865*, 1961
Christie's Sale Catalogue: *The Sir Albert Richardson Collection*, 1983
Kenneth Clark, *The Gothic Revival*, 1962 edition
Kenneth Clark, *Ruskin Today*, 1964
George Clarke, 'Grecian Taste and Gothic Virtue: Lord Cobham's

gardeningprogramme and its iconography' in *Apollo,* June 1973

H.M. Colvin, *A Biographical Dictionary of British Architects 1600–1840,* 1978

Olive Cook, *The English House Through Seven Centuries,* 1968

J.M. Crook, Introduction to Charles Eastlake's *A History of the Gothic Revival,* 1970 facsimile edition

J.M. Crook, *The Greek Revival: Neo-Classical Attitudes in British Architecture 1760–1870,* 1972

James Stevens Curl, *A Celebration of Death,* 1980

Anthony Dale, *James Wyatt,* 1956

Gillian Darley, *Villages of Vision,* 1978

Peter Davey, *Arts and Crafts Architecture: The Search for Earthly Paradise,* 1980

Terence Davis, *John Nash, the Prince Regent's Architect,* 1973

Terence Davis, *The Gothick Taste,* 1974

L. Dickins & M. Stanton, eds. *An Eighteenth Century Correspondence ... Letters to Sanderson Miller,* 1910

Memoirs of the Duchesse de Dino 1831–50, Princesse Radziwill, ed., 1909

Roger Dixon & Stefan Muthesius, *Victorian Architecture,* 1978

Kerry Downes, *Hawksmoor,* 1969

Kerry Downes, *Vanbrugh,* 1977

Ifor Edwards, *Davies Brothers Gatesmiths,* 1977

P. Ferriday, ed., *Victorian Architecture,* 1963

P. Frankl, *The Gothic,* 1960

Mark Girouard, *Sweetness and Light: The Queen Anne Movement 1860–1900,* 1977

Mark Girouard, *Life in the English Country House: A Social and Architectural History,* 1978

Mark Girouard, *The Victorian Country House,* 1979 edition

Mark Girouard, *Return to Camelot: Chivalry and the English Gentleman,* 1981

H.S. Goodhart-Rendel, *English Architecture Since the Regency,* 1953

Roderick Gradidge, *Dream Houses: The Edwardian Ideal,* 1980

Great Drawings from the Collection of the Royal Institute of British Architects, edited by J. Harris, J. Lever & M. Richardson, no date

Miles Hadfield, *A History of British Gardening,* 1960

John Harris, *The Artist and the Country House: A history of country house and garden view painting in Britain 1540–1870,* 1979

John Harris, *The Palladians,* 1981

David Hey, *The Buildings of Britain 1550–1750: Yorkshire,* 1981

H.R. Hitchcock, *Early Victorian Architecture in Britain,* 1954

Hugh Honour, *Neo-Classicism,* 1968

Christopher Hussey, *The Picturesque,* 1927

Christopher Hussey, *English Country Houses: Late Georgian,* 1958

Christopher Hussey, *English Landscapes and Gardens 1700–1750,* 1967

Gervas Huxley, *Victorian Duke,* 1967

David Jacques, *Georgian Gardens: The Reign of Nature,* 1983

David Jarrett, *The English Landscape Garden,* 1978

Barbara Jones, *Follies and Grottoes,* 1974 edition

James Lees-Milne, *Earls of Creation,* 1962

James Lees-Milne, *English Country Houses: Baroque 1685–1715,* 1970

James Lees-Milne, *William Beckford,* 1976

Nathaniel Lloyd, *A History of the English House,* 1976 edition

Lutyens, Arts Council Exhibition Catalogue, 1981

James Macaulay, *The Gothic Revival 1745–1845,* 1975

Stefan Muthesius, *The High Victorian Movement in Architecture 1850–1870,* 1972

Daniel O'Neill, *Lutyens Country Houses,* 1980

Nikolaus Pevsner, gen, ed., *The Buildings of England*

Nikolaus Pevsner, *Pioneers of Modern Design,* 1960 edition

Mario Praz, *On Neo-Classicism,* 1969

T.W. Pritchard, *The Wynns of Wynnstay,* 1982

Peter Reid, *Burke's and Savills Guide to Country Houses, Volume 2: Herefordshire, Shropshire, Warwickshire, Worcestershire,* 1980

Humphry Repton Landscape Gardener 1752–1818, Victoria & Albert Museum Exhibition Catalogue, 1982

Rococo: Art and Design in Hogarth's England, Victoria & Albert Museum Exhibition Catalogue, 1984

Helen Rosenau, *Boullée and Visionary Architecture,* 1976

Robert Rosenblum, *Transformations in Late Eighteenth Century Art,* 1969

Joseph Rykwert, *The First Moderns: The Architects of the Eighteenth Century,* 1980

Andrew Saint, *Richard Norman Shaw,* 1976

Alistair Service, *Edwardian Architecture,* 1977

Seven Victorian Architects, ed. by Jane Fawcett, 1976

Duncan Simpson, *C.F.A. Voysey: an architect of individuality,* 1979

Spirit of the Age: Eight Centuries of British Architecture, various authors, 1975

Gavin Stamp, *The English House 1860–1914,* 1980

Phoebe Stanton, *Pugin,* 1971

Roy Strong, Marcus Binney & John Harris, *The Destruction of the Country House*

1875–1975, 1974
Roy Strong, *The Renaissance Garden in England,* 1979
Dorothy Stroud, *The Architecture of Sir John Soane,* 1961
Dorothy Stroud, *Humphry Repton,* 1962
Dorothy Stroud, *Capability Brown,* 1975
John Summerson, *Architecture in Britain 1530–1830,* 1977 edition
Nigel Temple, *John Nash and the Village Picturesque,* 1979
The Torrington Diaries, ed. by C. Bruyn Andrews, 1935
David Verey, 'A Victorian Eclectic at Work: Samuel Whitfield Daukes' in *Country Life,* 13 December 1973
Horace Walpole's Correspondence, ed. by W.S. Lewis, 1973
Alfred Waterhouse 1830–1905, Exhibition Catalogue, RIBA Heinz Gallery, 1983
David Watkin, *Thomas Hope and the Neo-Classical Idea,* 1968
David Watkin, *The Life and Work of C.R. Cockerell R.A.,* 1974
David Watkin, *The Buildings of Britain: Regency,* 1982
David Watkin, *The English Vision,* 1982
Laurence Whistler, *The Imagination of Vanbrugh and his fellow artists,* 1954
Roger White, 'The Influence of Batty Langley' in *Proceedings of the Georgian Group's Gothick Symposium,* May 1983
C. Whitfield, *A History of Chipping Campden,* 1958
Michael I. Wilson, *William Kent: Architect, Designer, Painter, Gardener, 1685-1748,* 1984
Rudolph Wittkower, *Palladio and English Palladianism,* 1974
Kenneth Woodbridge, 'The Making of Stourhead: Henry Hoare's Paradise' in *The Art Bulletin,* March 1965

INDEX

Note: architectural terms can be found in the glossary, pages 219–223

Aachen, Bourcette at, 136
Abraham, Roger, 147
accommodation *see* living accommodation
Adam, James, 62, 65
Adam, Robert, 86, 91–2, 97–9, 100–1, 186–7
Aisholt Lodge, Over Stowey, 169
Aislabie, John, 84
Albert, Prince, 76, 146
Allen, Ralph, 155
Alscot Park, lodges, 128–9, Ill. 115
Althorp, lodges, 27–31, 39, 84, Ill. 23
Alton Towers, xii, 199; Pink Lodge, 147–9, Ill. 132
Ammerdown Park, lodges, 121, Plate XVI
Ancy-le-Franc, château, 6
Anet, château, 6
Anne, Queen and style, 19, 24, 174, 177, 216
antecedents of lodges, 1–15
Apleyhead Lodge, Clumber Park, 86, Ill. 72
Aqualate Hall, lodge, 162
Arbury Hall: Griff Lodges, 46–7, Ill. 36; Round Towers, 45–7, 52, Ill. 35
Archer, Thomas, 34
archways, 46–7, 56, 80; in pattern books, 56–7, 66, 69–70, 73, 76; *see also* triumphal arch
Armitage, Faulkner, 175
Armstrong, Lord, 195
Arnos Vale cemetery, 110–11, Plate XIII
Arts and Crafts movement, 144–5, 160, 173, 175–7, 197, 214
Ashley Lodge, 155
Ashton Court, Combe Lodge, 131–3, Ill. 119
asymmetry, 178–81
Aston, Sir Walter, 20
Atcham Lodge: Attingham Hall, 87, Ill. 73; Longner Hall, 161–2, Ill. 142
Atkyns, Robert, 12, 25
Attingham Hall, 162; Atcham Lodge, 87, Ill. 73; Tern Lodge, 105–6, Ill. 92
Audley End House, 6; Cambridge Lodge, 109, Ill. 95
Austen, Jane, xiv, 36
Aynho House, 16

Badminton House: Hermit's Cell, 138; Root House, 138; Slait lodges, 138–40, Ill. 124; Worcester Lodge, xi, 31, 33–5, 42, 190
Badminton village, *cottage orné*, 138–40, Ill. 125
Balfour, Arthur, 200
banquet houses, 7–9
Baroque style, 24, 28, 30, 39, 78, 116, 175, 177

Barry, Charles, 146, 150, 153
Basildon Park, Oxford Lodges, 107–8, Ill. 93
Bath, 153–5 *see* Bathwick Hill Cleveland Bridge; Kelston; Landown Cemetery; Lyncombe; Montebello; Prior Park
Bath Lodge: Dodington Park, 116–17, Ill. 102; Dyrham House, 22–3, 28, Ill. 18
Bathurst, Lord Allen, 18–19
Bath, 153–5 *see* Bathwick Hill,
Bayham Abbey, 72
Beaconsfield Lodge, Hall Barn, 175–6, Ill. 156
Beaufort, Dukes of, 34, 138
Beckford, William, 89, 158
Bedford, Dukes of, 17
Bedfordshire *see* Woburn Abbey
Belcher, John, 181
Belgrave Avenue Lodge, Eaton Hall, 194, 198–9, 203, Ill. 172
Belmont Park, 68–9, Ill. 56
Belwood, William, 101
Berkshire *see* Basildon House; Coleshill House; Hamstead Marshall
Berrington Hall, gatehouse, 81–2, Ill. 67
Berrydown House, 176
Berwick, Lord, 162
Bishops Fonthill gateway, Fonthill Splendens, 89–90, Plate X
Black Gate Lodges, Leeswood Hall, 28–31, 34, Plate IVb, Ill. 24
Blaise Castle: Coombe Hill Lodge, 54–5, Ill. 43; cottages, 140–1, 144; Timber Lodge, 55
Blaithwaite, William, 22
Blenheim Palace, 146; Ditchley Gate, 70; High Lodge, 71; Woodstock Gate, 78–9
Blithfield Hall, lodge, xiii–iv, Ill. 3
Blore, Edward, 127, 135–6, 146, 153
Blunt, Wilfred Scawen, 200
Bodt, Jean de, 39
Bottle Lodge, Tixall, 20, Plate II
Boughton House: forecourt gateway, 23–4, Ill. 19; Hawking Tower, 41, Ill. 32
Boullée, E.L., 71, 104–6
Bourcette, Aachen, 136
Bowden Park, east lodges, 49, Ill. 39
Bowood House, Golden Gates, 150–1, Ill. 134
box, classical (1740–1800), 95–106
Boycott Pavilions, Stowe House, 32, 80
Bramham Park, 58
Brettingham, Matthew, 31–2, 78, 86, 103
Bridgeman, Sir Henry, 101
Brierley, Walter, 180
Brington Lodges, Althorp, 27–31, 84, Ill. 23
Bristol *see* Arnos Vale; Ashton Court; Blaise Castle; Broomwell House
Brockhampton Park, lodges, 108–9, Ill. 94
Brockhampton Court, 174–5, Ill. 155
Brogyntyn, triumphal arch, xiii

229

Bromfield Lodge, Oakley Park, 182
Bromham House, gatehouse, 49
Brookfield, coach house, 155
Broomwell House, lodge, 141–2, Ill. 128
Brown, Lancelot ('Capability'), 48, 70, 187–8
Bruce, Lord, 58
Bryanston House, gateway, 91–2, Ill. 77
Brydges, James, 21
Bryn Kynallt, west lodge, 127–8, Ill. 113
Buckingham House, 56
Buckingham Palace, 146
Buckingham *see* Bury; Dropmore House; Hall Barn; Hartwell House; Nashdown House; Stowe House; Tyringham; Tythrop House; Waddesdon Manor; West Wycombe Park
Buckler, John, xiii, 52
Burlington, Earls of, 18–19, 27–8, 37, 216
Burn, Wiliam, 195
Burne-Jones, Sir Edward, 199–200
Burton, Decimus, 65
Burton Constable, gate tower, 4
Bury, The, 24
Buscott Park, lodge, 182
Butterfield, William, 153, 172
Buxted Place, lodge, 183
Byng, John, 188
Byres, James, 187

Caerhays Castle, lodges, 129–30, Ill. 117, Plate XVIII
Caernarvonshire *see* Penryhn Castle
Cambridge colleges, 4, 110
Cambridge Lodge, Audley End House, 109, Ill. 95
Camelford, Lord, 79
Campbell, Colen, 27–8, 31, 84
Campden House, banquet house and gate lodges, 8–9, Ill. 8, 9
canal lodges, 133
Canons Gardens, 11, 21–2; lodges, 28
Carden Hall, 81, 89; south lodge, Ill. 66; Honey Pots, 114–16, Ill. 100, 118; north lodges, viii
Carlisle, Earl of, 37–9
Carr, John, xii, 52, 97, 101–3, 155
Carr Glyn, Sir William, 142
carriages, 4–5
Carrmire Gate, Castle Howard, 38, Plate VI
Carter, John, 60–1, 66, Ill. 53
Castle Howard; Carrmire Gate, 38, Plate VI; Pyramid Gate, 27–8, 38, Plate III; outworks, 37–8
Castletown House, lodge, 58–9
castle-type lodges, 129–32, 138
Cavendish, Elizabeth, 4
Cecil, Thomas, 6
Cecil, William, 6
cemeteries, 107, 110–12, 157

Chain Bridge Lodge, Stuckeridge House, 142, Plate XXI
Chambers, Sir William, 97–101
Champneys, Sir Thomas, 134
Chandos, Duke of, 11, 74
Charborough Park, Cottage, 142
Charlecote, gate tower, 4
Charlton Park, lodges, 165–6, Ill. 147
Chatsworth House, lodges, 150–2, 170, Ill. 135
Cheere, John, 84
Chesham, Lord, 200
Cheshire *see* Carden Hall; Chester Castle; Cholmondeley Castle; Combermere Abbey; Crewe Hall; Dorfold Hall; Eaton Hall; Greenbank; Hooton Hall; Marbury Hall; Peckforton Castle; Tabley House; Tatton House
Child, Sir Richard, 28
Chillington Hall, Cross Lodge, 34
Chinthurst Hill, lodge, Plate XXIX
Chippenham Lodge, Dodington Park, 87
Chipping Campden House, banquet house and gate lodges, 8–9, Ill. 8, 9
Chirk Castle, 112, Ill. 98; Davies gates, 175
Chiswick, 19
Cholmondeley, Marquess, 129
Cholmondeley Castle: east lodge, 168–9, Ill. 151; Tower Lodge, 130, Ill. 116; west lodge, 129
Cirencester, 18–19
Claremont, lodges, 31, 33–4, 56, 61, Ill. 27
classicism and neo-classicism, 9, 185, 188, 215; box (1740–1800), 95–106; modern, 177, 182; pattern books, 61, 68–9, 71; triumphal arches, 77–8, 80; *see also* Greek; Roman
Clearwell Castle, 28, 38–9, 45, Ill. 29
Cleveland Bridge, 155
Clive, Lady Henrietta, 188
Cliveden, 153, 194
Clopton Bridge, toll house, 133
Clouds, 176
Clumber Park, Apleyhead Lodge, 86, Ill. 72
Clutton, Henry, 169
Cobham, Lord, 18, 32, 80, 199
Cockerell, C.R., 190–1
Codrington, Christopher, 87
Coleshill House, gate piers, II, Ill. 11
columned temples, 107–25
Combe Hay, cottage, 142
Combe Lodge, Ashton Court, 131–3, Ill. 119
Combermere Abbey, south lodge, 164
Conolly, Lady Louisa, 58
Constitution Arch, 89
Convent Lodge, Tong Castle, 48, 70, 190, Plate VII
Coombe Hill Lodge, Blaise Castle, 54–5
Corinthian order, 86, 108, 216
Cornbury Park, lodges, 181–2, Ill. 162

Cornwall *see* Caerhays Castle; Port Eliot; St Germans; Tregothan House; Trelissick House
Cothelstone House, lodge, 123, 137, Ill. 110
cottage orné, 136–43, 146
Couchman, Henry, 46–7
Covent Garden, St Paul's, 61
Cowick Hall, lodges, 103
Cragside, 179, 195
Crane, Walter, 203
Craven, Lord, 11
Crewe, Sir Randulphe, 8
Crewe Hall, lodges, 7–8
Crook, Mordaunt, 155
Cross Lodge, Chillington Hall, 34
Cumberland, Highhead Castle, 78

dairy lodge, 64
Dashwood, Sir Francis, 95
Daukes, Samuel, 152
Davies, Robert, 29, 175, 195
Dearn, T.D.W., 72–4, Ill. 59, 60
Deepdene, 146–7, 149, 155
Denbigh Castle, Porter's Lodge Tower, 1–3, Ill. 4
Denbighshire *see* Bryn Kynallt; Chirk Castle; Denbigh Castle; Wynnstay Park
Derbyshire *see* Chatsworth; Hardwick Hall; Kedleston Hall; Kinmel Park
Destailleur, Hippolyte, 170
Devey, George, 172
Devonshire, Duke of, 186
Devonshire *see* Flete House; Saltram House; Silverton Park; Stuckeridge House; Tapeley House; Tawstock Court; Ugbrooke Park
Dino, Duchess de, 16
Ditchley Gate, Blenheim, 70
Dodington Park: Bath Lodge, 116–17, Ill. 102; Chippenham Lodge, 87
Dolgorouki, Princess, 182
Donowell, John, 95
Dorfold Hall, north lodge, 169–70, Ill. 148
Doric order, 107–13, 117, 136, 179, 216; in pattern books, 56–7, 65, 74; triumphal arches, 78, 80, 88–9, 91–4, Glossary Ill.
Dorset *see* Bryanston House; Charborough Park; Gaunt's House; Lulworth Castle; Milton Abbey; More Crichel House; Motcombe; West Bay
Douglas, John, 174, 195, 197–9, 202–3, 205
Dowdeswell Court, lodge, 149–50, Ill. 133
Downing College, Cambridge, 110
Downton Castle, 48
Downton Hall: cottage, 47, Ill. 38; lodges, 47–8, 51, 183
Drayton House, gatehouse, 11, 77
Dropmore House, lodge, 175
Drybridge Lodge, Mostyn Hall, 132–3
Duncombe Park: Helmsley Lodge, 109; Nelson memorial arch, 78

Dunraven, Countess, 39
Durant, George and son, 48
Durham, Raby Castle, 52
Dyrham House, Bath Lodges, 22–3, 28, Ill. 18

Eaton Hall, 184, 191–205, Ill. 171; Belgrave Avenue Lodge, 194, 198–9, 203, Ill. 172; Eccleston Lodge, Ill. 176; Eccleston Hill Lodge, 194, 198–9, 202–3, 204, Plate XXXII; Gardener's Lodge, 199, 203, Ill. 174; Golden Gates, 195, 197; North Lodge, 199–201, Ill. 173; Overleigh Lodge, 204; Paddocks, the, 199, 203; Pulford Lodges, 194, Ill. 170; River Lodge, 205; Stud Lodge, 199, 203–4, Ill. 175
Eccleston Hill Lodge *see* Eaton Hall
Echo, Kingsweston House, 26
Edensor village lodges, Chatsworth, 170
Edge, William, 182
Edgehill Tower, 42–5, 55–6, 190, Ill. 34
Edward, Prince of Wales, 160
Edwards, William, 89
Egerton, Wilbraham, 88
Elizabeth, Empress of Austria, 89
Elizabeth I, 6–7
Elizabethan *see* Tudorbethan
Elsam, Richard, 68–9
Ermine Lodge, Fillingham Castle, 52
Esher Place, lodges, 30, 32–3, 56, 92, Ill. 26
Essex *see* Audley End House; Mistley Hall; Wivenhoe Park
Estcourt, Walter, 12–13
Euston Hall, lodges, 34, 70, 61, 97
Euston Station, Propylacum, 93–4, Ill. 79
Evans, John, 188
Evans, William, 142
Everard, William, 78

Falmouth, Earl of, 164
Faringdon, Lord, 192
Farleigh House, gatehouse, 134
Farr, Thomas, 55
ferme ornée, 60
Fillingham Castle, Ermine Lodge, 52, Ill. 41
Fletching village lodge, Sheffield Place, 49
Flete House, lodge, 178
Flintshire *see* Halkyn Castle; Leeswood Hall; Mostyn Hall
follies *see* mock buildings
Fonthill Gifford, 194–5
Fonthill Splendens, Bishops Fonthill gateway, 89–90, Plate X, Ill. 75
Forcett Park, lodges, 99
fortifications, 38–9; *see also* castle-type
French style and movement, 104–6, 161, 170, 197, 202

Gandy, Joseph, 56, 70–1, Ill. 57

231

Gardener's Lodge, Eaton Hall, 199, 203, Ill.
Gardenesque style, 75–6
gardens *see* parks and gardens
Garrett, Daniel, 27
Garrick, David, 186
gate lodges, establishment of, 17–35
gatehouse towers, 1–4, 11, 14
Gaunt's House, lodge, 142, 144–5, Ill. 131
George, Ernest, 172, 179, 181
George III, 186
George IV, 191, 216
Gibbs, James, 32
Gisburn Park, lodges, 49–51, Ill. 40
Glamorgan, St Fagan's Castle, 200
Gloucestershire *see* Badminton House; Chipping Campden House; Clearwell Castle; Dodington Park; Dowdeswell Court; Dyrham House; Kingsweston House; Lypiatt Park; Newark Park; Rendcomb House; Sherborne House; Shipton Moyne; Siston Court; Stanway House; Westonbirt House
Glyn, Elinor, 200
Goodrich Court, Monmouth Gate, 135–6, Ill. 123
Goodwin, Edwin, 172, 178
Golden Gates: Bowood House, 150–1, Ill. 134; Eaton Hall, 195, 197
Gothic Temple, Stowe House, 34
Gothic(k) style, xiii–xiv, 215; *cottage orné*, 138, 140–3; early, 33–55; in Eaton Hall lodges, 191, 194–5, 197, 201, 205; in pattern books, 58–62, 68, 76; Regency, 126–35; Victorian, muscular, 159, 161–2, 164, 167; in Wynnstay Park, 185, 188–90
Grafton, Duke of, 34
Grand Lodge, Heaton Park, 92–3, Ill. 78
Grange, lodge, 112
Grantley Hall, lodge, 181, Ill. 161
Greek style, 107–25, 136
Greenbank, triumphal arch, 81–3, Ill. 68
Greenwich Palace, 4
Griff Lodges, Arbury Hall, 46–7, Ill. 36
Grosvenor family, 184–6, 191–6
Grosvenor, Hugh Lupus, 185, 192–5, Ill. 169
Grosvenor, Lady Sibell, 200
Gummow, Benjamin, xiii, 189–91

Hackwood Park, lodges, 96–7, Ill. 81
Hagley Park: garden temple, 107; sham castle, 45, 138
Halfpenny, William and John, 59, 62, 128, Ill. 49
Halkyn Castle, lodge, 52, 194
Hall Barn, Beaconsfield, Lodge, 175–6, Ill. 156
Halswell House, lodge, 142, 144, Ill. 130
Ham House, lodge, 20–1, 165, Ill. 17
Hamstead Marshall, gate piers, 9–10, Ill. 10

Hampshire *see* Berrydown; Grange; Hackwood Park
Hampton Court Palace, 4; gatehouse, 7; Great Round Arbour, 6; Water Gate, 6
Hanmer, Sir Thomas, 10
Hanover Gate, Regent's Park, 118–19, Plate XIV
Hardwick, Philip, 93–4, 152
Hardwick Hall, gatehouse and lodges, 4–6, Ill. 6, 52
Harewood House, triumphal arch, 80, Ill. 65
Harrison, Henry, 164
Harrison, Thomas, xii
Hartwell House: lodge, 84, Plate IX: Star Lodge, 177–8, Ill. 157
Hatfield House, 7
Hawking Tower, Boughton Park, 41, Ill. 32
Hawksmoor, Nicholas, 78–9
Haycock, Edward, xiii
Hazeldine, John, 205
Heath House, lodge, 123–4, Ill. 111
Heaton Park: Grand Lodge, 92–3, Ill. 78; Smithy Lodge, 117–18, Ill. 104
Helmsley Lodge, Duncombe Park, 109
Henley Lodge, 155
Henry VIII, 10
Herefordshire *see* Belmont Park; Berrington Hall; Brockhampton Court; Goodrich Court; St Briavels Castle; Stoke Edith
Hermit's Cell, Badminton Park, 138
Herstmonceaux Castle, 4
Hicks, Sir Baptist, 8
Highhead Castle, arch, 78
historicism, Victorian, 159–71
Hitchcox, William, 42
Holkham Hall: East Lodge, 103–4, Ill. 90; Triumphal Arch Lodge, 31–2, 78, 96, Plate V
Holland, Henry, 17, 81–3
Honey Pots, Carden Hall, 114–116, 118, Ill. 100
Hooton Hall, lodges, 104–5, Ill. 91
Hope Dale Lodge, Millichope Park, 124–5, Ill. 112
Hopper, Thomas, 127, 146–7, 149
Hudson, Edward, 183
Hulls, Richard, 129
Humbert, A., 160
Hunt, T.F., 74–6, 149, Ill. 61, 62
Hyde Park: Queen's Gate lodge, 120–2; Screen, 65, 89
Hylton, Lord, 134
Hyslop, Geddes, 182

Ickenham House, cottage, 142
Ince Blundell Hall, Lion Gate, 78, Ill. 63
Ionic order, 78, 89, 108, 121, 216
Ionides, Basil, 182

Island Temple, West Wycombe, 95, 118, Ill. 80
Isleworth screen, Syon House, 85–6
Italianate style, 75, 146–58

Jacobean/Jacobethan style, 47–8, 161–2, 164–5
James of St George, 1
Jersey, Earl of, 44
Jesus College, Cambridge, 4
Jones, Inigo, 56, 61, 89, 216
Jones, John, 187

Kedleston Hall, lodges, 65, 91–2, 97, Ill. 76, 82
Keene, Henry, 42, 45, 84, 96
Kelmarsh Hall, lodges and gate piers, 182
Kelston: Knoll Lodge, 155–6; Park Lodge, 155–6, Plate XXIII
Kennels Lodge, Wynnstay Park, 109, 187–8, Ill. 165
Kent, William, xi, 18, 31–5, 56, 61, 78, 80, 92, 96–7
Kew, 202
Kildare, County, Castletown House, 58–9
Kingston Lodge, Ham House, 165
Kingsweston House: Echo, 26; gardens, 24–5, Ill. 21; Penpole Gate, 25–7, Ill. 22, 84
Kinmel Park, 195; lodge, 176–7
Kip, Johannes, 1, 11–12, 14–16, 22, 25, 27
Kitty's Lodge, West Wycombe, 95, Ill. 80
Knoll Lodge, Kelston Park, 155–6
Knutsford Lodge, Tatton Park, 87–9, Ill. 74
Knyff, Leonard, 1, 15–16, 29

Lacy, Henry de, 1
Lancashire see Heaton Park; Ince Blundell Hall; Low Hill cemetery; Manchester Town Hall
Landmark Trust, 53
Langley Park, lodges and triumphal arch, 69
Langley, Batty, 31, 38, 56–60, 65, 78, Ill. 44, 45, 46, 47
Lansdown cemetery, 157, Ill. 139
Lansdowne, Marquess of, 150
Lascombe, 179
Law, E.F., 168
Leasowes, cottages, 140
Ledoux, C.H., 71, 104, 191
Ledston Hall: pavilions and gateway, 23–4, Ill. 20
Leeswood Hall, 96; Black Gates, 28–31, 34, Plate IVb, Ill. 24; White Gates, 29–30, Plate IVa
Leicester, Earl of, 18, 31, 37
Leicester gaol, 83
Leland, Thomas, 36
Leoni, Giacomo, 30
Leveson-Gower, Constance, 192
Lewis, Sir John, 24

Lightoler, Timothy, 59–60, 63–4, Ill. 50, 51
Lincolnshire see Fillingham Castle; Norton Place; Redbourne Hall; Scrivelsby Park
Lion Gate, Ince Blundell Hall, 78, Ill. 63
Lion Lodge; Welbeck Abbey, 165, 167, Ill. 149
Littlecote, gate tower, 4
Llandegai lodge, Penrhyn Castle, 159-61, Ill. 140
London, George, 22
London see Buckingham House; Buckingham Palace; Covent Garden; Euston Station; Hyde Park; Kew; Regent's Park
Longleat, 4
Longner Hall, Atcham lodge, 161–2, Ill. 142
Loudon, J.C., 147, 149
Louis XVI, 62
Louis XVIII, 84
Love Peacock, Thomas, 127, 135–6
Low Hill General cemetery, 112
Lowndes, William, 24
Lucknam Lodge, 150
Lullington gatehouse, Orchardleigh Park, 134–5, Plate XIX, Ill. 122
Lulworth Castle: gatehouse, pavilions, garden house, 14–15, 21; lodges, 52–4, 158, Ill. 14, 41
Lune Bridge, 81
Lutyens, Edwin, 172–4, 176, 179, 183
Lyncombe, 123
Lypiatt Park, tower lodge, 132
Lyttelton, Lord George, 44, 187

Macky, J., 11, 21
Manchester Town Hall, 197
Mannerist style, 91, 215
Marble Arch, 56
Marbury Hall, lodge, 175
Market Drayton lodge, Pellwall House, 122–4
Matthews, John, 68
Mausoleum Lodge, Trentham Park, 115–16, Ill. 101
May, Hugh, 9, 181
Mere Lodge, Tatton Park, 117, Ill. 103
Merfield House, lodge, 156, Ill. 138
Middlesex see Canons; Ickenham House; Syon House
Middleton Stoney, lodge, 44–5
Midford Castle, lodge, 130–31, Ill. 118
Milford Lodge: Shugborough, 119–20, Plate XV; Witley Park, 179–80, Ill. 159
Miller, John, 61–2, 65, 103, 181
Miller, Sanderson, 41–2, 44–7, 52–3, 55, 138–9, Ill. 33
Millichope Park, Hope Dale Lodge, 124–5, Ill. 112
Mills, N., 179
Milton, John, 97
Milton, Lord, 97

233

Milton Abbey, 53; lodges, 97–8, Ill. 83
Mistley Hall, lodges, 99
Mitchell, Robert, 100
mock buildings and follies, 39, 45, 60, 138, 215
modern style, 83, 177, 181–2
Moneypenny, George, 83
Monmouth Gate, Goodrich Court, 135–6, Ill. 123
Montacute, 200; pavilions, 8
Montebello, lodge, 154–5, Ill. 137
Moor Place, lodge, 181
More Crichel House, lodge, 175
Moreton Pinkney Manor, gateway, 168
Morris, John, 84
Morris, Roger, 28, 31, 38–9, 59, 84
Morris, William, 172–4, 214
Mostyn Hall, Drybridge lodge, 132–3, Ill. 120
Motcombe, 194–5
Muschamp, John, 80
Mylne, Robert, 27, 54
Mythe Bridge, toll house, 133, Ill. 121

Nansawn Lodge, Tregothnan House, 164–5, Ill. 146
Nantybelan tower, 188–9
Nash, John, 56, 71, 87, 130–1, 141, 161–2, 164, 216
Nashdown House, lodges, 182
Nelson memorial arch, Dunscombe Park, 78
neo-classicism *see* classicism
neo-Georgian style, 181–2, 216
Nesfield, Eden, 172, 176, 195, 202
New College, Oxford, porter's lodge, 3, Ill. 5
Newark Park, north lodge, 128, Ill. 114
Newbridge Lodge, Wynnstay Park, 190–1, Ill. 168
Newby Hall, Skelton Lodges, 100–1, Ill. 87
Newcastle, Dukes of, 33, 86
Newdigate, Sir Roger, 45
Newton, Isaac, 18
Norfolk *see* Holkham Hall; Langley Park; Overstrand; Raynham Hall; Rousham; Sandringham House; Tendring Hall
Norman style, 159, 161, 170
Norney Grange, lodges, 177–8, Plate XXVII
Northamptonshire *see* Althorp; Boughton House; Drayton House; Kelmarsh Hall; Moreton Pinkney Manor; Rushton Hall; Thenford
Northumberland, Duke of, 86
Northumberland, Cragside, 179, 195
Norton Place, lodges, 102
Nottingham Castle, 148
Nottinghamshire *see* Clumber Park; Nottingham Castle; Welbeck Abbey

Oakley Park, Bromfield Lodge, 182
Onslow Hall, lodge, xiii, Ill. 2

Orchardleigh Park, Lullington gatehouse, 134–5, Plate XIX, Ill. 122
origins of lodges, 1–15
Osborne House, 146; towered lodge, 76
Ottershaw Park, lodges, 118–21, Ill. 105
Outwork tower, Stainborough Castle, 40, Ill. 31
Over Stowey, Aisholt Lodge, 169
Overleigh Lodge, Eaton Hall, 204
Overstrand, Pleasaunce House, 176
Oxburgh Castle, 3
Oxford Gate, Stowe House, 29, 32, 80, Ill. 25
Oxford Lodges, Basildon Park, 107–8, Ill. 93
Oxfordshire *see* Buscott Park; Cornbury Park; New College; Phyllis Court; Shirburn Castle; Stonor Park

Packington, Sir John and grandson, 11, 70
Paddocks, The, Eaton Hall, 199, 203
Paine, James, 96, 100–1, 103
Painshill, lodges, 100, Ill. 86
Palladian style, 19, 26–30, 34, 37, 61, 84, 92, 146, 216
Palladio, Andrea, 33, 92, 216
Papworth, John, i, iii, 72, 145, Ill. 58
Park Hatch, lodge, 179, Plate XXVIII
Park Square, lodges, 119, 121, Ill. 106
Park Village West, Regent's Park, 148
Parkyns, George J., 65–6, 69, Ill. 56
Parry, John, 186
pattern books (1740–1830), 56–76
Paul, Rowland, 149
pavilions, 1, 4, 6–8, 11–12, 14–15, 23–4, 32, 47, 80
Paxton, Joseph, 170
Payne Knight, Richard, 48, 66, 191
Pleasaunce, Overstrand, 176
Peckforton Castle, gatehouse, 166, Plate XXV
Pellwall House, Market Drayton Lodge, xiv, 122–3, Ill. 109
Pennethorne, James, 148
Penpole Gate, Kingsweston House, 25–7, 84
Penrhyn Castle, Llandegai Lodge, 159–61, Ill. 140
Peper Harow, gatehouse, 166–8, Plate XXIV, detail Ill. 150
Perrycroft House, 177
Peterborough, Earl of, 11
Petworth House, 16
Pevsner, Nikolaus, xii, 173
Philips, John, 129
Phyllis Court, lodges, 100, Plate XI
Picturesque style, 126–7, 141, 161, 170, 179, 203; Italianate, 148, 150
piers, 10–11
Pink Lodge, Alton Towers, 147–8, Ill. 132
Piranesi, Giambattista, 156, 158, 191
Pitt, Thomas, 79–80

234

plans, pattern books, 63–4
Plumpton Place, gateway and lodges, 183, Plate xxx
Pope, Alexander, 18–19, 21, 76
Porden, William, 194–5, 198
Port Eliot, gatehouse, 164, Ill. 145
porters' lodges, 1–3, 31, 56–7, 59
Pratt, Sir Roger, 9, 11
Pre-Raphaelites, 192, 199
Price, Sir Uvedale, 66, 148–50, 152–3, 156, 158
Prior, Edward, 176
Prior Park, lodge, 154, Plate xxii
privacy, 7, 16–17
Proctor, Sir Thomas Beauchamp, 69
Propylaeum, Euston Station, 93–4, Ill. 79
Pugin, Augustus Welby, 52, 164, 166–8
Pulford Lodges, Eaton Hall, 194, Ill. 170
Pyramid Gate; Castle Howard, 27–8, 38, Plate iii

Queen Anne style see Anne, Queen
Queens College, Cambridge, 4
Queen's Gate Lodge, Hyde Park, 120–2, Ill. 107

Raby Castle, 52
Radcliffe, Ann, 36, 54, 137
Radway Grange, 42, 44; cottage, 138
Ramsbury Manor, lodges, 100
Raynham Hall, lodge, 182–3, Ill. 163
Rea, John, 10
Red House, 172–3
Redbourne Hall, lodge, 52, Plate viii
Regency style, 83, 216; Gothic, 126–35
Regent's Park: Hanover Gate, 118–19, Plate xiv; Park Square Lodges, 119, Ill. 106; Park Village West, 148
Reilly, Professor, 81–3
Rendcomb House, lodge, 152–3, Ill. 136
Rendlesham Hall, Woodbridge Lodge, Ill. 2
Repton, George Stanley, 137, 141
Repton, Humphry, 1, 49, 54–6, 68, 71, 80, 137, 141, 144, 161
Repton, John Adey, 71, 105–6
Reynolds, Sir Joshua, 148
Rhos y Madoc Lodge, Wynnstay Park, 188, Ill. 166
Ribblesdale, Lord, 49–51
Richardson, Sir Albert, 182
Richardson, George, 62–3, 65–7, 69, Ill. 54, 55
Richmond Palace, 4
Rickman, Thomas, 52
River Lodge, Eaton Hall, 205, Ill. 177
Robertson, John, 150, 170
Robinson, Sir Thomas, 40
Rococo style, 96, 216
Rockingham familiy, 101
Rode, lodge, 158
Roman style, 108–9, 114–15; triumphal arches, 77, 79–80, 87, 91
Romano, Guilio, 191
Root House, Badminton, 138
Rostherne Lodge, Tatton Park, 109–10, Ill. 96
Rothschild, Baron Ferdinand de, 170
Round Towers, Arbury Hall, 46–7, 52, Ill. 35
Rousham, 19
'Rundbogenstil', 153
Rush Meyrick, Samuel, 135–6
Rushton Hall: lodges, 135, Plate xx; Triangular Lodge, xv, Plate i

St Briavel's Castle, gatehouse, 136
St Fagan's Castle, 200
St James's Palace, 4
St Paul's, Covent Garden, 61
Saltram House, Stag Lodge, 99, Ill. 85
Salvin, Anthony, 159, 166–8
San Giorgio Maggiore, 92
Sandringham House, lodge, 161, Ill. 141
Scarisbrick Hall, lodge, 52
Scott, Sir George Gilbert, 153
screens, 65, 67, 85–6, 89, 99
Scrivelsby Park, lodges, 141, Ill. 127
sedan chair lodges, 154
sentryhouse lodges, 1
Setteringham, John, 24
Shaftesbury, Earl of, 18–19
Shakespeare, William, 7
Shavington Hall, lodges, 178–9, Ill. 158
Shaw Norman, Richard, 160, 165, 172, 175–9, 181, 195
Sheffield Place: east and west lodges, 126, Plate xvii; Fletching village lodge, 49
Shenstone, William, 140
Sherborne House, 170–1, Ill. 153
Shere Manor House, 179; lodge, 173, Plate xxvi
Shillinglee Park, lodges, 34
Shipton Moyne: gardens, 25; gatehouse, 12–14, Ill. 13
Shirburn Castle, lodge, 132
Shrewsbury, Earls of, 147, 199
Shrewsbury Abbey, 48
Shropshire see Attingham Hall; Downton Castle; Downton Hall; Longner Hall; Millichope Park; Oakley Park; Onslow Hall; Pellwall House; Shavington Hall; Shrewsbury Abbey; Stokesay Court; Tong Castle
Shugborough, 20; garden buildings, 107; Milford Lodges, 119–20, Plate xv
Sidney, Sir Philip, xv, 6, 8, 59
Silverton Park, 122
Siston Court, lodges, 46–7, 53, Ill. 37
Skelton Lodges, Newby Hall, 100–1, Ill. 81
Slait Lodges, Badminton, 138–40, Ill. 124
Slater, John, 52
Smith, Charlotte, xiv

Smith, Francis, 30, 186–7, 190
Smithy Lodge, Heaton Park, 117–18, Ill. 104
Smoothway Lodge, Ugbrooke Park, 142–3, Ill. 129
Smythson, Robert, 6
Soane, Sir John, xiv, 69, 83, 92
Somerset *see* Ammerdown Park; Combe Hay; Cothelstone House; Halswell House; Kelston Park; Merfield House; Midford Castle; Montacute; Orchardleigh Park; Over Stowey; Rode
Southwell, Edward, 25, 27
Spenser, Edmund, 7
Spiers Lodge, Warwick Castle, 60, 65, Ill 52
Spye Park Lodge, Bromham House, 49
Staffordshire *see* Alton Towers; Aqualate Hall; Blithfield Hall; Chillington Hall; Heath House; Shugborough Park; Tixall Hall; Trentham Hall; Weston Park
Stag Lodge, Saltram House, 99, Ill. 85
Stainborough Castle, 39–41; Outwork tower, 40, Ill. 31
Standen House, 176
Stanley, Sir William, 104
Stanway House, gatehouse, 4–5, Ill. 7, 77
Star Lodge, Hartwell House, 177–8, Ill. 157
Steel, Thomas, 34
Steeple Lodge, Wentworth Castle, 39–41, 43, Ill. 30
Steuart, George, 106
Stoke Edith, west lodge, 114–15, 119, Ill. 99
Stokesay Court, lodge, 179
Stonor Park, gatehouse, 52
Stowe House, 199; Boycott Pavilions, 32, 80; Corinthian arch, 79–80, Ill. 64; Gothic Temple, 34; Oxford Gate, 29, 32, 80, Ill. 25
Strafford, Earls of, 39, 41
Strawberry Hill, 41
Street, G.E., 153
Stuckeridge House, Chain Bridge Lodge, 142, Plate xxi
Stud Lodge, Eaton Hall, 199, 203–4, Ill. 175
Studley Royal, screen and lodges, 84–6, Ill. 70
Suffolk *see* Rendlesham Hall
Summerson, Sir John, 19
Sunderland, Earl of, 28
Surrey *see* Chinthurst Hill; Claremont; Deepdene; Esher Place; Ham House; Moor Place; Norney Grange; Ottershaw Park; Painshill; Park Hatch; Peper Harow; Shere Manor House; Sutton Place; Witley Park
Sussex Castle, 179
Sussex *see* Buxted Place; Glynde Place; Plumpton Place; Sheffield Place; Shillington Park; Standen House
Sutherland, Dukes of, 174, 192

Sutton Place, lodge, 20, Ill. 16
Swift, Jonathan, 17, 19
Sydney Hotel, 123
Syon House, Isleworth screen, 85–6, 99, Ill. 71

Tabley House, south lodge, 81, 83–4, Ill. 69
Tallard, Marshal, 10
Talman, William, 23, 31
Tapeley House, lodge, 149
Tasker, John, 53–4
Tatham, C.H., xii
Tatton Park: Knutsford Lodge, 87–9, Ill. 74; Mere Lodge, 117, Ill. 103; Rostherne Lodge, 109–10, Ill. 96
Tawstock Court, cottage, 142
Taylor, Sir Robert, 96
Telford, Thomas, 133
Temple, Lord, 80
temple, columned, 107–25
Tendring Hall, lodges, 69
Tern Lodge, Attingham Hall, 105–6, Ill. 92
Terry, Quinlan, 181
thatched cottages, 136–43
Thenford, garden changing room, 181
Theobalds, banquet houses and summer house, 6
Thornton-le-Street Hall, east lodge, 98–9, 101–2, Ill. 84
Timber Lodge, Blaise Castle, 55
Tittenley Lodge, Shavington Hall, 178
Tixall Hall: Bottle Lodge, 20, Plate ii; gatehouse, 20
toll lodges, 133, 155
Tong Castle, Convent Lodge, 48, 70, 190, Plate vii
Tottenham Park, portico and lodges, 58, 61, Ill. 48
Tower Lodge, Cholmondeley Castle, 130, Ill. 116
towers, 1–3, 132, 188–90; gatehouse, 1–4, 11, 14; Gothic, 40–55
Tregothnan House, Nansawn Lodge, 164–5, Ill. 146
Trelissick House, lodge, 109, Plate xii
Trentham Hall, 146, 153; altar-type lodges, xii; Mausoleum Lodge, 115–16, Ill. 101; west lodge, 173–4, Ill. 154
Tresham, Sir Thomas, xv
Trevor, Richard, 84
Triangular Lodge, Rushton Hall, xv, Plate i
triumphal arch lodges, xiii, 31–2, 77–94; at Holkham Hall, 31–2, 78, 96, Plate v; in pattern books, 57, 66, 69, 76; *see also* archways
Tudor Lodge, Woburn, 161
Tudorbethan/Elizabethan style, 75, 161–2, 164–5
Twickenham, garden, 18
Tyringham, gateway, 92
Tythrop House, lodge, Plate xxxi

Ugbrooke Park, Smoothway Lodge, 142–3, Ill. 129

Van Wyngaerde, Anthonis, 6
Vanbrugh, Sir John, 25–8, 31, 37–8, 148, 153, 156
Vanbrugh Fields, 38
Vardy, John, 97
Vavasour, Sir Thomas, 20
Victoria, Queen, 146
Victorian style, 145–6; historicism, 159–71
Voysey, Charles A., 172, 174, 177
Vulliamy, Lewis, 162

Waddesdon Manor, lodge, 169–70, Ill. 152
Wakefield, Court House and Library, 111–12
Walker, Romaine, 180
Walpole, Horace, 41, 53, 79, 137
Wanstead House, lodge, 28
Ware, Isaac, 96
Warwick Castle, Spiers Lodge, 60, 66
Warwickshire see Alscot Park; Arbury Hall; Edgehill Tower; Radway Grange; Warwick Castle
Waterhouse, Alfred, 195, 197–8, 201–3
Waterloo Tower, Wynnstay Park, 189, Ill. 167
Watkin, David, 190
Watson, H. Paxton, 179
Watson-Wentworth, Thomas, 39
Watts, G.F., 192
Webb, Aston, 146, 172
Webb, Philip, 172–3, 176, 195
Webbe, John, 20
Welbeck Abbey, Lion Lodge, 165, 167, Ill. 149
Welburn Hall, lodge, 180
Weld, Mrs Humphrey, 14–15
Weld, Thomas, 53–4
Wentworth, Thomas, Earl of Stafford, 39
Wentworth, Thomas, Lord Raby, 39–40
Wentworth Castle, Steeple Lodge, 39–41, 43, Ill. 30
Wentworth Woodhouse, lodges, xii, 102–3, 111, 155, Ill. 89, 97
West Bay, 176
West Wycombe Park: Kitty's Lodge, 95; Island Temple, 95, 118, Ill. 80
Westminster, Dukes of see Grosvenor
Weston Park, lodges, 101–2, Ill.
Westonbirt House, lodges, 162–3, Ill. 143, 144
Westwood Park, gatehouse, 11–13, 77, Ill. 12
White Gates, Leeswood Hall, 29–30, Plate IVa
Wilkins, William, 71
William IV, 126, 153

William of Orange, 20, 22
William of Wykeham, 3
Wiltshire see Bowden Park; Bowood House; Charlton Park; Cirencester; Clouds; Fonthill; Lucknam; Ramsbury Manor; Tottenham Park
Wimbledon, banquet house, 6
Winchester gaol, 83
Windsor, Lady, 200
Witley Court, 152; Milford Lodge, 179–80, Ill. 159
Wivenhoe Park, lodge, 140–1, 143, Ill. 126
Woburn Abbey, lodge, 16–17, 161, Ill. 15
Wollaton House, pavilions, 6
Wood, Henry, 132
Wood, John, 155
Woodbridge Lodge, Rendlesham Hall, x–xi, Ill. 2
Woodstock Gate, Blenheim Palace, 78–9
Worcester Lodge, Badminton House, ii, 31, 33–5, 42, 56, 96, 190, Ill. 28
Worcestershire see Hagley Park; Westwood Park; Witley Court
Wordsworth, William, 137
Wrelton, 121–2, Ill. 108
Wren, Sir Christopher, 11, 172
Wrest Park, 34
Wright, Stephen, 86–7
Wright, Thomas, 137–40, 142
Wyatt, James, 49, 68, 87–8, 92, 126, 132, 155, 188, 191
Wyatt, Lewis, 87–9, 92
Wyatt, Samuel, 104
Wyatville, Sir Jeffry, 132, 189
Wykeham Abbey, east lodge, 180, Ill. 160
Wyndham, George, 200
Wyndham, Thomas, 38–9
Wynn family, 184, 186–91
Wynn, Watkin William, Sir (3rd) 185–6, Ill. 164
Wynn, Watkin, Sir (4th), 186–9
Wynn, Watkin, Sir (5th), 188, 190–1
Wynne, Sir George, 30
Wynnstay Park, 184–91; Kennels Lodge, 109, 187–8, Ill. 165; Newbridge Lodge, 190–1, Ill. 168; Rhos y Madoc Lodge, 188, Ill. 166; Waterloo Tower, 189, Ill. 167

Yorkshire, North Riding see Castle Howard; Duncombe Park; Thornton-le-Street Hall; Welburn Hall; Wrelton; Wykeham Abbey
Yorkshire, West Riding see Bramham Park; Cowick Hall; Gisburn Park; Grantley Hall; Harewood House; Ledston Hall; Newby Hall; Stainborough Castle; Studley Royal; Wakefield; Wentworth Castle; Wentworth Woodhouse

D C B

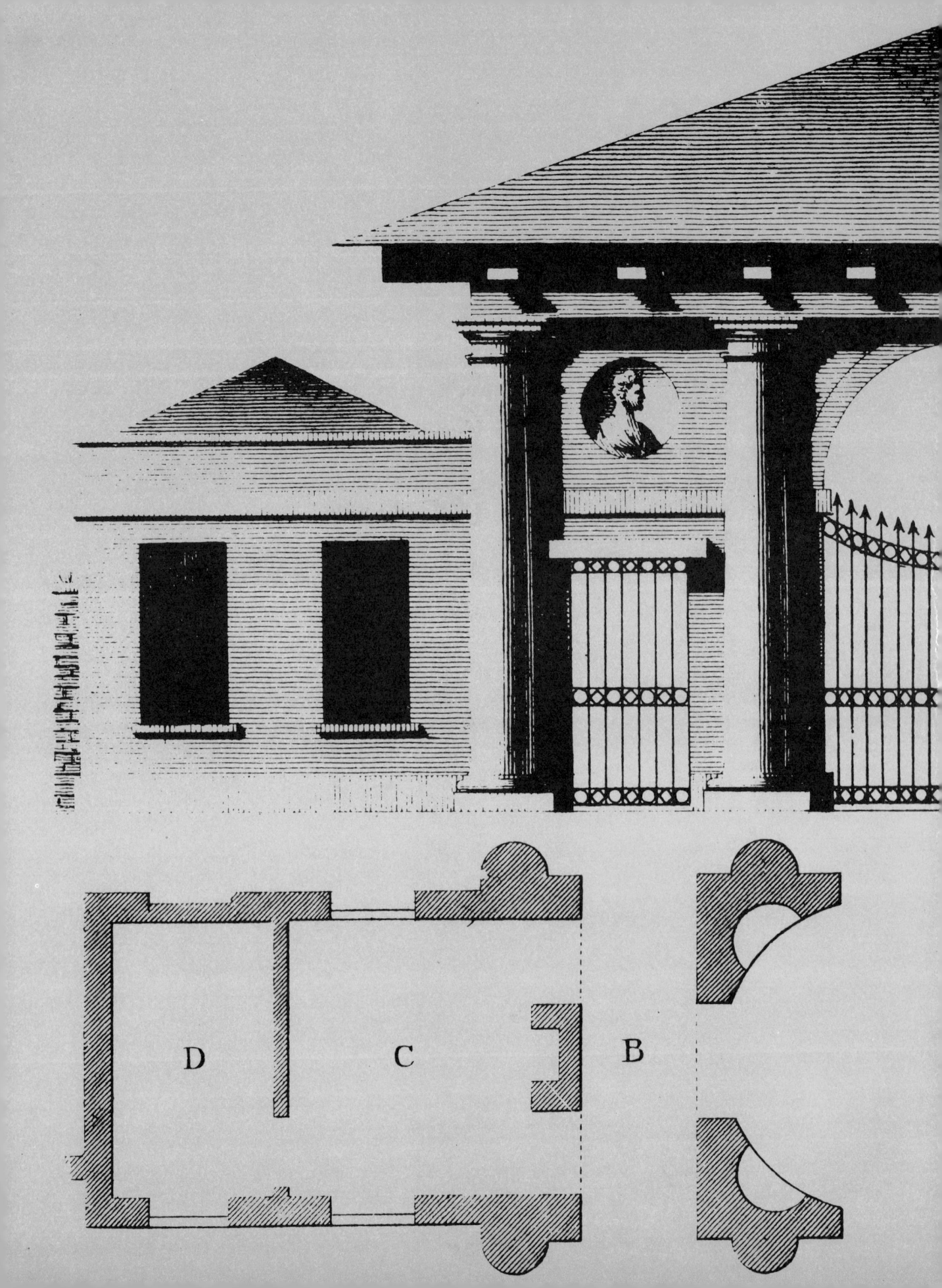